Privacy and the In-
surance Industry

Privacy and the Insurance Industry

Harold D. Skipper, Jr.

Department of Insurance
College of Business Administration
Georgia State University

Steven N. Weisbart

Research Director
Teachers Insurance and Annuity Association
New York, N.Y.

1979

Research Monograph No. 83

Publishing Services Division
College of Business Administration / Georgia State University
Atlanta, Georgia

Library of Congress Cataloging in Publication Data

Main entry under title:

Privacy and the insurance industry.

    (Research monograph — College of Business Administration, Georgia State University; no. 83)
    Based mainly on papers presented at the National Conference on Privacy and the Insurance Industry held in Atlanta, Oct. 13-14, 1977.

    1. Confidential communications—Insurance—United States—Congresses. 2. Insurance Companies—Records and correspondence—Congresses. 3. Privacy, Right of—United States—Congresses. I. Skipper, Harold D., 1947- II. Weisbart, Steven N. III. National Conference on Privacy and the Insurance Industry, Atlanta, 1977. IV. Series: Georgia State University, College of Business Administration. Research monograph — College of Business Administration, Georgia State University; no. 83.

HG8535.P74   368   79-21197

ISBN 0-88406-123-X

Georgia State University is an equal educational opportunity institution and an equal opportunity/affirmative action employer.

Published by:
Publishing Services Division
College of Business Administration
Georgia State University
University Plaza
Atlanta, Georgia 30303

Cover design by Richard Shannon

To John W. Hall for his leadership and dedication to excellence in insurance education and research.

Table of Contents

Preface

This book is an outgrowth of presentations made and issues discussed at the *National Conference on Privacy and the Insurance Industry* held in Atlanta on October 13-14, 1977. The Conference was sponsored by the Department of Insurance of Georgia State University in its continuing efforts to provide a forum for insurance executives and others to discuss openly major issues facing the insurance business. The great interest in privacy matters, evidenced by the presentations and discussions at the Conference, suggested the need to capture many of the remarks in book form.

It is hoped that through the diversity of opinions expressed herein, reasonable solutions to privacy problems will be promoted.

Many individuals are responsible for the success of the Conference and, therefore, this book. The authors of the chapters were selected because of their expertise in their respective area. Theirs is the significant contribution, of course, and their splendid work is deeply appreciated. The reader will see clearly the importance of each person's contribution.

The individuals who served as panelists in the various informal workshops at the Conference added immensely to the attendees' understanding of privacy issues. Their adroit presentations and discussions are appreciated. Included as panelists in the various workshop sessions were:

Marketing and Underwriting in Life and Health Insurance Session

Steve Weisbart — Moderator
Associate Professor of Insurance
Georgia State University

Robert Blevins
Senior Vice President
Southland Life Insurance Company

Neil M. Day
President
Medical Information Bureau

L.B. Kennedy
Vice President
Equifax Services, Inc.

Charles N. Walker
Vice President
New England Mutual Life Insurance Company

Marketing and Underwriting in Property and Liability Insurance Session

William Feldhaus — Moderator
Assistant Professor of Insurance
Georgia State University

William O. Bailey
President
Aetna Life and Casualty Company

R.L. Kennedy
Vice President
Equifax Services, Inc.

James McTurnan
Vice President
MFA Mutual Insurance Company

Claims in Life and Health Insurance Session

Donald Hankin — Moderator
Senior Vice President
Occidental Life of California

Thomas F. McDermott
Vice President
Metropolitan Life Insurance Company

William Waters
Vice President
Aetna Life Insurance Company

Claims in Property and Liability Insurance Session

John Hall — Moderator
Chairman, Department of Insurance
Georgia State University

W.T. Browning
Vice President
Equifax Services, Inc.

M. Croydon Johns
Chairman, Johns-Eastern Company

Jules H. Marckmann
Vice President
Chubb and Son, Inc.

Operations in Life/Health and Property/Liability Insurance Session

Bernard Webb — Moderator
Professor of Insurance and Actuarial Science
Georgia State University

A. Douglas Murch
Senior Vice President
Prudential Life Insurance Company

Irwin Sitkin
Vice President
Aetna Life and Casualty Company

Employment and Personnel Session

Stuart Schwarzschild — Moderator
Professor of Insurance
Georgia State University

Edward Cabot
Associate General Counsel
The Equitable Life Assurance Society

Allen Knautz
Vice President
Equifax Services, Inc.

Ronald L. Plesser
Partner
Blum and Nash

Other individuals whose less visible, although no less valuable, work contributed greatly to the success of the Conference include: Hal Arnold, Equifax, Inc.; Fred Beck, Alliance of American Insurers; Mason Connell, Life Insurers Conference; James Foley, Life Office Management Association; and Otto Meletzke, American Council of Life Insurance.

The encouragement and participation of Kenneth Black, Jr., Dean of the College of Business Administration at Georgia State, the participation of Michael Mescon, Chairman of the Management Department at Georgia State, and the administrative guidance of John Adams, Director of the Center for Insurance Research at Georgia State, are gratefully acknowledged.

Without the direction and level-headed guidance of Annette Colie and Sue Peters of Georgia State University, the Conference would have been doomed to failure. Their assistance was invaluable.

Irene Cook, the editors' secretary, shouldered more than her share of the burden of the Conference and this book. She is due our appreciation and has our affection.

John Hall, Chairman of Georgia State University's Insurance Department, is the guiding light behind, and the reason for, both the Conference and this book. His mission—to use the best in insurance academics to help achieve a better insurance industry—was the inspiration for the Conference. Our appreciation for his encouragement, excitement, and insight in these undertakings cannot be expressed adequately.

Introduction

The release of the report of the Privacy Protection Study Commission (PPSC) signaled the beginning of extensive debate about how best to achieve fairness to individuals regarding the use of personal information in activities involving private sector organizations. Insurers and their support organizations have a vital stake in the outcome of this debate. Initial reaction from insurers, insurance trade associations, and organizations which provide services to insurers to the insurance recommendations of the PPSC report has been mixed, ranging from full to partial to no support. But the focus of the debate should not be on the PPSC report alone. State insurance commissioners, state legislatures, the U.S. Congress, and federal agencies also have views on needed changes in privacy protections which are either more or less stringent than those proposed by the PPSC.

Moreover, confusion and uncertainty seems to exist within the insurance industry about privacy issues. The concept of what constitutes adequate personal privacy protection appears to be undergoing fundamental change. If changes are forthcoming, alterations in the way the insurance business is conducted will likely follow.

The papers included in this book represent a cross-section of thoughts and opinions of those within and outside the insurance industry who would likely be affected by or would effect privacy-related changes in information practices. The book is divided into three parts, each of which is intended to provide a different perspective on privacy issues.

Part I gives, in two chapters, the Privacy Commission's perspective. The Commission's recommendations have provided and will likely continue to provide the primary basis for advocating changes in insurers' information practices.

The report of the Commission is viewed by many as a benchmark in the evolution of privacy protection. Consequently, it is imperative that the Commission's purpose and recommendations be understood fully. Commission Chairman, David F. Linowes, authored the paper presented in chapter 1. In this paper, Mr. Linowes speaks to the changing concept of privacy and provides an overview of the Commission's work. As the Commission's work went far beyond an investigation of the insurance industry, Mr. Linowes addresses many issues from a broad perspective.

Ronald L. Plesser, the General Counsel of the PPSC, presents and discusses the seventeen insurance recommendations of the Commission in chapter 2. Included in this paper are the Commission's justifications for its recommendations. In reading Mr. Plesser's paper, one should be mindful that while the author addresses only insurance recommendations, insurance and related organizations could also be affected in other-than-insurance areas (for example, employment).

Part II, which consists of five chapters, gives a potpourri of perspectives on privacy issues facing the insurance business from those who would be most directly affected. Chapter 3 is William O. Bailey's view of the PPSC findings. As a member of the Commission and President of Aetna Life and Casualty Company, Mr. Bailey is uniquely qualified to provide insight into why he and Aetna consider privacy as a positive force.

Francis Gregory, attorney with Sutherland, Asbill and Brennan, has been deeply involved in insurance-related privacy issues. Chapter 4 gives a view somewhat in contrast with Mr. Bailey's about the possible impact that implementation of the PPSC recommendations would have on the insurance business.

As publisher of the *Privacy Journal*, Robert E. Smith's consumer perspective provides what many readers will consider an interesting, yet different, perspective in insurance-related privacy issues. In chapter 5 Mr. Smith implies that changes beyond those recommended by the PPSC are needed.

W. Lee Burge writes in chapter 6 of his concerns regarding privacy issues. As President and Chief Executive Officer of Equifax, Inc., his perspective is that of a firm which provides services to insurers.

Chapter 7 is a condensation of the thoughts and concerns of several insurance executives. Life, health and property/liability executives' views are presented from a marketing, underwriting, claims, and personnel standpoint.

Part III presents, in three chapters, the perspectives of those in government who would likely play a significant role in shaping any new privacy legislation or regulation. In chapter 8, two state insurance regulators—Illinois' Director Richard L. Mathias, and Indiana's Commissioner H.P. Hudson—share their concerns with the reader.

Lewis H. Goldfarb, Director of Special Statutes for the Federal Trade Commission, presents, in chapter 9, his ideas regarding changes needed within the insurance industry to protect better individual privacy. A particularly interesting aspect of his presentation is the comparison of the FTC-recommended changes with the PPSC-recommended changes.

Representative Barry Goldwater, Jr., writes in chapter 10 that changes are needed. Congressman Goldwater was a member of the PPSC, is co-sponsor of two insurance-related privacy bills, and was co-sponsor of the Privacy Act of 1974.

The final chapter gives the editors' views of developments in the field of privacy to date.

Part I

The Privacy Commission's Perspective

The Privacy Protection Study Commission (PPSC) was created by the U.S. Congress to determine the adequacy of existing privacy protections in the private sector and, if necessary, to recommend changes needed to strengthen these protections. In its report, *Personal Privacy in an Information Society*, the Commission made numerous recommendations which, if implemented, would change the information collection, use, and disclosure practices of organizations and individuals in the insurance business.

The first chapter of this part, "The Changing Concept of Privacy," was written by David F. Linowes. Mr. Linowes highlights the events in society that have caused a rethinking of the more traditional view of privacy. He then presents an overview of the purpose, functioning, and findings of the PPSC. Following Mr. Linowes' paper are questions which were directed to him at the Privacy Conference and his responses.

The second chapter, written by Ronald L. Plesser, is "The Privacy Protection Study Commission's Insurance Recommendations." Mr. Plesser provides detailed information about the PPSC's insurance-related recommendations and shares with the reader the Commission's logic for each recommendation. The discussion period that followed Mr. Plesser's presentation is included and sheds additional light on the recommendations.

1

The Changing Concept of Privacy

David F. Linowes

It is a pleasure to be here with you today. As Chairman of the Privacy Protection Study Commission, I welcomed the opportunity to meet with various groups of American business leaders during the past two years, when we were seeking answers to many of the complex problems with which we had to grapple. Now that our report has been completed, it is imperative that our recommendations be understood and debated by those institutions in the private sector that will be affected by them.

I will address three areas. First, I will attempt to give you, very briefly, an overview of the phenomena that brought about the need for the kind of investigation that we undertook. Next, I will comment on our general findings and will address the broad recommendations in all areas. Finally, I will touch on those areas that deal directly with the insurance industry. I

David F. Linowes was Chairman of the Privacy Protection Study Commission and is Bloeschenstein Professor of Political Economy and Public Policy at the University of Illinois. He is the author of several books, including *The Corporate Conscience* and *Strategies for Survival*. A certified public accountant, he has headed missions to Turkey, Pakistan, India, and Greece on behalf of the U.S. Department of State and the United Nations. Mr. Linowes has served as Chairman of the Trial Board of the American Institute of Certified Public Accountants, Chairman of the City Affairs Committee of the New York Chamber of Commerce and Industry, and as a member of the New York State Governor's Task Force on Human Services. He serves on the boards of directors of numerous corporations.

think it is appropriate that we deal with matters beyond those within the insurance industry because all of you are not only insurance executives or executives of insurance-support organizations but you also are Americans, you are spouses, you are parents, you are loyal citizens—you are as much concerned about our democracy, our freedoms, the direction in which we are going, as others. We all carry credit cards, we all need bank credit, we all need life insurance.

In our developing computerized society, most Americans are unaware of the record-keeping practices of private organizations and the uses made of the personal information that is supplied to those organizations. Because people are largely unaware of what happens when they apply for credit, take out insurance, open a bank account, or go to the doctor, they are unable to exercise control, or even determine if they want to exercise control, over that information. If more Americans were better informed about the collection, maintenance, and dissemination of personal information, they very well might seek to exercise stricter controls over its use.

Information about people obviously has become a valuable commodity in today's society. It is used not just to help manage and control an organization's operations, but it has become a product in itself. It is transferred, it is exchanged, it is rented, and it is sold. Chronic problems of previously minor dimensions have become major social policy questions, as the efficiencies of modern record-keeping technology have eased the task of compiling, comparing, and retrieving information for use in administrative decision making and as an instrument of surveillance.

The advent of the computer has served to underscore the fact that in most societies today the holder of a collection of records about individuals has considerable freedom to decide how those records will be used. In both government and the private sector, there are organizations that keep records about persons without the individuals ever knowing the records exist, let alone the uses to which they are put. Indeed, until quite recently, it has been unusual for any organization in this country, whether public or private, to be willing even to describe its record-keeping practices to the public. Today, moreover, there is still no way for any of us to find out all the organizations that maintain data on us and how they use them to make decisions that directly affect our private lives.

Before the advent of the computer, the bulk of personal records accumulated by a particular agency or company stayed with that institution. There was no mass transfer of information, if for no other reasons than those of cost and physical inaccessibility. Also, because it always has been costly to accumulate and keep data, most of it was promptly destroyed. Today, however, almost unlimited amounts of personal data are being accumulated by scores of organizations and fed into data banks, and much of it is being shared with others, often without the knowledge of the person concerned.

With split-second retrieval, anything that is ever recorded about a person becomes immediately available, and with computer-to-computer linkage—which, incidentally, is the fastest growing dimension of computer technology—anything put into the data bank of one organization could be tied together with another organization's data bank. It is this linkage that has the potential for creating one of the greatest threats to our way of life. Little by little, by silent encroachment, individuality and freedom of enterprise are being eroded. It should be made clear, however, that the threat is not the computer itself, but rather the person or the organization that controls this electronic masterpiece.

As you know, the Constitution is vague on "privacy"; the term is not even mentioned there. The courts have been interpreting the "right of privacy" for the individual through the Fourth Amendment dealing with "the right of the people to be secure in their person, houses, papers and effect, against unreasonable searches and seizures"; the Fifth Amendment against self-incrimination; the First Amendment dealing with freedom of the press and assembly; and the Ninth Amendment, which reserves to the people all rights not specifically delegated to the federal government and the states.

The Privacy Act of 1974 for the first time in history gave statutory recognition to a so-called "right of privacy," and nobody is quite sure what that means. It established a uniform set of fair information standards governing the record-keeping practices of federal agencies. It requires such agencies to disclose the existence of records they maintain on individual Americans; it establishes procedures for the disclosure of those records to third parties; and it requires agencies to assume their fair share of responsibility for the accuracy, completeness, timeliness, and relevance of the records they maintain on people. Most important, it provides the individual with a right to inspect and request correction of records that an agency maintains about him or her.

The Privacy Protection Study Commission was created by this Act to conduct a two-year study of all actual or potential invasions of privacy in the public and private sectors. Our work began in the summer of 1975, and we presented our final report to President Carter and the Congress a few months ago. The significance of our findings for each of us is not difficult to understand. They cover a broad spectrum of issues.

Individuals who undertake some normal, everyday action, such as subscribing to a magazine or buying something through the mail, should be fully aware of the almost automatic follow-on of their acts. When you subscribe to a magazine or buy a shirt through the mails, you can expect, within a year, to receive 25 additional solicitations based on that one action. That is indicative of the speed with which your name and address are circulated once you indicate the nature of your actions and interests. The probable further results of such an act could be that the nature of the magazine or book or the organization to which you made a contribution through the mail will be entered into a data bank to be matched with other publicly and privately available data to create a profile about you.

This profile helps identify you, along with others of similar profiles, for any specific purposes an organization or individual might have in mind. Thus a person for his or her own purposes can rent lists of names of people classified as inquisitive children, staunch liberals, American foreign-policy hawks, conservative anti-communists, women conservatives, persons who inquired about beating the dice tables, home addresses of learned persons, and so on.

In the use of credit cards, these systems are becoming the thread which weaves through a person's life, linking together what he or she reads, where he or she travels, with whom he or she associates. The number of credit cards in circulation—and, incidentally, there are some 400 million cards, carried by 100 million people—and the frequency and varied purposes of their use, make card-related record-keeping operations a rich source of information about the movements, purchases, associations, and life-styles of individual Americans. Abuses can be, and to some extent already are, associated with these practices. We learned that governmental authorities, particularly those with investigatory or law-enforcement responsibilities, have access to customer records maintained by credit-card issuers.

Americans have long believed that the details of their personal finances are nobody's business but their own. They generally have faith that the information they disclose to banks does not travel much further. When you and I sit down with a banker to negotiate a mortgate loan or a student loan or for any other reason, we have an expectation of confidentiality: we expect the information to stay there. That expectation of confidentiality is not a fact, nor, of course, as you know, is it legally enforceable. Nevertheless, we as Americans continue to do business with these institutions, on the assumption that the information we give stays there.

Several agencies of government have intruded themselves into private-sector data banks. The Internal Revenue Service has acquired lists from commercial list compilers to use for verification of whether or not persons have filed tax returns. The Federal Bureau of Investigation has obtained lists for law-enforcement purposes. Where does the private sector end and the public sector begin? In the converse, over the years the tax return files of the Internal Revenue Service have become so widely used as a source of personal data by various agencies that they have been characterized as a "generalized governmental asset" and used as a financial lending library on individuals.

On the subject of medical records, every American is the subject of one or more medical files. These records are highly personal. Each person expects his or her medical information to be used exclusively by his or her physician or by those who have a direct and legitimate need for access to it. It has always been assumed that such data is held in strict confidence. Clearly this is not so today.

Recommendations

As we talk about the complex privacy problems that are evolving, and the recommended solutions, two concerns are understandably uppermost in people's minds. One is that everyone is wary of any increase in government regulation of the private sector of a democratic, free-enterprise economy. The other is that the report is ominously thick. It runs to 654 pages and includes 162 recommendations, and many of them call for federal or state legislation. The first thing I want to say is that the multiplicity of recommendations does not add up to an elaborate program for government regulation of private-sector record-keeping. In fact, the large number of recommendations reflects the Commission's determination to keep government regulation to a minimum. For example, at no place in any of the recommendations do we require any reporting.

No doubt it would have been simpler for us to lay out a program of tight, across-the-board controls to protect the interest individuals have in the innumerable records about them, which organizations maintain and disclose to each other. This interest grows more critical every day, as organizations more and more are driven to rely on records in arriving at decisions about the individuals they deal with. In earlier days, and simpler days, most decisions about us were made on a face-to-face basis. Very seldom were significant records maintained. Today we live in a very complex, mobile, and large society. Therefore, these same decisions are now being based on records that organizations have about us. Therefore, record-keeping practices become critical in our dealings with organizations.

Instead of trying to devise broad controls, however, the Commission looked for ways to increase the individual's participation in the record-keeping process in order to establish a fair balance in one's record-keeping relationships with organizations. This meant examining record-keeping practices not only in the private sector as a whole but more specifically in each of the main areas we explored. Then we tailored the recommendations to the specific problems in each area. Hence the multiplicity of recommendations, but also, we hope, an overall approach that is least burdensome because it takes account of the peculiarities of each area.

The Commission also adopted a general policy of recommending objectives to be achieved, and then leaving it to each organization to find its own best way of achieving them. We were very much concerned about not developing the type of recommendation that would permit an inexperienced, bureaucratic administrator to substitute his or her judgment for the seasoned judgment of an experienced business executive.

Of course, this general policy could not be followed in every instance. In some cases, there will have to be specific legislation. In the consumer-credit relationship, for example, most credit bureaus have a clause in their contracts with subscribers that forbids the subscriber from disclosing to an individual what the bureau reports about him or her. Since the subscriber is bound by the contract, only legislation can assure the individual access to this information at the point where it may cause him or her to be denied credit unfairly.

After 60 days of public hearings and meetings, and after hearing testimony from some 350 witnesses, the Commission took its bearings on three main public policy objectives: (1) to minimize intrusiveness; (2) to maximize fairness; and (3) to create legitimate expectations of confidentiality where such expectations are warranted. Even though these may be esoteric-sounding objectives, I do not suppose anyone would quarrel with them in principle. But in practice, they inevitably come up against conflicting interests. The important thing to keep in mind, however, is that, for the most part, the legitimate interest of the individual and the legitimate interest of the organization that keeps records about him or her run in parallel, with both trying to achieve the same thing. An insurance company wants to sell policies; the applicant wants to buy. The banker wants to make that loan; the customer of that bank needs and wants that loan. So it is important to keep that in mind, and we can assure you we kept that foremost in our deliberations.

Take the matter of *intrusiveness*. When a person wants something from an organization—perhaps a job or promotion, insurance, or a welfare benefit—that individual must provide the organization with enough personal information to substantiate a claim for consideration. And the person may be uncomfortable about answering some of the questions from the organization.

But what are the real interests on both sides here? In theory, both the individual and the organization have a strong interest in curbing the tendency to accumulate or spread any more information than is necessary for the stated purposes. It is a financial burden on the organization to collect and maintain more records than it needs, and it is dangerous for the individual to have intimate details of his or her personal life put into a record that can be retrieved by anyone who has access to a terminal. In practice, however, the individual's interest sometimes gets short shrift.

When it comes to *fairness* in record-keeping practices, there are a great many problems, but the starting point for solving them is that an organization's records about an individual be as accurate, and complete, and up-to-date as necessary for the purposes for which the records are to be used. Here again, the legitimate interests of individual and organization are theoretically the same. On the one side, an organization that bases its decisions about individuals on inaccurate, incomplete, or obsolete information is not acting rationally. No individual with a legitimate purpose wants an organization's record on him or her to be distorted. I suspect that many of us know of one or more unfortunate consequences resulting from record-keeping mistakes. Suffice it to say that such mistakes are today a greater threat than ever before, because they can be propagated at the speed of light throughout the nation and throughout the world by use of satellite—from credit grantors to credit bureaus, from one insurer to another through an organization like the Medical Information Bureau (MIB), from an employer to an insurance company, and from one government agency to another. Victims of such mistakes often are helpless to stop the damage, even if they can manage to identify the original error and its source.

I also should point out that this and other problems of fairness are compounded by the fact that, in arriving at decisions about individuals, organizations are more and more being driven to substitute recorded information for the face-to-face interview. Face-to-face encounters offer both sides some leeway in adjusting their mode of communication to the other's mode of comprehension. With computers talking to computers, not infrequently relaying records alone, which leave no allowance for such adjustments, the result can be unfairness.

Since both organizations and individuals have a strong interest in the accuracy, completeness, and timeliness of the record, the question is how best to assure those qualities. The Commission's answer is to make use of the concerned individual himself or herself. Our main fairness recommendation is that the individual should have a right of access to an organization's records about him or her and should have some way of getting errors and other deficiencies in them corrected.

Turning now to the matter of *confidentiality*, the main point I would like to make is that individuals, by and large, have little concept of how seriously their expectation that certain records about them will be held in confidence has been compromised. Here we can profitably take an example from the banking area. For most people, their checking account constitutes, in effect, an economic and social diary, which they assume their banks hold sacred. However, the principle that our personal financial transactions are nobody else's business unless we choose to disclose them is not honored in practice.

Gaping holes in the confidentiality of bank account records have been opened by the banks' rapidly deepening penetration of the open-end credit field. This exposes their records on individuals to organizations that recognize no duty of confidentiality to the individual, such as employers and landlords, and to organizations, like independent authorization services, that have no direct relationship with the individual.

The situation for other types of credit grantors is even worse. Our survey of independent credit-card issuers confirmed testimony that perhaps as high as 99 percent of some government agency requests for access to the records they maintain about individuals are made informally—either over the telephone or in the course of an informal visit—and are granted just as informally. The result is that most of these inspections happen without the knowledge of the individual and leave no trace in the record at either end. Individuals may wonder how a government agency came by some particular piece of information about their spending or whereabouts, but they have little chance of finding out, even if they can show that the information itself is in error.

In fact, as the law now stands, even if a government agency goes through the formal procedure for gaining access to bank credit records or insurance records, and even if the organization conscientiously notifies the individual of the agency's request for access, there is little he or she can do about it. A person has no legally recognized grounds for either challenging the government's right to access or preventing the disclosure, no matter how unjustly the mere fact of disclosure may damage him. Under the law of the land, affirmed by the Supreme Court of the United States as recently as April 1976, an individual has no legitimate expectation of privacy in his or her bank records, and thus presumably no legitimate expectation of privacy in the records his or her credit-card issuer, insurer, or employer keep about him or her.

The court, interpreting existing law, said that when such records are kept by someone else, such as the bank (and we can extend that to the credit-card issuer or insurer), they belong to the bank or card issuer or insurer, not to us. Hence, we have no interest to assert in what happens to them.

Against this background of general policy considerations, let me now sketch in the major general recommendations regarding the insurance industry. With the impressive growth in all lines of insurance over the past half century, no segment of the private sector was more complex for the Commission to deal with.

We learned a great deal from the many formal and informal contacts we had with spokespersons for the various institutions that, taken together, we think of as the insurance "industry." Hopefully, our recommendations reflect our concern for balancing the protection of individual privacy with the legitimate information needs of your industry. We believe they also reflect our awareness of various regulatory mechanisms already in place—particularly at the state level—and they seek to strengthen, rather than replace, such mechanisms.

With regard to the three major policy objectives, we sought to advance our goals against a background that takes cognizance of existing practices. To minimize intrusiveness, the Commission recommends that decisions about the relevance of certain categories of information, such as sexual preference, living patterns, and so on, be dealt with—either directly or by specific delegation—by a government mechanism. There is no clear line separating that information which *per se* is relevant to an insurance decision and that which public opinion may consider relevant. Yet, as our recent history suggests, when sufficient pressure does exist, difficult judgment questions can be dealt with through the appropriate political channels.

With the background of the experiences of such operations as Factual Services Bureau, Inc., which were revealed to the Commission, we recommend that pretext interviews be prohibited and that insurance institutions exercise reasonable procedures in the selection of outside investigating agencies. We believe these would not place unduly burdensome restrictions upon the industry.

With regard to the question of fairness in the relationship between an insurance institution and a client, our primary concern was to make certain that the individual is involved and made knowledgeable about the information practices of the company with which he or she is dealing. This turned, in our view, on three major steps: (1) a clearly delineated notice concerning information-collection practices, including indication of the techniques to be used and the types of sources to be contacted; (2) a relatively specific—in terms of dates, individuals to be contacted, nature of information to be divulged—authorization form that would limit data-collection practices; and (3) amendment to the Federal Fair Credit Reporting Act that would provide, upon request, complete access by individuals to recorded information held by insurance institutions and insurance-support organizations; allow the individual the right to see and copy such information; and provide procedures for correcting, amending, or deleting information in such records.

Additionally, in the case of adverse decisions, we recommend that federal law require that the company disclose in writing the specific reasons and items of information that led to the adverse decision. The Commission recommends that no decisions be based on previous declinations or exclusively on information generated by industry-supported clearinghouses, such as the Medical Information Bureau.

With regard to the Commission's third policy goal, namely, legitimizing an expectation of confidentiality, we recommend that a federal law be enacted to provide that each insurance institution and insurance-support organization be considered to owe a duty of confidentiality to individuals about whom they collect information. Although specific exemptions are recommended, moving beyond these would create a liability on the insurance institution or support organization that would run from court costs and actual damages to—in cases of willful or intentional violation—general damages of between $1,000 and $10,000.

Conclusion

We recognize that not all of these recommendations will be universally popular within the insurance industry. There is no question that, in varying degree, they will create some additional administrative burdens for different companies.

On balance, however, the Commission sought to weigh its concern for the privacy rights of individuals with its clear recognition of the legitimate need of the insurance industry for developing a great deal of personal information. It is our conviction that the recommendations I have outlined to you strike the appropriate balance and, in the long run, will strengthen the relationship between insured and insurer while promoting appropriate public policy objectives.

Questions and Answers

Question: *In what areas would you say that your Commission's findings differ from the earlier HEW report on privacy in general? And something I have heard from a lot of people in our industry is that privacy is really a governmental agency problem and that is where the abuses mainly are centered. How do you feel about that?*

Answer: First, with reference to the HEW report and all other reports and Congressional studies, we built on the shoulders of what went before us. We decided not to reinvent the wheel. As a matter of fact, the Privacy Act specifically says we should take these into consideration. I am not aware of anything in our recommendations that is different from or counters anything that has gone on before. As a matter of fact, many of our findings confirm much of what is in the Congressional record, in terms of their own hearings and in terms of the data that was available to HEW. I should add further that not only did we have a very select, well-informed commission but our staff was tops. Further, any person in this country who had any significant background in privacy participated in this study in one way or another. So we do feel we have the benefit of everything that has gone on before us.

The second part of your question—perhaps I should stress here, our mandate was very broad. We decided, because so little has been done in the private sector, that we should give priority to that area. None of the other studies gave attention to any significant extent to the private sector. We found a number of abuses there, and if I had the time I could dwell on some. But one major thing that troubled me more than anything else was how easily government agencies could inject themselves into the private sector data. Constantly! There is a complete blur, no separation between the public and private sectors in many instances. Information was shared informally, without subpoena. As a matter of fact, senior executives of companies testified before us that they were proud they responded so quickly to a request from government agencies. They believed they were being loyal Americans, not aware that it was just the reverse. They were helping build power and authority in a bureaucratic department of government, which brings you right on the track to totalitarianism. If you just let that continue, then where do you end?

Many of the abuses were as a result of errors (and I think our reporting points out some of the elements involved there—e.g., people get names mixed up). Many of the abuses were because of investigative reporting—somebody would go talk to a neighbor. In one case, a woman said her neighbor was a weird character, unsavory, not very good. She was angry at his children for destroying her flower beds. He happened to be a respected journalist, who wore a beard, which of course was a mark against him. She said she suspected that he used drugs, which he did not. He never knew it was in his record. Often you do not know what adverse decisions are being made about you from information in a record that nobody has told you about. In another case, a woman applied for a teaching job and was turned down. A person substantially inferior to her got the job. She was incensed and had the determination and the funds to pursue it. She found out the prospective employer had access to her medical record. In her medical record she learned that her mother visited a psychiatrist. In this society we associate a visit to a psychiatrist with mental instability. The prospective employer said if the mother is unstable, most likely the daughter will be. We won't give her the job.

Question: *What is the status of privacy protection in other countries?*

Answer: Internationally the problem is great. A couple of weeks ago I returned from an international conference in Vienna. Representatives from 26 nations were there, and they all were concerned and alarmed. Let me just recount one thing that I have learned about something that is going on in Britain now (and I am sure it will come here). It can be frightening. In Britain the medical field is now working with a computer in diagnosis and in interrogating a patient. They set a computer up in a room. The patient sits alone in a small room and talks to the computer. The computer is programmed for about 200 questions. The patients like it so much that, on the average, they sit in there for an hour and a half and tell the computer everything about themselves, their troubles with their husbands or lovers, their money, everything. They just keep spewing it all out. Reportedly this is for the doctor to hit his or her terminal and then identify what he or she wants to hear. What the patient does not know is that it goes right into a data bank. Everything going into that computer goes into a data bank, retrievable by anyone who has access to a terminal. This has been quite successful as a diagnostic tool, and it will spread, but how do you build in adequate controls?

Question: *I was just wondering, now that your Commission has issued its report, what do you see as the role the Commission will play in the short run?*

Answer: It is entirely voluntary. Bill Bailey is here, as is Ron Plesser, each aggressively asserting himself in these areas. I made it very clear before I accepted this appointment from the president that we all were aware that very often Commissions' reports gather dust and are forgotten. I was assured at the time by the White House (of course, it was a different administration) that under no circumstances would that administration permit it to gather dust. I was given the same assurance by a couple of senators with whom I spoke before I accepted the appointment. Since that time, the assurance has been even stronger from President Carter. He has appointed some of the brightest White House staff to this work. As for the senators, there was a resolution commending the Commission on its work and findings and urging that Congress adopt our recommendations. It was co-introduced by some 15 or 20 of the leading senators of the country.

The House already has, I understand, 12 bills, 10 of which were introduced by Congressmen Goldwater and Koch. Representative Goldwater will be here tomorrow, I understand. They are now in the hopper, and I have every indication that they will be given encouraging attention and enactment once President Carter finishes with a few small things like Panama, the Middle East, welfare, energy, and the like.

Question: *Recommendation Number 1 on relevance troubles me. Doesn't it basically call for the creation of a governmental regulatory agency?*

Answer: We do not call for the creation of a regulatory agency. We call for the creation of a Privacy Board. And this is the one point that we were challenged the most on in the joint meeting of the House and Senate committees. They questioned why we made a recommendation to create a Board that was so weak. In effect, the proposed Privacy Board would serve in the private sector as an ombudsman so people would have someplace to go to complain. Currently you have no place to go. To complain about privacy problems if your privacy is abused by a bank, by a credit-card company, you can try the Federal Trade Commission if they are not busy with other bigger problems, or you can get your own lawyer and try to do something. But the problem is that there is no place to go. We feel that it is appropriate to have an ombudsman.

You may be unaware of what some other countries are doing. Sweden has a data-inspection board. It has been in effect about a year and a half now. Every organization, public or private, that has a data bank or individually identifiable data must register and be monitored each year.

West Germany just passed an act—it will not take effect for another year—that will require all data to be destroyed in five years or be locked up if it is needed for research or historical purposes after five years.

So far as the government is concerned, HEW has issued regulations and the Privacy Act already is in place. As for the "relevance" portion of Recommendation 1, we suggest that insurance commissioners, perhaps, be given that authority in this area. It seems to me the industry should welcome that kind of cooperation from a group that is so knowledgeable about the industry.

Question: *Aren't the Commission's recommendations based mainly on potential, rather-than actual, abuses of individuals' privacy?*

Answer: Yes, to some extent. Do you know this is the first time in history that any government has created a body to investigate potential abuses to a new, revolutionary technological development? Our Congress is to be commended for having the great wisdom to do that. If Congress had had the wisdom to do that for the automobile industry, we would not have had the tremendous burden being thrown on that industry today to avoid pollution. Sixty years ago, if Ralph Nader's grandfather had gotten upset about what was going to happen to pollution and had said, "Let's build in constraints," the auto industry would likely have had engines that did not pollute and maybe could have even been produced cheaper. The same is true whenever there is a new technological breakthrough, whether it is a steam engine, a printing press, an electric light, or, today, the computer. Society has to readjust. We are now readjusting to it. The whole tenor of our recommendations is that this is a revolution in our society. We must give the system an opportunity to catch up with it. But where we do see abuses, then we have to be specific. That is a long answer to your question. But I think it deserves it because it was one of the most sensitive, agonizing questions we had to deal with as a Commission.

2

The Privacy Protection Study Commission's Insurance Recommendations

Ronald L. Plesser

In reading the report of the Privacy Protection Study Commission, it is important to look at the chapter headings. They are significant in that they give a particular insight into what the report is about. The Commission, in its Chapter 5 heading, purposely did not use the titles "record keeping in insurance" or "privacy in the insurance industry." The chapter refers to the "insurance relationship." The concept of relationship is a central concept to the report. I would like to discuss this concept in terms of the mandate of the Commission and how we came to it.

Mr. Linowes very clearly has said that the biggest problem is the general Privacy Commission finding that records mediate the relationship between individuals and institutions. The Commission found that individuals have less and less ability to control and to participate in what records say about them. Therefore, their relationships with institutions that make decisions on the basis of records are becoming more and more attenuated. Decisions are being made on the basis of records of which there is very little control and very little input by the affected individual. As a result, there can be

---

Ronald L. Plesser was the General Counsel of the Privacy Protection Study Commission and is a partner in the Washington law firm of Blum and Nash. He is a graduate of George Washington University and George Washington University Law School. He began his legal career with the New York firm of Lond, Buttenwiesser and Chalif. He came to Washington as a staff attorney with the Center for the Study of Responsive Law. His main work has been in the field of freedom of information and privacy. He has served as Director of the Center's Freedom of Information Clearing House.

intrusive activities, there can be unfair results, and there can be violations of an expectation of confidentiality.

The mandate of the Commission was to determine in a short period of time whether or not the principles and requirements of the Privacy Act of 1974 should be applied to the private sector and to state and local governments. The answer to that was yes and no—yes to the principles; no to the requirements. And it is important to understand this, because the Commission did not recommend that other institutions be subject to what the federal government did to itself in establishing the Privacy Act. The Commission did not recommend an omnibus approach to solve all the problems in the private sector. Neither did the Commission recommend a data registration kind of statute with extensive reporting requirements. The thrust of the Commission report was to strengthen the role of the individual in record-keeping relationships. So rather than having the government regulating abstract standards, what the Commission has done is attempt to come up with recommendations and an implementation strategy that give incentives and the tools to the individual to become the fighter in the relationship. By putting individuals back into the relationship, it hoped that the problems that exist will be resolved.

The Commission determined that principles should be applied separately to each record-keeping area. The recommendations should be tailored to each of the relationship areas identified by the Commission. That is why the report is set up in separate chapters, and, in reading the report, you will understand why we have approached each one differently.

The Commission conducted extensive hearings in the insurance area and found abuses as well as systemic problems with the way information is managed. The Commission recommendations are not simply reactive to those abuses. These recommendations are not necessarily there just because we had a particular horror story brought in front of the Commission. Some of the stories that were brought are solved by existing law.

The primary thing pointed out by the Commission's hearings was the systemic problems with the system of information collection in the insurance industry. We had hearing notices that posed the questions. The industry and public representatives discussed the problems with the Commission. For example, there are problems with how the Fair Credit Reporting Act (FCRA) operates. The Commission saw a problem in the Fair Credit Reporting Act in which it separates the rights of the individual from the organization with which that individual is doing business—namely the insurance company. If an individual goes to an insurance company and gets turned down on the basis of an erroneous consumer-investigative report, he or she should be able to sit down with the underwriter, or perhaps with the agent, and discuss it and get some understanding about why they made that decision. The FCRA sets up a separation so the individual immediately has to go to the investigative agency or to a local field office to be informed of the nature and substance of the report from the reporting agency.

The consumer-investigative agency can discuss the report, they can show you the report, but they cannot tell you why you were turned down. They do not know the reasons, because they did not make the decisions. Then, an individual has to go back to the insurance institution to discuss the reason for the turn down. This is a procedure that will weed out all but a few who have the time and money to go through these stages.

As to the recommendations, I would like to go through them briefly. The first recommendation is the one that develops a great deal of excitement. It gets the award for being the recommendation that gets the most excitement for the least reason. However, before discussing Recommendation 1, it may be helpful to "set the stage" by discussing Recommendation 4.

Recommendation 4 states that each insurance institution and insurance-support organization, in order to maximize fairness in its decision-making processes, should have reasonable procedures to assure the accuracy, completeness, and timeliness of information that it collects, maintains, or discloses about an individual.

Section 3(e)(5) of the Privacy Act (of which we were supposed to extend the principles and requirements) says that government agencies should collect, maintain, use, and disclose all records that are used by the agency in making any determination about an individual with such accuracy, relevance, timeliness, and completeness as is reasonably necessary to assure fairness to the individual in the determination. There is one word in the second paragraph (the one from the Privacy Act of 1974) that applies to the private sector, which is not in the recommendation that the Commission has suggested be extended to the privacy sector, and that word is "relevance." The word "relevance" is not in Recommendation 4. The Commission suggests that Recommendation 4 be applied to the private sector. In effect, it is the same recommendation as the Privacy Act of 1974. But one word is missing from Recommendation 4: *relevance*.

This is important to note. Relevance is not in this general recommendation nor in the rest of the recommendations. A standard of relevance (in terms of assuring the fairness of the record) is not a recommendation of the Privacy Commission. There is nothing in the recommendations that allows an individual to challenge the relevancy of the information.

The concept of the Privacy Commission report is that the best way to cure the relevancy question is to allow the individual to use the record and not to have an external standard so that business judgments can be second-guessed. It is in there as an attendant feature to the disclosure recommendation in that if you are making declinations for irrelevant purposes, hopefully, the marketplace, public embarrassment, or other reasons will be sufficient disincentive. But there is no affirmative requirement on relevancy except in Recommendation 1.

Recommendation 1 is not an affirmative requirement in the same way as the other recommendations. It states that government mechanisms should exist for individuals to question the propriety of information collected or used by insurance institutions and to bring such objections to the appropriate bodies which establish public policy. Legislation specifically prohibiting the use, or collection and use, of the specific item of information may result. Or an existing agency or administrative body may be given the authority, or use its currently delegated authority, to make such a determination with respect to the reasonableness of future use, or collection and use, of a specific item of information.

What the Commission intends is that, except where there are existing regulatory structures (such as in California where there are some relevancy mechanisms), there be a mechanism by which people who have complaints that irrelevant or improper information is being collected or used can register such complaints. An example (not in the insurance area right now but in the credit area) is that in the Equal Credit Opportunity Act the Congress decided that sex should not be used as a factor in determining eligibility for credit. This is the type of prohibition at which the Commission is looking. The Commission, however, does not take that approach to vitiate or to interfere with the California approach. California really has pioneered certain aspects of privacy. For example, under California regulation, in underwriting automobile insurance information may be collected by insurance companies on cohabitation of two adults, because it may be relevant for automobile insurance. If you have someone sharing your apartment with you, the chances are that person will be a second driver on your car, and it is then important for that purpose. But it is not theoretically relevant to your life expectancy and, therefore, should not be used in connection with life insurance.

Why "propriety" and not "relevance"? Society can make judgments as to the propriety of the collection of certain information, even if the information may be relevant to a decision. The one that is referred to in the report is the question of minorities, particularly blacks, in terms of underwriting decisions. The mortality tables indicate that a black person has a shorter life expectancy than a white person. It may be relevant, but is it proper to collect race information? There should be a means to allow consideration of these types of problems.

Congress has made a decision that asking individuals about their marital status is improper even though it may be relevant. It was not what Congress believed should be done under the circumstances because of the interest in equal opportunity and equal rights, and so the Commission used the word impropriety or propriety rather than the word relevancy. I am sure that this will generate a great deal of controversy over the years.

The second recommendation, also in the area of intrusiveness, is a prohibition on pretext interviews. The equivalent recommendation in the medical-records area states that "federal and state penal codes be amended to make it a criminal offense for any individual knowingly to request or obtain medical information from a medical care provider under false pretenses or through deception." That is really a refinement of the pretext interview recommendation in the medical case. The recommendation calls for a penal code violation in that particular context. The use of pretext interviews does not call for criminal violations as does the general prohibition in the insurance recommendations.

The genesis of these two recommendations was the Commission's study of the Factual Services Bureau case. The Commission's analysis, as a result of that case, was that there were no adequate laws to deal with the problems of obtaining medical records without authorization and with the broader question of obtaining information from individuals through the use of pretexts. The Commission recommended that both actions be subject to controls.

The third recommendation is the "reasonable care in selection of the support organizations" one and is very broad. It recommends that the FCRA be amended to provide that each insurance institution and insurance-support organization must exercise reasonable care in the selection and use of insurance-support organizations, so as to assure that the collection, maintenance, use, and disclosure practices of such organizations comply with the Commission's recommendations. This also came out of an analysis that resulted from some of the Factual Services Bureau's findings, as well as some of the others. The conclusion was that contractor theory of not being responsible for the acts of the persons performing as a contractor was not appropriate in this kind of activity. However, the person letting the contract should not be absolutely liable.

An insurance company cannot exercise absolute control and, therefore, cannot be liable in all cases. However, if the support organization is entering into a course of conduct of performing practices that are illegal, the insurance company should not be able to escape its responsibilities under the recommendations. Although the Commission does not recommend absolute responsibility, it does recommend some type of responsibility for reasonable care in the selection and use of support organizations. If the insurance institution would have reason to believe, through either actual or constructive knowledge, that they are using the services of a contractor violating the law, they should not be able to escape liability totally.

Recommendation 5 deals with fairness in the collection and use of information and has to do with the general notifications that we think an insurer should give before it collects information. In terms of implementation, this is one area in which we see the state insurance commissioners as having the primary role in working out what format application and notification forms should take. There are likely hundreds of questions about the form of the notifications. This will be a difficult area with which to deal, but I think it can be handled affirmatively and effectively.

The sixth recommendation is very much related to Recommendation 5. Recommendation 6 states that an insurance institution, in asking others to collect information, is limited to those types of information set forth in the notification.

I am not sure that I completely understand Recommendation 7. It says that any insurance institution or insurance-support organization must clearly specify to an individual those items of information desired for marketing, research, and other purposes not directly related to establishing the individual's eligibility for an insurance benefit or service being sought, which may be used for such purposes in individually identifiable form. This resulted from a concern that insurance application forms were collecting a lot more information than was needed in terms of making the particular underwriting decision. This recommendation requires an insurance company to tell an applicant that it is asking certain questions even though it does not need it to make a determination.

The eighth recommendation deals with authorization statements. There are a lot of questions in terms of what it means and what the expiration dates are. It resulted from our analysis of many application and authorization forms that were vague and unclear. How long could they be used? To whom were they directed? The Commission felt that there should be some clearer basis for authorization statements. Again, this is something to be implemented primarily through the insurance commissioners.

Recommendation 9 is another one that may be a little confusing. It advocates giving an individual the right to be interviewed by the consumer-investigative agency that is doing an investigative-consumer report. The concern here came out of the findings in hearings that investigative reports were being written and everybody was being asked to comment about the applicant except the applicant. The only person who was not within the scope of an investigative agent's investigation was the applicant. Therefore, if the applicant requests, the insurance company should give him or her an opportunity to input and to answer the same questions that are asked to other people. There is a caveat that says once an individual requests an interview and cannot reasonably be contacted, the obligation of the institution preparing the investigative report can be discharged by mailing a copy of the report, once prepared, to the individual.

Recommendation 10 advocates the general right for an individual to be able to see and copy records maintained about him or her by insurance institutions or insurance-support organizations. Such organizations must inform the individual, after verifying his or her identity, whether it has any recorded information pertaining to him or her. The individual may see and copy any such recorded information either by person or by mail, or the institution or organization may apprise the individual of the nature and substance of any such recorded information by telephone. Finally, the individual must be permitted to use one or the other of the methods of access provided or both if he or she prefers. This recommendation provides a clear policy question. We found that in the insurance area, unlike other areas such as banking and credit, there is a great deal of personal information maintained. There is information about an individual's life-style, about his or her family, about facts in his or her background, and so on, all of which may reside someplace within an insurance company. Individuals should have a right, irrespective of an adverse action, to have access to see them.

Recommendations 11 and 12 deal with the rights of correction and amendment, both of the insurance record itself as well as medical records. Obviously, with medical records, the right of correction posed very particular kinds of problems. An insurance company cannot correct the opinion of a doctor. Therefore, the Commission recommended that medical records be sent back to their medical source for correction.

Recommendation 13 stipulates that, when an individual is the subject of an adverse underwriting decision, the individual should be told the reasons why and the specific items of information that support the reasons, except that medical-record information may be disclosed either directly or through a licensed medical professional designated by the individual, whichever the insurance institution prefers.

This was a very difficult problem, both at the Commission staff level as well as at the Commission level. How do you create the balance in the relationship so someone can know why he or she is being treated in a certain way and how information is being used? It was only through a disclosure of the reasons and then a listing of the items. It does not state that you must give the items right away. It states that you must list the reasons, and the individual has a right to come back later and request access to the items. The insurance institution must list the reasons and the items. It seemed to the Commission that was the way to get full disclosure without the bureaucratic layering that is contained currently in the Fair Credit Reporting Act.

The rights of access, both the general right of access and the rights to obtain the reasons for a declination pursuant to this section, would result by amendment to the Fair Credit Reporting Act, with the individual having an ability to obtain specific performance. Failure to do this is not going to result in windfall recoveries. An institution would have as a defense for failure to do so that reasonable procedures and reasonable steps were taken to comply. Second, if an individual wins, he or she will be able to collect the attorney's fees. There are legitimate reasons for attorney's fees. If individuals do not obtain attorney's fees, no one is going to test these recommendations because generally there is little financial incentive for the individuals to do so.

The company that complies with these recommendations, if enacted, and takes affirmative steps really has very little exposure; and it is intended for them to have very little exposure. The company that does not comply, that takes an intransigent position in terms of these recommendations, is subject to litigation. It is up to the court, which may award up to a thousand dollars to the individual as a bounty for prosecuting a successful case, as well as collecting attorney's fees. This creates incentives for the institution, but not so much pressure that, if a company, in good faith, complies with these recommendations but makes a mistake or a technical error, it will be slapped with a great judicial recovery.

Recommendations 14 and 15 have to do with making inquiries as to previous adverse decisions. The interest here was that if there is accurate information on somebody's background, then "yes," the decision can be or should be made on the basis of those facts. But one institution should not caboose onto another institution's decision to deny.

Recommendations 14 and 15 are somewhat awkward. I think they need to be smoothed out, but the intent of those two sections was to prevent one company's denial from automatically resulting in another company taking an adverse selection. Hopefully, that is something that can be taken care of through self-regulation and by the state insurance commissioners.

Recommendation 16 is another very interesting one and states basically that there be no disclosure of medical information that is not from a medical source or the individual or spouse or guardian. The concern that led to this one was that a great deal of information was being transferred between insurance companies about the medical conditions of applicants (primarily), and that it was not always clear from where that information came. Therefore, the reliability of that information was sometimes suspect. Maybe a neighbor has said, "Mr. Doe looks very florid, therefore, I think he may have high blood pressure." It is not from a medical source and, therefore, is not reliable information; but it gets into the system that way.

The Commission has found that medical information is exchanged between companies particularly through the Medical Information Bureau, as well as in other manners. Such exchanges have a great effect on the individual and his or her future insurability. One of the really important requirements is that the information that is exchanged be obtained either from the medical source or from the individual directly. Hopefully, this will increase accuracy and reliability in the system. If I can be so bold, I think this recommendation works to the industry's, as well as the individual's, advantage.

Finally, Recommendation 17 is the frosting on the cake. It deals with expectations of confidentiality and it appears complicated. As background, I will discuss *Miller v. U.S.*

In *Miller*, the Supreme Court went further than necessary, because it said not only that the individual could not raise objections to government access requests but also it said, point blank, that the individual had no interest in those records. Those records were the property of, and under the control of, the institution, and only the bank could raise some procedural objection. The Supreme Court stated that an individual has no standing and, therefore, cannot even talk to a court about those records because they do not belong to the individual. Once an individual goes into a bank, he or she has entered into the flow of commerce; if anybody wants to complain about how those records were obtained, the bank must do it.

It is their responsibility; they are their records. I think the answers would be the same if the government requested insurance records.

The Commission felt that individuals should have some expectation of confidentiality when they enter into the record-keeping relationship. The first questions relate to creating property interests. Does the applicant have a property interest in the application form, in the medical record, in the family history that he or she completes? Does he or she have a property interest in the consumer-investigative report? I think not. I think it is a very difficult concept to think of information in eighteenth-century property terms. The Commission did not think that anything would be resolved by saying that an individual "owns" the application form that an insurance company has in its file drawer. The question of property becomes even more elusive when one starts talking about property interest in the electronic impulses or magnetic configurations on tape. Who owns them?

Being somewhat creative, we just said we do not need to worry about property, but what we really want to say is that when someone enters into a relationship with an insurance institution, that person should have an assertable interest in records maintained about him or her. There was a need for a new concept, and it is that an individual should be able to have continuing expectations of confidentiality when he or she enters into the relationship. That means the institution must notify the individual about what uses it intends to make of the information (including disclosure), and it must abide by that notification. To the extent the information travels outside of that institution, the individual should be able to maintain some kind of interest in it.

Questions and Answers

Question: *You mention that you approved of attorney's fees in support of actions to assert the rights that ended up in recommendations of the Commission. Would you support what seems to be a slowly emerging counter-trend which is attorney's fees being assessed against individuals who bring frivolous actions under such recommendations?*

Answer: It depends. The federal rules of civil procedure provide (I forget which number) that an attorney can be penalized severely for bringing frivolous actions. As an attorney, I would like to think that my professional standards and being subject to disbarment from the federal courts are pretty strong disincentives to bringing frivolous actions. But I think that attorney's fees—reasonable ones—should be paid.

I am not sure that a company should be responsible for paying senior-partner time in a major law firm if obviously there is some harassment going on. There should be some concept of fairness. I think you understand, as well as I, the potential danger of this kind of thing if it is not severely limited to areas in which a course of harassment really could be shown. I do not think insurance institutions, or anyone else, should be harassed.

Question: *Why didn't you mention or feel that Recommendation 10 (Right of Access) might be tough on the industry? And don't you feel that, depending on how it is interpreted, it would seem to place a great burden on searching files and that companies might not have the mechanisms to do that easily in many cases?*

Answer: I think that is basically a question of start-up costs. It likely will be an initial problem. I do not believe it will be an ongoing problem, such as the "reasons and items" will be. I think the "reasons and items," and also the second part of Recommendation 10, should be subject to some kind of good management control and oversight, and that you are going to have trouble with it but you can establish your system. There are going to be some problems but, initially, set it up so that it can be accessed and used easily.

When you start talking about the items of information and reasons for disclosure, the start-up costs (and I am not comparing one against the other) are only part of it. Because on an ongoing basis, you must make sure, first of all, that professionals are making these decisions in the rejection letters. This is true because not only do these rejection letters have to say that you have been declined but they have to be very substantive, as well. They have to list the reasons, and you have to be careful about the reasons. It could get you in trouble with state insurance commissioners. It may get you in trouble with your individual customers. The exposure and liability of the items (the liability is limited in the recommendations) and the care with which the reasons and items must be dealt with on an ongoing basis is why I have picked it as being the most burdensome. That is not saying the start-up costs will not be more burdensome.

Question: *Some people do not want to receive certain mail that may be opened by people other than themselves in the household. So wouldn't the possibility of a two-step process in Recommendation 13 (Disclosing Reasons for Adverse Underwriting Decisions) be more workable for many people? Such a procedure would seem to save the insurance company much in the way of administrative expenses and would protect better the individual's privacy. I wonder if you would mind enlarging on this question?*

Answer: I think that the strong feeling of the staff was that, without the items, the reasons really would not be very meaningful. The two together were the significant disclosure. Reasons alone, on the basis of our experience in reviewing the disclosure statements under the Equal Credit Opportunity Act in which they have to disclose reasons, are not very helpful. They become very categorical, and they do not really become very insightful. It is from the reasons connected to a listing of the items that one, hopefully, can get more insight into why a particular decision was made. That is what the staff's reasoning was on that issue.

Question: *What about the uses of the telephone for disclosure? Doesn't that increase the potential of justifying the kinds of abuses you are trying to prevent?*

Answer: First of all, the recommendation is not meant to say that someone can call up and say "I'm Ron Plesser. Give me the form and substance of what you have on me." The telephone, in some circumstances, can be used. But the institution still can use appropriate procedures to establish the identification. In writing to you, I might say that I would like to call you on the telephone and these are some key questions that you can ask me to identify that it is, in fact, me. Some other kind of procedure could work, also. We are not suggesting that telephone disclosure be done without some kind of verification procedure to protect the rights of the individual.

Question: *One problem I have had in trying to handle the procedural implementation of the Commission's recommendations relates to the definition of an "individual." Recommendation 10 assumes that an institution is dealing with a single individual, when, in reality, many times we are gathering information on numerous members of the family. A situation might be on a child; it might be on the wife whose husband does not know that she is really a go-go dancer, and he thinks that she is busy with her mother every night. This is an actual case. The glossary is not clear on where the duty lies.*

Answer: I think that there was a feeling that it was really the principle insured—the one who had the relationship—that we were dealing with. We did recognize that there would be some difficulties in terms of getting information that he or she might not otherwise know. If a man is rejected for automobile insurance because his wife has a poor driving record, shouldn't one person know that it was information about the other person that affected the decision about him or her? I think that in the staff thinking about those problems, the way we resolved it is that there would not be a separation between family members in such situations. The principle insured then could get access. It could be husband or wife.

Question: *Recommendation 13 requiring the disclosure of "reasons and items" continues to trouble me but mainly from a cost standpoint. Wouldn't it be sufficient simply to identify the reasons and, if the individual desired, submit the items of information that support the reasons? This would greatly simplify the administrative burden, as well as the cost. How would Congress react to that?*

Answer: I suggest that is a legitimate argument for you to make. I am sure Congress will consider your argument very carefully when they are deliberating this. We thought that ours was the proper solution. But I think that what you say is a legitimate argument, which I am sure will be considered.

Question: *The thing that bothers me is that you say Congress will consider it very seriously. I wonder whether you have more credibility than I—because I supposedly am biased and you supposedly are not?*

Answer: I don't think so. I think Congress has been responsive to questions. Of course, in some cases, they have not. I would suggest, and I say this quite seriously, that you know as well as I that the far-flung argument that, "This is going to cost us $10 billion to implement on an industrywide basis," is not very well received in Congress because it has just been said too many times. If you really want to make a cost argument, you should get some very good cost-accounting people and do some very careful analysis. Maybe you should establish a model that really fits this and see what the real costs are. Or perhaps try to project what real costs would be incurred in setting up a shop to operate in this manner. I think Congress would be far more responsive to that kind of documentation than they will be with the usual type of blanket statement.

Question: *On Recommendation 10 (access), was any consideration given to the extent to which, in the terminology, "see and copy" might force violations of Recommendation 17 (confidentiality) in situations in which a single document has personal information on two individuals?*

Answer: I think I have answered that question already. In some circumstances, perhaps, there should be some modification of the right of access to accommodate the right of confidentiality. I am not sure. But, in general, we are talking about the right of the individual, and in most cases there probably will not be a problem. In the group area, you could get into more difficulty. Also, in the business relationship—we did not really cover business insurance. How do you deal effectively with key-man insurance or partnership policies or business policies on executives? I believe the kind of problem you mentioned is likely to be no more difficult to resolve in that area. Our recommendations apply to personal lines only. I think our solution is workable. There could be some limitations placed on such access questions where there, in fact, would be a violation of the expectation of confidentiality of other persons.

Question: *In Recommendation 16 (Disclosure of Medical-Record Information), why didn't you come right out and say that insurers may not use any kind of underwriting information that does not come directly from an individual or his physician? This is the ultimate effect of 16. When you speak of not disclosing the information, in effect, you are making a* *judgment that you should not be using the information, so why not simply say so?*

Answer: How do you control use? How do you unring a bell? Once you have this information—once it is in front of you—how do you say it is not relevant, it should not enter into your decision-making process? The human mind (and I understand that underwriting is still done by humans and not by machines) is not like a machine. You cannot hit a key and say "Don't take that fact into consideration." Some lawyers think juries can do that sometimes, but people really cannot do it.

Recommendation 16 really was established with the Medical Information Bureau in mind, I think. The transferring and the quality control transfer points in the exchanges, I think, the Commission felt could bring about the best results without getting into the use question. For if you say that it is a "use" restriction, aren't you really getting into the relevancy argument, and then you have to look at how particular information was being used. Our solution in Recommendation 16 just seemed to be a cleaner way of resolving the issue.

Question: *Aren't you saying in effect that you are really concerned about relevancy?*

Answer: No. In this area it is not relevancy—it is accuracy. I think there was a feeling that medical information not obtained from a medical source was inherently, or at least had the great potential of being, inaccurate. It is not saying that you cannot collect information directly from a nonmedical source and use it. It allows that. It says, in terms of the interindustry exchanges, that only information that is highly reliable should be used.

Question: *What I am concerned about are reinsurance transactions, which are really one transaction occurring at the same time. The reinsurer may require all the information. Aren't you suggesting a serious change in that traditional relationship?*

Answer: I do not think it interferes with that. I think that, if you read the other parts of the report, the reinsurer situation is considered within the insurance relationship.

Part II

The Affected Parties' Views

The members of the Privacy Protection Study Commission (PPSC) were selected to provide representation of the many interests affected by privacy issues. The staff also sought input from consultants specializing in particular applications of privacy principles to aspects of American life. At Commission meetings all viewpoints were aired and argued, and the resulting report and recommendations represent a consensus of the full Commission.

That the recommendations and accompanying discussion would not please all affected parties thoroughly is to be expected. As the following presentations show, some of the disagreement with the Commission's recommendations is with the principles embodied in them; some with the methods recommended to achieve these principles; and some with the regulatory structure required to oversee the implementation of the recommendations. As is common in situations where major revisions in practice are proposed, questions are raised about the need for change, the wisdom of change, and the capacity to change. Attendees at the Conference expressed concern about the ultimate impact of the cost of implementing the proposed changes. At least in part, this is because the PPSC left the details of the methods of complying with its recommendations with those responsible for doing so, and some of those people were estimating costs based on worst-case implementation plans.

The following five chapters are an effort to survey responses to the perceived impact of the PPSC insurance recommendations on the affected parties. Chapter 3 presents a unique view—that of William Bailey, a prominent insurance company executive who served as a PPSC Commissioner. Chapter 4 presents the views of Francis Gregory, an attorney who frequently represents the interests of insurers. His remarks were not made to the Georgia State University Insurance Department Conference on Privacy and the Insurance Industry, but because of his special involvement in privacy and the insurance business, his views are insightful and relevant. Since the opinions he expresses differ from others presented at the GSU Conference, the editors invited the paper for inclusion in this volume. We believe it is particularly instructive to contrast Mr. Bailey's presentation with Mr. Gregory's.

Outside the insurance industry, at least two other parties can be said to have a substantial interest in privacy—the investigative reporting industry, which supplies insurers with the information to carry on insurance transactions, and the general public. Representing the investigative reporting industry, W. Lee Burge, Chairman and Chief Executive Officer of Equifax, Inc., the largest investigative reporting firm in the world, is an articulate spokesman for its viewpoint. His presentation and the question-and-answer period which followed appear as chapter 6. The task of selecting someone to speak for the general public was more difficult, and some will undoubtedly disagree with the choice represented here. Robert Ellis Smith, a lawyer and editor of *Privacy Journal*, a newsletter on privacy matters, makes it his business to keep abreast of public opinion on privacy matters. Mr. Smith's presentation constitutes chapter 5.

A significant portion of the GSU Conference time was devoted to workshops—unstructured, open discussions led by a panel of executives from the insurance industry and related fields who had thought carefully about implications of the PPSC recommendations for specialized applications. Workshops in marketing and underwriting, claims, employment, and operations were conducted. Although the discussion that transpired was not recorded, written statements of industry panelists and summaries by workshop moderators permit the editors to re-create the concerns and tone of the workshops. This re-creation appears as chapter 7.

3

Privacy Problems as a Positive Force

William O. Bailey

One of the interesting experiences one has in serving on a Commission like this after the openness craze in Washington is that the Commission's deliberations for the most part were open to the public, and people tended to get to know you as you are, rather than perhaps as you would like to have them visualize you. The title of this paper—certainly a description of my experience as a member of the Privacy Protection Study Commission—might better be "A Pilgrim's Progress."

At the time of my appointment to the Privacy Commission, my concern, probably not unlike most Americans, about privacy intrusions and misuse of personal information related primarily to government—its licit, as well as illicit, interest in our activities, expressions, and thoughts. Watergate, the Ellsberg case, and other incidents left many of us uneasy about government surveillance, the use of tax reports for other than tax

William O. Bailey is President and Director of Aetna Life and Casualty Company, Hartford, Connecticut and was a member of the Privacy Protection Study Commission. He is responsible for all of Aetna's insurance and mutual fund operations. He is a graduate of Dartmouth and received his master's degree from the Wharton School of Finance, University of Pennsylvania. In addition to serving as a member of the Privacy Commission. Mr. Bailey has served as a member of the Flood Insurance Advisory Committee, U.S. Department of Health, Education and Welfare, and on the Advisory Committee of the U.S. Department of Transportation. He is considered to be one of the country's experts on privacy matters as they relate to the insurance industry.

purposes, and the sometimes intentional leaks of personal information to discredit or harm individual Americans.

Two years later, I have broader insight into what personal privacy is all about. My original concern remains, but it has been joined by an equal concern about the intrusions of business into the details of one's personal life and the resulting misuse, or potential misuse, of personal information by private institutions, as well as by government.

We live in an information society in which records about individuals largely have become a substitute for direct knowledge and contact between an individual and his government or a business with which he has, or seeks to establish, a relationship. We cannot reverse this nor should we want to do so. While none of us likes the thought of a predominantly "impersonal society," we necessarily have had to sacrifice some of our desire to deal only with those we know personally and who know us. But in spite of this fact, most Americans still do not wish—and rightfully so—to be judged by unknown strangers without an opportunity to be considered as an individual and dealt with on the basis of our own unique characteristics.

When one seeks insurance, opens a bank account, borrows money, needs medical care, or utilizes any of a variety of social services, he typically is asked to divulge a wide amount of personal information about himself and often, knowingly or not, opens himself to inquiries from others to verify or supplement the information he provides. The disclosure of personal information to others or its subsequent use for a purpose different from that for which it was provided is quite common today. In effect, the individual often loses control over such information and, as a result, may be harmed without knowledge or explanation. To the Commission and its fine staff, the need for safeguards was clear.

The Privacy Commission Mandate

The Privacy Act of 1974, which established the Privacy Protection Study Commission, sought to give citizens some control over the collection, use, and dissemination of federal government agency records about them. It established eight principles to guide the making and keeping of records by federal government agencies:

1. There should be no system of records whose very existence is a secret.

2. An individual should have access to a record maintained about himself, including the right to obtain a copy of it.

3. An individual should be able to get an inaccurate record corrected.

4. The information an agency collects about an individual must be necessary and relevant to a purpose the agency is required to perform by statute or executive order.

5. The government should not collect information about an individual's exercise of his First Amendment right unless the collection falls within the scope of legitimate law-enforcement activity.

6. There should be limits on the uses that are made of records collected by government agencies about individuals—limits on their disclosure both within agencies as well as to other agencies or to members of the public.

7. A federal agency should assume its fair share of the responsibility for keeping records about individuals accurate, timely, and complete and should have reasonable procedures to safeguard its records about individuals from unauthorized use.

8. A set of arrangements should be established whereby the record-keeping institutions, in this case agencies of the federal government and certain categories of its contractors, could be held accountable for their compliance with the law.

These principles, and the Act's specific requirements for implementing them, applied only to agencies of the federal government. The mandate of the Privacy Commission was to explore whether or not, and to what extent, they should be applied to state and local government agencies and to organizations in the private sector.

The Commission concluded that the eight principles are basically sound but that the Privacy Act's specific requirements were both inadequate and too rigid for state and local governments and the private sector. We concluded that balances needed to be struck between the interests of record subjects and those of record-keepers, but the specific requirements of the Privacy Act did not achieve the necessary balance. In attempting to balance these competing interests, we were guided by three objectives:

1. To minimize intrusiveness by constraining what an individual is expected to divulge about himself or herself, or is asked to permit others to divulge about him or her when seeking either a service or a benefit.

2. To maximize fairness by creating incentives for organizations to manage their records about individuals so that they will not become a source of unfairness in any decision based on them.

3. To create enforceable expectations of confidentiality.

Within this framework, the Commission had to determine how to protect individual privacy interests without overburdening business or government with restrictions on the flow of personal information essential to the equitable treatment of individuals.

The Commission's General Approach

We recognized at the outset that the problem cannot be solved by restricting the collection or use of information without regard to the cost to society of denying to an institution information it needs to perform its function. On the other hand, we also felt the need to develop a set of ground rules that would allow the individual to use the marketplace pressures to control the content and consequences of the disclosures he or she makes about himself or herself, or allows others to make about him or her in return for a service or benefit.

The Commission considered and rejected the approach taken by the Privacy Act, which imposed a single set of requirements on all federal government agencies. Instead, the Commission's recommendations take into account the special circumstances of each major type of record-keeping relationship. We thus separately examined information practices relating to the consumer credit, banking, insurance, employment, medical care, and education areas and suggested somewhat different rules for each. One of the unique contributions of the Commission was to resist the temptation to oversimplify both the problem and the solution. It is the hard way, particularly in Washington, but it is the honest way to measure cost/benefit relationships.

The Commission also tried to build on existing statutory and regulatory structures, such as the Fair Credit Reporting Act and the system of state insurance regulation. Finally, we relied to the extent possible on voluntary compliance with a number of our recommendations, and, where this was not practical, we focused on desired results rather than on detailed procedures and requirements, which so often produce more form and little substance.

It is really interesting that some of the questions from the audience today amounted to an assertion that the Commission's report does not provide details for implementing the recommendations. We purposely did not do so. Had we done so, you would criticize us for putting you in a straightjacket. Our failure to do so leads us to the criticism that we have not answered all your problems. I strongly prefer the route that we went. I hope that as we go through these two days you will come to the same conclusions.

Looked at another way, the Commission's objective was to open to public scrutiny the record-keeping practices of both the private and government sectors—to reveal how record-keeping mechanisms work, to give individuals the right to learn what information is kept about them, and to provide them with the opportunity to correct erroneous information. In this way, the Commission sought to develop solutions to the privacy problem that would constitute a positive force in dispelling skepticism about the motives and practices of both public and private institutions.

Privacy and the Insurance Business

Although I did not join the Commission with the thought of representing my company, and certainly not with the presumption of representing the insurance industry, I was confident that the insurance industry could bear—and indeed would benefit from—scrutiny of its practices.

I always have been proud to be a part of the insurance industry, and the evidence developed by the Commission in the course of its 18-month study reinforced that pride. As with other businesses, however, we get blamed for a lot of things—some because they are our responsibility and we do not discharge them very well; others because, while they are not our responsibility, we are caught by them as participants in the system or they arise through misconceptions about how we conduct our business and deal with the public.

In my view, the principal reason we are suspected of unduly intruding into people's personal privacy is that our record-keeping systems and decision-making processes, by and large, are not understood by consumers. The public is not aware of the imperatives that govern the insurance business, nor does the public see all of the fair things we do on its behalf. Often, only the negative things seem to rise to the surface through complaints to public bodies and the press.

I suspect that at the heart of some of our problems concerning products liability or automobile insurance availability or affordability is the fact that this industry has not explained adequately the rationale for the decisions it has been required to make. Few industries have. The same is also true where issues of personal privacy are concerned. If one couples the need for more openness in explaining decisions and decision-making processes with the knowledge that life, health, and property and casualty insurers probably gather more personal information about individuals than almost any other part of the public or private sector, it is not surprising that the Privacy Commission would find it necessary to make a number of recommendations relating to the insurance relationship.

More surprising may be my support for recommendations that are to be implemented through statute rather than by voluntary compliance. I started out strongly supporting voluntary compliance but changed my views over time. I finally was convinced that there is great public skepticism about whether or not institutions, be they public or private, will behave in a desired manner without some legal sanction to compel their good behavior. I guess one can only chalk this up to my realization that I live in a real world, not necessarily the one in which I would most wish to live. It also reflects the sad truth that limited immunity protections are required today to avoid claims and suits that otherwise would arise in a litigious society.

I will now comment on a few of the recommendations that I suspect give you some concern.

I would hope that the right of an applicant or insured to see his or her underwriting file and to request correction or amendment of a record, which is believed to be in error, would not cause real concern. File notes perhaps will have to be made with more care, but all of us recognize the need to base our decisions on accurate information, which will be enhanced by the right of access and correction.

I rather suspect that the government's experience with the right of access will carry over to the private sector. Relatively few individuals will seek to exercise their right of access, because their concerns will be relieved by the mere knowledge that they can do so if they wish. In our judgment, the cost of compliance with these related recommendations will be minimal and the benefits of openness in terms of public confidence will far outweigh the cost.

The recommendations dealing with reasons for declination or nonrenewal and other adverse underwriting decisions undoubtedly give you much more trouble. I would remind you that, in a number of states, reasons are now required for nonrenewal of certain policies, but the information on which the decision is based is not required. Our decision to require that information, as well as the reason, be disclosed is based on a concern that the information may well be inaccurate or incomplete and, therefore, needs to be disclosed if the information process is to be cleaned up.

Many of you may be concerned that the need for disclosure will severely reduce your ability to exercise your underwriting judgment responsibly. I would hope that this would not be the case. Remember that the decision remains yours alone, and if your information is correct and the decision reasonable in terms of these facts, few applicants will choose to dispute it or question your right to decide whether or not you wish to do business with them.

Often your negative decision will be based on reasons that are not personal to the individual, and candid disclosure will avoid the stigma that often surrounds unexplained declinations or nonrenewal today. I like to think that this is the way each one of us would like to be treated, but our industry has fallen into the habit of dealing impersonally with the public. Beyond the issue of fairness, I am convinced that opening up our processes to public awareness, on balance, will be positive in terms of public support for our business.

But I am not totally naive, and I do recognize that some of our decisions will not be supported or accepted by the public. I do believe, however, that the failure to disclose the basis for our decisions costs us more today in public attitudes than secrecy is worth. Private institutions of all kinds—including insurance companies—will prosper and, in fact, survive only to the extent that the public believes they conduct their business in a fair and responsible manner. To the extent that we are not open, we are suspect in today's environment. We have much to gain and little to lose by making our decisions known and by being sure that they are based on accurate and complete information.

It was in this context that the recommendation concerning the mere fact of prior declination or nonrenewal was developed. In my judgment, this is one of very few bad business practices we as insurers engage in. An underwriter who bases a decision on the mere fact of a company's declination or nonrenewal is just not being fair to the applicant.

There are many reasons besides personal qualifications that govern whether or not a company will underwrite a risk. Many of us decline business in a state because the rates are inadequate. We also may decline or refuse to renew business because we have terminated our relationship with an agent or because of capacity problems. These serve to illustrate that no fair decision can be arrived at without asking what the reason for declination or nonrenewal was. Obviously, as a matter of fairness, if the question is to be asked, we also must be required to provide the reason when we decline or nonrenew so the applicant can answer future inquiries completely. This recommendation .can, and should, be implemented promptly, and all parties will be better off when this is done.

Finally, let me address the question of relevance. The Privacy Act applies a relevance test to inquiries made by federal agencies, which requires them to certify that they have a legitimate and relevant need for the information in order to carry out their functions. As you may well imagine, there was considerable initial support by the Commission and its staff for applying a relevance test to information used by the insurance industry, the credit industry, the banking industry, and in the employer-employee relationship. I argued strongly, and ultimately successfully, that the mechanism for testing the propriety of information should involve interaction over time between concerned consumers and those groups in our society charged with making judgments on issues of public policy. Unlike federal agencies, an insurer's responsibilities are not set out in statute or regulation. There are no set criteria against which the "relevance" of information collected by insurers can, or should, be assessed. In our view, no simple relevance rule would prove workable, and the Commission certainly was not competent to dictate what items of information are or are not relevant to particular decisions. In a competitive society, the marketplace can, and should, be the vehicle for correcting abuses and bringing those who seek sensitive information of questionable value into line with other business.

The compromise in this area is a proposal that a governmental mechanism be created through which individuals could question the reasonableness of particular items of information. The mechanism would consider the frequency of those complaints and criticisms and would make periodic reports to legislatures and regulatory bodies, which then could decide issues of public policy to be applicable to all insurers. The obvious vehicle for doing that in the insurance industry is state insurance departments, and that is the recommendation of the Commission—although we did acknowledge that federal policy is an alternative here and, therefore, provided that the federal insurance administrator could gather complaints directly or through individual state reports and periodically report to Congress.

Accusations that insurance companies ask very personal questions about life-style—accusations that are difficult, if not impossible, to justify on a relevance, as well as on a propriety, basis for most forms of insurance—are not going to go away. Clearly, one of the risks that we assume by opening up the system is that we will put the spotlight on the reasonableness and propriety of gathering items of information. But I, at least, believe that in today's society we must stand public scrutiny rather than attempt to avoid it by keeping our system closed from public view. By dispelling the mystery that surrounds a lot of record-keeping activities within the insurance industry, we may well head off much of the skepticism, loss of confidence, and bad regulation that otherwise might come with respect to such activities.

If you have not already read the Commission's full report, I hope you will do so. The recommendations are fairly detailed and specific. Your reaction might well be, "They are too much of both." However, the industry groups that participated in the hearings and those that reviewed the tentative recommendations offered many valuable suggestions for making the final recommendations workable and practical. I believe that the representatives of the insurance industry who worked with us, and who came to understand the objectives and the public issues involved, are in support of the final recommendations.

One always is concerned when completing a report that it will mark the end of his task but the start of someone else's. With that in mind, the Commission sought to document the reasonableness of its recommendations and the foundation on which they were based. Importantly, we also sought to anticipate those who would place the private sector under much greater restriction by providing the rationale for not going beyond our recommendations. We increase the risk of more stringent restrictions to the extent that we resist reasonable reforms.

The issue of privacy really may be defined as one of openness and fairness in the collection, use, and dissemination of personal information by institutional record-keepers. Our society increasingly expects this, and, viewed in this light, the Commission's recommendations can be a positive force in building the essential public confidence in business without which we cannot succeed. Our industry can be a leader within the private sector in fulfilling public needs and expectations with respect to privacy considerations.

The Commission's recommendations are not without risk or cost, but I hope you will come to my conclusion that they represent fair and workable business practices, which will improve our image and preserve our essential freedom to conduct our business on a sound basis.

Before I go to questions, let me deal with a few that already have come along. Somebody asked, "Aren't you really making these recommendations against a backdrop of potential, or theoretical, abuses, rather than actual ones?" No matter how you decide this kind of issue, you find people on the other side. I think the Commission wisely made the decision very early in the game that we were not going through the witch-hunt process that is so typical of Congressional committee investigation, and that we would operate under the assumption that, where abuses were possible, we surely could find them if we looked for them. We did gather a few abuses, but we did not try to document a laundry list and a litany of abuses in support of our recommendations. As Ron Plesser said, we were dealing with systemic problems—with questions of openness and fairness—and I am satisfied that, for anybody who believes that we have not done an adequate job of developing abuses, I can look within his shop and mine and get more documentation of abuses than either one of us would be comfortable with. So I do not think the report should be criticized for its lack of documentation of abuses. They are out there, we know many of them ourselves, and we really do not have to go through that kind of an exercise.

Also let me comment on the complexity of some of our recommendations. We tried to deal with objectives rather than procedures. We tried to deal with concepts and what we thought society expected in the way of reasonable behavior without telling people exactly how they were to accomplish that. Clearly, some of the recommendations are not specific in terms of knowing exactly to whom you should disclose information in the case of a multiple inquiry about several people with respect to either a life insurance or a property-casualty insurance application.

I would urge you to back away from the details of the words and to think about what we really are trying to achieve. Then I think you can answer your own questions as to whether or not there is a conflict between this recommendation and that one. I also remind you that there is substantial protection for a company that operates within the confines of these recommendations. Protections exist in certain instances only when statutory provisions are enacted and cannot be achieved fully with respect to voluntary compliance. A great many of these recommendations can be implemented voluntarily with little or no real risk with respect to claims for mishandling or coverage claims, which some of you may visualize will arise.

There are cost implications to a number of these. The most important one is obviously the requirement of notifying individuals, in the case of adverse decisions, of the reasons and the items of information. This is going to take considerable education within my company, and I suspect within yours, in the handling of this information. Those costs, I am afraid, are inherent in the kind of recommendations that we have made. But one would open up the process with some concern if they did not train their people adequately in terms of how to respond, because oftentimes people communicate with others on the basis of their feelings rather than on how it is going to be received by the third party.

In our own instance, we are going to implement the employment recommendations first (those few that we have not implemented already within our company) for two purposes. First, it seems reasonable that you deal with your own people first and with the outside world second, as a matter of priority. Second, by implementing the employment recommendation we will have started the education process of our own people, sensitizing them to the concern that others might have about the abuse of personal information about them. I hope this is successful. We are going to implement a number of recommendations before there is legislation. For some of them we are going to wait for legislation. This is an issue that presumably will not go away, and I think it behooves us all to get ready, whether we decide to wait for legislation or go ahead on our own. In either event, something is likely to happen in this area in the foreseeable future.

Questions and Answers

Question: *Mr. Bailey, our company has been wrestling with a problem. It came up when we were about to start our telecommunications program, in which facilities in our agency and branch offices would have direct access to our computer information on policyholders. We wanted to set up some rules with respect to that usage, and the question arose, should we attempt to incorporate some of the recommendations from the Privacy Protection Study Commission report? The answer was that, "I don't want to install a system now and have to change it later when the statutes are enacted or the regulations are enacted." And that was the decision that was made. I am not quarreling with it, but I am raising a practical question that might be helpful to all of us. What is your opinion on this?*

Answer: I recognize the frailties of the legislative process no better than any others in this room and not as well as some, who I recognize are more constantly involved in that process. As I said, we tried to develop our recommendations as a practical balance between some obvious conflicting interests. And we tried to be concerned for the cost considerations, as well. One always has the fear, as I suggested, that somebody will use this as a starting point and will go substantially further. My contribution, if any, to the final report of the Commission was to try to build documentation of our rationale in two ways: (1) in support of the recommendations and (2) subtly at times and directly at other times, to build a case against doing something substantially more. I would have concern that the Proxmires might very well look at this as a starting point and try to go further. There are two ways one deals with this. I prefer the way that says "go out and get some support for these recommendations that will also oppose extensions beyond them." The other way is to go undergound and hope the thing goes away. The latter has some peril to us all, but the first one has some risks, as well. There is no answer here. Legislation obviously is required for the reasons I mentioned, and the legislative process is somewhat tricky at times. I would suggest that the best defense is a good offense. Let's go out and try to get this done before some Factual Service case bursts on the scene, and we find people wanting to go a lot further. That is a judgment call, and each one of you will have to make that for yourself.

Question: *In terms of the extent of involvement and commitment by the Commission, where did employment fall, and also, did you recommend much legislative action in that area?*

Answer: No. Let me answer the last part first. In almost all employment recommendations, we did not go the legislative route for two very good reasons. One, there was no handle available in the employment thing—no existing regulatory agency that would be appropriate to try to implement that. Second, the employer-employee relationship is by its very nature a personal one, in which an intermediary cannot perform a useful role, and, therefore, to go the regulatory route seemed to us to be totally inconsistent with the very nature of the relationship. The employment area has a number of sensitive aspects to it and was not low on our priority list. But as we tried to do, hopefully with some success, in all areas, we tried to tailor-make our recommendations, and what we thought of as our implementation strategy, to the requirements and to the needs of the particular relationship. There was almost unanimous agreement. The report was a unanimous one, although Ed Koch differed with the balance of the Commission with respect to the question of whether or not we should create some intermediary relationship around the employer-employee situation. The balance of the Commission felt differently. The final report reflected that view and acknowledged the minority view. There was no dissent from the Commission's report.

Question: *I notice the recommendations in the report are the same as those in the appendix volumes. Is that correct?*

Answer: Well, yes. All of the appendix volumes repeat identically the recommendations in the main report, but they give a lot more background and history about our findings and the problem areas, or potential problem areas, than does the main body of the report. There are five appendix volumes, and they really are substitutes for making the main report any longer than it was. There are no changes in the recommendations. Those recommendations are just carried over into the appendix volumes.

Question: *You are suggesting, I believe, that we ought to seek some kind of legislation based on this report rather than run the risk of having something much worse at a later date. Should we seek that at the state or the federal level?*

Answer: I obviously am an advocate of the Commission's findings. My answer is that I would favor the levels at which we recommended that a particular recommendation be implemented. I think we tried to preserve the existing mechanisms wherever we could find a logical one, and we tried not to create any new ones because, as you might suspect, I am not a devotee of greater and greater layers of regulations. I would repeat the comment that both the Chairman and Ron Plesser made: There is no reporting requirement in any of these recommendations. I think we were conscientious in trying not to build a monster here. The issue does not require this, in my own judgment. "Reporting" is a lousy way to do a lot of things that we do now. Someday this society will mature to the point where public institutions will tell the private sector what it expects of them, will establish some incentives for those who conduct themselves in a proper manner and some penalties for those who do not, and then will let the system kind of operate itself. Regulation, in most respects, has a tremendous amount of form over substance; it creates a bureaucracy for no real purpose. We tried to chart some new ground here, which, if in fact it is adopted and proves workable, may be a more significant contribution by this Commission than wrestling with the particular subject matter that we did. That is a little blue sky, I am sure, but we are going to mature as a society one day and recognize that oversight by a government agency is really not worth the cost.

Question: *You mentioned the importance from the fairness standpoint of allowing someone to see and review the material in their underwriting file. I am sure there are times when a company might want to refuse to do business with someone based upon suspicion or the lack of concrete information. They really do not have it in writing, but they do not want to issue a large policy, for example, where they suspect there is a criminal element that they cannot establish. Back in the days when relationships were on a personal basis, two people standing next to each other dealing, one could say, "I just don't want to do business with you," and walk away from it. Do you think the impact of these recommendations is going to be, in effect, to require companies to underwrite risks unless they have concrete evidence that would allow them to decline, or would you say that the company would still have the right to refuse to do business with a person without evidence?*

Answer: Absolutely yes! The answer is yes. The one condition is that if we all do it in the extreme and society does not like the way we are treating them, they will institute a process of correction. I fondly hope that all the recommendations get adopted but one, and that is the first one. All I was supporting in that first recommendation, about setting up a mechanism, is that every one of us lives by public policy. We have antidiscrimination statutes, and we all live by them. That is the way that our government and our processes ought to develop do's and don'ts, not by second-guessing individual decisions or setting up proscriptions or relevancy tests in a vacuum. Let the process be opened up and, then, if society finds it offensive and changes the rules of the game for the future, we all will learn to live with them, just as we have learned to live with those very few areas in which society has proscribed our freedom of action up to now. With respect to a particular case, you do not have to have any reason. You can say, "I don't have any reason, but I don't want to do business with you." That meets every one of these tests here.

Whether society will let you continue to do that over time is another kind of a question, but my suspicion is that it will. This is a competitive business. You are not the only game in town. If you do not offend people and stigmatize them by your actions, why should people want to do business with somebody who does not want to do business with them? I think we are seeing a ghost in this area, unless the practice is far more widespread than I believe it is, in which case you may have some political pressure to change your ways.

Question: *Realistically, no one would accept a company's statement that "We don't want to do business with you for no reason at all." There must be a reason that can be indicated rather than saying, "We suspect there are external activities that we can't prove."*

Answer: I am not sure you have to give them a reason if you do not know whether it is true or not. If you have a reason, then I think openness and fairness require you to tell them. If you have a suspicion of a reason, I would put it in that context: "I'm not quite sure why, but I just don't want to do it."

Question: *Many of the recommendations exclude information in preparation of claims settlement or investigation of criminal or civil acts. However, Recommendation 2 about pretext interviews seems to include investigation of claims. It is difficult to prove fraud. Do you believe that a liberal interpretation of a pretext interview will take away some of the information sources that we presently have in investigating claims? Mainly surveillance items and such as this that could be construed as a possible pretext.*

Answer: I think we defined pretext more precisely than we did almost anything else. What it says, really, is that there are certain things that you cannot do. Everything else you can. For example, you do not have to disclose voluntarily the purpose of your inquiry. But if asked, you cannot lie. I think if you look at those words closely, you will find that in this case we really tried to pin down exactly what we meant. The reason is that we made this a criminal offense, therefore we were not casual in our definition. We originally had thought of exempting the claim area in this regard too, and, on further reflection, we said this is kind of a dirty practice and in our judgment no cause was such that this ought to be permitted.

Question: *In terms of implementation and without revealing any secrets, would you comment on the areas of the report where you would wait for specific legislation before moving to voluntary compliance?*

Answer: Yes, those in which there are penalties, such as the declination area, principally, in certain instances. The concern would be that, if you decline somebody for life insurance on the basis of erroneous information that you did not know was erroneous and that person dies, do you have liability for the requested policy limit? Without legislation, that is a very fuzzy area, and in our minds the legislation clarifies that question, or the recommendation does, and we would wait in that kind of an area. There are three or four recommendations, or parts of three or four of them, that we will not implement without legislation. If you look at them, it is the area of exposure for an innocent mistake.

Question: *In examining a report of this nature, you have to examine it for the immediate livability, but you also have to be concerned about what might happen to the implementation later on. There is a concrete example in this proposal that goes directly to the heart of the concern about what the initial program may be expanded to do and thereby become unlivable. Recommendations 2, 3, 9, 11, and 13 already propose an expansion of the Fair Credit Reporting Act. Now, most of the arguments that were made to protect against an overzealousness in amending the Fair Credit Reporting Act will have been discarded, and much of the enthusiasm for these arguments (for its being too strenuous) has been exhausted. But now we come in somewhat through a back door of other proposals and strengthen those (and I am not debating whether they are proper or improper) without maybe giving the existing Act the attention that it ought to have in an area and in ways that probably would not have been approved initially, and in some cases were not approved initially.*

Answer: I think two issues are involved here. One: did the Commission exhaust the options and really consider them, or will we find two years from now that we left something out that somebody will consider important? That is a real-life possibility. We obviously did not knowingly do so, but I suspect being seven common people, even with a fine staff, something probably got lost in the shuffle. Concerning the suggested amendments to the Fair Credit Reporting Act and thinking about what we did, the problems we identified were obviously poor drafting kinds of things. Number one, when Equifax does something, it is subject to the Fair Credit Reporting Act. When Aetna does the same thing on its own behalf, we are not subject to it. That is irrational and inconsistent, and I am surprised Equifax has not proposed that amendment a long time ago. So we blanketed in those. We were dealing with practices and procedures rather than with types of organizations. That is one of the amendments. With the other couple of amendments, as Ron Plesser says, we are closing the loopholes. For example, somebody comes to an underwriter and says, "Why did you decline me?" And he says, "I did it on the basis of an investigative report, and here is the name of the organization. Go to them." The individual looks at the report and sees something that is wrong or he believes to be wrong or misstated, or doesn't find anything wrong, and he asks that agency, "Why was I declined?" They say, "I don't know. That's the insurance company's decision." He's chased back, and the insurance company still will not tell him, because it has satisfied its obligation under the FCRA. That is obviously an unintended process. If the purpose was to clean up "bad" information and let people understand, then the present practice does not work. We fixed that.

I think if you look at each one of those recommendations and if you agree with our intent and purpose, then you will see that all we were doing was fixing up inadequacies in the FCRA.

I am sure there are inadequacies in our recommendations. Somebody has suggested that insurance companies give the reasons, and, then, if the individual wants the facts, give them too. That is a perfectly logical modification, and I would not be offended by a very strong effort to make that a two-step process. There is another little goof in the recommendations. We require, as part of the notice, that you spell out the ability to correct. Why tell everybody that they have a right of access and all the details of their correction-right procedures? Why not tell them they have a right of access, and if they exercise that right, then tell them their right of corrections? Simplify the process that way. There is refinement here that I think it totally logical and rational. As I said, maybe we have overlooked something. This is an evolving concept.

Question: *On the other side and in all fairness, I have to say they could have been much worse.*

Answer: I honestly have to say that I think a bad reason for supporting these recommendations is the fear of something worse. That is a negative view and potentially may be true. I think the evaluation of these recommendations in the first instance has to be done on the basis of whether or not you think the costs involved—and there are costs—are worth it from the standpoint of fairness (which is tough to criticize since openness, whether we like it or not, is going to be demanded by society) and whether or not you think we have done a reasonably balanced job. If you think we have, then I would hope you would support the recommendations. If you think we have not, then I would expect you to oppose them.

Question: *One thing you mentioned that you people seem dissatisfied with is that business about plodding back and forth between the insurance company and the organization that furnished the information. I have always taken the position of the underwriters. I can show you the information, but I cannot do anything to correct it.*

Answer: That is right, and we clearly said that the responsibility for correcting erroneous information was on the gatherer not the user.

Comment: *Right. So we will show it to you, but we will send you back to the organization that supplied us with the information.*

Answer: Right, but at that point, the individual knows the consequences of correcting a mistake. It either is not going to make any difference to you, or it is. Second, he also now knows that information going to others will be correct. If he does not correct it, that is his decision.

Question: *What responsibility does the insurer have in the correction process?*

Answer: All you have a responsibility to do is either try to correct your records or file his statement of disagreement. You have no responsibility to be sure that everybody else does the same. The provider of that information has that responsibility. I think the reason the investigative agencies have this restriction on them is that very reason. They accept the responsibility for the accuracy of their own information, and for you to correct it and not involve them may help you but it does not help them. They are ultimately accountable. We fixed that accountability, recognized it, and set up a mechanism whereby they could fix it for themselves.

Question: *A procedural question. How do you see the role of the Commission from now on? You have sort of given the impression that the Commission is going to self-destruct now that the report is out.*

Answer: The Commission has self-destructed. The participation of individual members of the Commission in the evolving process—in meetings like this or in the legislative process—is totally up to each individual. I can only say for myself, having spent sixty days in the last two years, that I am not going to walk away from it totally. I will do my share to be certain that those who I think are influence-makers understand the rationale of what we were about and the specifics of our recommendations. I do not plan on testifying when the banking industry recommendations get before a committee of Congress, but I sure expect to be involved with respect to the insurance recommendations. I have gone back to my old job, in effect.

Question: *I was wondering about Congressman Koch. He has suddenly decided to go a different way. He is out of the picture.*

Answer: My sense of the Congress is—and I get this from a number of sources—that there are a lot of people in favor of these recommendations, but there is nobody out there championing them yet. In order for something to happen, you have to find a congressperson (or three or four) and a senator or two to really kind of take up this crusade. Barry Goldwater may remain one of those people on the House side. The particular combination of senators has not yet been identified on the Senate side. Koch and Goldwater were identified with this issue by their prior submission of bills and by their presence on this Commission. This is going to be a cause for somebody other than them. They kind of preempted the ground. I suspect somebody will come along and fill half of a vacuum that has been created by Ed Koch, who is in his successful candidacy to be mayor of New York City.

4

The Privacy Protection Study Commission Report and the Insurance Industry: Some Reflections

Francis M. Gregory, Jr.

> The insurance industry is highly dependent upon recorded information about individuals. This dependence creates a number of privacy protection problems, some of which are inherent in the insurance system, but can be controlled, and some of which present real or potential abuses that need to be eliminated.[1]

The preceding quotation from the Report of the Federal Privacy Protection Study Commission (PPSC) concisely summarizes its basic finding with respect to insurance companies and privacy. (The use of the term "privacy" here generally refers to "informational privacy" or, more appropriately, "fair information practices." This concept of informational privacy is concerned with the control or regulation of practices pertaining to the collection, use, maintenance, and dissemination of personally identifiable information.)

The PPSC was created by Congress as part of the Privacy Act of 1974, which regulates federal agency information practices, to study the information practices of private businesses and state and local governments

---

Francis M. Gregory, Jr., a partner in the Washington office of Sutherland, Asbill and Brennan, is a frequent author and lecturer on issues affecting insurance companies. A member of the District of Columbia Bar and the American Law Institute, Mr. Gregory served as Law Clark to Carl McGowan, U.S. Court of Appeals for the District of Columbia Circuit (1966) and to William J. Brennan, Jr., U.S. Supreme Court (1967). He received his J.D. degree from Notre Dame Law School.

and to recommend whether or not there should be additional legislation to control the practices of such organizations. (The history and background of the PPSC are discussed in more detail in a subsequent section of this paper.) This paper has a threefold purpose:

1. To summarize the PPSC insurance recommendations. (There are 17 specific recommendations pertaining to the insurance industry. Other PPSC recommendations, not discussed herein due to limitations of time and space, related to medical records and employment and personnel record practices will be of substantial interest to the insurance industry and should be examined carefully. Still other PPSC recommendations of general application propose the creation of some form of independent federal entity, which may be a Federal Privacy Board or other unit in addition to the Federal Trade Commission.[2] This board or entity, to which Congress may well grant rule-making powers, would monitor privacy issues and could initiate proceedings related to privacy in other agencies. The PPSC also recommends the establishment of substantial rights for individuals to sue for civil damages and to obtain attorney's fees.)

2. To analyze briefly some of their potential effects on the industry.

3. To consider various levels of responses to the PPSC recommendations and related legislative proposals.

To understand better the significance of the PPSC Report and the relationship of its insurance recommendations to its overall scheme for a national information policy, it is helpful to reflect briefly on the history of the PPSC first.

Background of the PPSC

The PPSC was established by the Federal Privacy Act of 1974 (P.L. 93-579) and was charged with the general task of making a "study of the data banks, automatic data processing programs, and information systems of governmental, regional, and private organizations, in order to determine the standards and procedures in force for the protection of personal information." (The Privacy Act of 1974 established numerous so-called fair information practices to regulate the collection, maintenance, use, and dissemination of personally identifiable information maintained by federal agencies, and to a limited extent by certain federal agencies and certain federal governmental contractors. During the legislative debate on the Privacy Act, many congressmen wanted to include the private sector in its coverage. However, it ultimately was concluded that the legislative record did not document adequately the record-keeping practices of such organizations or the effects of extending the bill's coverage to these private companies. Therefore, a compromise position was adopted to create the PPSC to study private firms' practices and to recommend what legislation, if any, was needed.) The Commission then was required to recommend to the President and Congress the extent, if any, to which the requirements and principles of the Privacy Act of 1974 should be applied to such organizations and to make such other legislative recommendations that it determined were necessary to protect individual privacy while meeting the legitimate information needs of government and society.

The PPSC undertook to fulfill this mandate over a period of 2 years, by conducting 60 days of hearings and receiving testimony from over 300 persons.[3] Its final Report and recommendations address a number of specific areas in addition to insurance, including, for example, consumer credit, the depository relationship, mailing lists, employment record-keeping practices, medical records, and the use of the social security number.

In general, the PPSC concluded that we live in an "information society," with little option for avoiding relationships with record-keeping organizations. In its opinion, records increasingly are replacing face-to-face contact and today *mediate* relationships between organizations and individuals. Moreover, the PPSC concluded that there is an "overwhelming imbalance against the individual in the record-keeping relationship between an individual and an organization."[4] It found that there are five systemic features of personal data record-keeping in America:

> First, while an organization makes and keeps records about individuals to facilitate relationships with them, it also makes and keeps records about individuals for other purposes, such as documenting the record-keeping organization's own actions and making it possible for other organizations—government agencies, for example—to monitor the actions of individuals.
>
> Second, there is an accelerating trend, most obvious in the credit and financial areas, toward accumulation in records of more and more personal details about an individual.
>
> Third, more and more records about an individual are collected, maintained and disclosed by organizations with which the individual has no direct relationship but whose records help shape his life.
>
> Fourth, most record-keeping organizations consult the records of other organizations to verify the information they obtained from an individual and thus pay as much or more attention to what other organizations report about him than they pay to what he reports about himself; and
>
> Fifth, neither law nor technology now gives an individual the tools he needs to protect his legitimate interests in the records organizations keep about him.[5]

To deal with what it considered the problems these "systemic" features of American record-keeping create, the PPSC calls for a national information policy guided by three objectives: to minimize intrusiveness; to maximize fairness; and to create legitimate, enforceable expectations of confidentiality.[6]

Another significant finding by the PPSC, which permeates many of its recommendations, deals with the need to regulate problems that have not been shown to exist currently:

> As information in systems is used more and more to take preemptive action against individuals, institutional record-keeping policies and practices must become preventive rather than curative. Emerging information system capabilities and uses are making irrelevant the FCRA approach of rectifying errors made on the basis of inaccurate information after the "adverse decision" has been made.[7]

This preventive approach to the privacy issue requires substantial emphasis at this point. A basic theme found throughout the Report is that "potential" problems must be dealt with. Theoretical difficulties are raised, and preventive measures are recommended, embodying theoretical solutions to these perceived difficulties. Once the theoretical validity of this approach is accepted, anyone who objects to what is perceived as unreasonable legislation is placed in the position of negating a future hypothetical event—hardly a pleasing prospect from a tactical point of view.

The PPSC also identified the following competing societal values, which must be taken into account in formulating a national information policy: e.g., First Amendment interests; freedom of information interests; the societal interest in law enforcement; cost; and federal-state relations.[8]

Ultimately, the PPSC proposed 162 recommendations to control the collection, use, maintenance, and dissemination of information by various organizations. It suggested that these recommendations be implemented through a combination of federal and state laws and voluntary actions consistent with the principles that incentives for systemic reforms should be created; that existing regulatory and enforcement mechanisms should be used insofar as possible; and that unnecessary costs should be avoided. (A determination of whether or not costs are "unnecessary" often calls for difficult value judgments that are debated hotly.)

The preceding brief overview of the PPSC's history, objectives, and guiding principles demonstrates that the PPSC was given a tremendous task and was motivated by high purposes. Most people will agree readily with such PPSC goals as fairness, minimal intrusiveness, and confidentiality, but reasonable men, upon careful study and reflection, in a number of cases may reach far different conclusions as to whether or not particular problems exist, what new procedures should be established to deal with them, and what cost is acceptable for their solution.

Major PPSC Recommendations
Pertaining to the Insurance Industry

Many of the recommendations of the PPSC Report in the section entitled "The Insurance Relationship" are directed *specifically* at the business practices of both the insurance industry and insurance-support organizations,[9] such as consumer-reporting agencies, the Medical Information Bureau, and the various claims indexes. (Although many of the PPSC recommendations discussed in this paper would apply equally to insurance-support organizations, this discussion will focus primarily on the proposals as they relate specifically to insurance companies.) The thrust of the PPSC must be contrasted with the federal Fair Credit Reporting Act (FCRA), which in effect regulates insurance underwriting *indirectly* by imposing numerous restrictions on the ability of consumer-reporting agencies to furnish information for differential underwriting to insurance company customers. Because of the work of the PPSC, the legislative focus now is on *direct* regulation of the information practices of insurance companies, particularly with respect to underwriting and claims.

For ease of analysis, one can view the PPSC recommendations relating specifically to the insurance industry as falling within three general areas of information practice: access to and correction of information; collection and use of information; and requirements of confidentiality against disclosure of information to third parties. These categories will be considered seriatim.

I. Access to and Correction of Information

A. Statutory Access Rights: Four of the PPSC's recommendations propose that federal law require insurance companies to establish mandatory access and correction procedures. Insurance policy recommendation 10 proposes that the FCRA be amended to require an insurance company to inform "any individual" upon request whether it has "any recorded information pertaining to him" in its files, and to give the individual a right to see the information and at his discretion to secure a copy of the information, either in person or by mail, or at his option to be told the nature and substance of the information by telephone.[10] The disclosing organization could charge a reasonable copying fee, but the PPSC does not propose to allow a charge for the possibly substantial retrieval cost of finding the data requested.

This recommendation is supplemented, and to some extent duplicated, by insurance policy recommendation 13(b), which proposes that the FCRA be amended to require that insurance institutions establish "reasonable procedures" to permit an individual, upon request, to see and copy "all recorded information pertaining to him" used to make an adverse underwriting decision, to the extent that such recorded information continues to exist.[11]

Significantly, the PPSC proposes that companies could *not* protect institutional sources of information, nor could individual sources be protected from disclosure unless they have provided information *on the specific condition* that their identity be kept confidential. Special provisions are suggested for medical-record information, which, although subject to disclosure, could be disclosed through a licensed medical professional designated by the individual.

This access and disclosure procedure could have a great impact on many companies. As drafted, apparently *anyone* could ask a company if it had *any* information pertaining to him, and the company would be forced to search its various files to determine if it had any such information, so long as the individual reasonably described the nature of the information.[12] In many instances, it could be very difficult under current manual or EDP file procedures for a company to comply, since information frequently is scattered through various company and agents' offices and often is not indexed for easy retrieval.

Increased mandatory disclosure of institutional and individual sources of information logically will "dry up" underwriting information. Sources understandably are reluctant to expose themselves to harassment or possible lawsuits. Similarly, one wonders whether physicians, many of whom already are preoccupied by malpractice considerations, will be willing to provide full and candid medical information if their medical opinions can be released easily to the patient through another physician.

Although the proposed disclosure of information by mail often would be convenient to the consumer, it could be burdensome and costly, particularly to smaller companies. Many consumers may ask whether or not increased costs are worth the additional benefits. It also should be remembered that consumers may find that mail disclosure results in invasions of their privacy, since letters containing very sensitive information might be misdirected or opened by business associates or family members.

Additional costs can be expected from lawsuits. Consumers could sue to compel disclosure, and the PPSC suggests in the narrative text accompanying the recommendations that systematic denials of access by insurance companies could be addressed by FTC enforcement, or alternatively by state insurance commissioners, if states enacted amendments to the unfair trade practices sections of their insurance laws.[13] Although the PPSC seeks to limit the number of consumer lawsuits by suggesting a qualified privilege as to information disclosed under these recommendations, which generally would impose liability only for false information furnished to third parties with malice or willful intent to injure the individual,[14] the effectiveness of such an immunity provision, or indeed whether any legislature would ever adopt it, is open to serious question.

It is significant also to note that the narrative text suggests that the disclosure recommendation should not apply to records compiled in "reasonable anticipation" of a civil or criminal action or for use in settling unresolved claims. After a claim is settled, the PPSC recommendations would not apply to any records relating to third-party claimants, except as to portions disseminated or used for purposes unrelated to claims processing.[15]

B. Statutory Correction Procedures: After the individual receives access to data, the PPSC proposes in insurance policy recommendation 11 that the FCRA be amended to mandate detailed procedures to permit the individual to request correction or amendment to his record if the individual believes information is not "accurate, timely or complete."[16] Moreover, it would require an insurance company to delete from its files information that was not within the scope of data which the individual originally was advised would be collected about him.

Companies would have to furnish the correction, or fact of deletion, to persons designated by the individual who may have received such information during the preceding two years and automatically furnish such information to support organizations that furnished the information originally, as well as to support organizations, such as the Medical Information Bureau (MIB), whose primary source of information is insurance institutions, if such support organizations systematically had received such information from the company within the past seven years (unless such support organization no longer maintains the information).

If the insurance company refused to correct or amend a record, the PPSC proposal would require the company to so advise the individual and provide the reasons for its refusal. The individual must be allowed to file a statement of dispute, which the company would be required to provide in subsequent disclosures pertaining to the disputed information, as well as to certain past recipients or providers of the disputed information.

In addition to these general correction procedures, insurance policy recommendation 12 suggests a special provision for correction of medical-record information.[17] Upon request, an insurance company would be required to disclose to a consumer, or "medical professional" designated by him, the identity of any medical-care provider who provided the medical-record information. The consumer would be free, of course, to recontact that individual. If the provider agreed that information was inaccurate or incomplete, the insurance company would have to correct the information in its files promptly. If an individual believes medical-record information about him is inaccurate or incomplete, procedures must be established in order that the individual may provide limited supplemental information for inclusion in his file.[18]

The correction procedures proposed by the PPSC are similar to those contained in the FCRA. Although it is eminently reasonable to establish procedures for correction of inaccurate data, because no insurance company wants incorrect information in its files, the question arises whether procedures should be spelled out in detail in statutes or regulations or whether each company can best devise its own process to ensure that its files are accurate. An opportunity for an individual company to tailor its procedures to meet its particular needs would seem to be a far more flexible and less costly way to proceed, yet such flexibility is hardly the touchstone of federal regulation.

Statutory compliance would require revisions in, or preparation of, detailed company procedural manuals, staff training time, and additional personnel to handle disputes. Moreover, the proposed statutory correction process allows challenge if the individual believes a record is not "accurate, timely or complete"—hardly an objective standard. Even if subjective "accuracy" may be determined with minimal difficulty in most instances, companies may expect frequent consumer disagreement over the elusive terms "timely" and "complete."

With limited exceptions, the Report's narrative text proposes that the FCRA be amended to allow consumers to sue to force compliance with the access recommendations. The consumer would be entitled to "reasonable" attorney's fees and other litigation costs "if he substantially prevails." The PPSC also suggests that up to $1,000 in punitive damages would be appropriate for intentional or willful refusal to comply. The Federal Trade Commission (FTC) or, alternatively, state insurance commissioners are proposed as the governmental enforcement authorities.[19]

II. Collection and Use of Personal Information

A. *Controls on Collection of Information*: The largest number of PPSC recommendations relate to the collection and use of information. Insurance policy recommendation 4 states that, in order to maximize fairness, every insurance company should have "reasonable procedures" to assure the "accuracy, completeness and timeliness" of personal information the company collects, maintains, or discloses.[20] The PPSC indicates in the narrative text of the Report that it does not propose that this recommendation be incorporated into a statute. It envisions the recommendation as being implemented automatically as a consequence of its other recommendations.[21] However, the thrust of this recommendation is well known generally to legislators, and the industry should expect proposed legislation to include this provision. It also should be remembered that insurance policy recommendation 11, discussed previously, which would be implemented by amendment to the FCRA, would allow a consumer to challenge information as being inaccurate, untimely, or incomplete. Therefore, the concepts of recommendation 4 would be given statutory force.

Insurance policy recommendation 4 greatly expands FCRA section 607(b), which requires reasonable procedures to ensure accuracy (there is no comparable FCRA requirement with respect to timeliness or completeness), and it could cause substantial compliance problems if implemented by statute. For example, it is likely that the FTC would step in frequently to determine if procedures are "reasonable"; likewise, the FTC staff undoubtedly would put forth their own views as to whether or not information is complete or timely. Consumers, of course, also would be able to argue in lawsuits that they were injured because information was not accurate, timely, or complete.

Company officials, in considering this recommendation, undoubtedly will ask questions, such as, "Is complete information usually needed or even desirable? How often will my company be required to seek additional information or purge old information to meet these requirements?" Given the difficulty of defining the concepts in recommendation 4 by statute, it is quite possible that Congress would allow the FTC to "clarify" the meaning of these terms through detailed regulations. This might remove most of the questions as to what is required for compliance, but such regulations could be quite burdensome and could place substantial additional controls on the underwriting process.

Another PPSC proposal to regulate companies' collection of information is contained in insurance policy recommendation 5, which states that, before collecting any information about a principal insured or applicant from another person, the insurance company should be required to provide the individual applicant with a very detailed prenotice concerning its information practices.[22]

This recommendation is supplemented by insurance policy recommendation 6, which would limit a company's own information and disclosure practices to those specified in the prenotice required by recommendation 5.[23] Moreover, recommendation 6 would require insurance companies to limit their requests to other organizations collecting information on the company's behalf to information, techniques, and sources specified in the disclosure notice. The Report's narrative text states that neither recommendation should apply to information collected for first- or third-party claims purposes or for marketing purposes where the information is collected prior to the initial application.[24] However, the PPSC expressly states that the notice should specify that information may be disclosed to loss indexes and the Insurance Crime Prevention Institute.[25]

The procedures proposed by these two recommendations, without question, limit a company's present ability to obtain information. From both a company and consumer point of view, questions arise as to the practicality of the PPSC's proposals. Because it is not possible always to know the collection techniques that will be utilized before an investigation has begun, or to know in advance many of the other detailed items that must be disclosed, a complex "laundry list" type notice of every conceivable situation probably would be necessary. Based on "truth in lending" and similar disclosure experiences, the conclusion that few consumers will read lengthy disclosures is not unbridled skepticism. Thus it is possible that the proposed disclosure form may be of little practical value to anyone, although it may be cumbersome and expensive to prepare.

Aside from the issue of whether or not the prenotice disclosure would be useful or desired by most consumers, companies may encounter substantial problems in complying with the requirements. The Report text is unclear as to whether or not the PPSC envisions implementation of the prenotice requirement through amendments to the FCRA, state insurance commissioners' actions, or voluntary procedures.[26] In any case, it is virtually certain that some legislators will propose that this requirement be mandated by statute, as was in essence proposed in the 95th Congress in S.1840, the FCRA amendments bill that ultimately was not reported by the Senate Banking Committee. (Assuming the prenotice requirement is enacted into statute, companies undoubtedly would be subject to consumer lawsuits alleging failure to properly disclose and failure to limit collection practices to those described as required by recommendation 6. The main compliance problem, however, might well come from the FTC, which might have authority to challenge the propriety of a company's notices or practices.)

Companies also may experience compliance difficulties due to the requirement that they limit their investigatory requests to support organizations to the information, techniques, and sources specified in the prenotice. If companies are required to particularize their procedures, support organizations may find it difficult to interface their own practices with the unique practices of individual insurance companies.

Insurance policy recommendation 3 calls for the FCRA to be amended to require that insurance companies "exercise reasonable care in the selection and use of insurance support organizations, so as to assure that the collection, maintenance, use and disclosure practices of such organizations comply with the Commission's recommendations."[27] The narrative text indicates that, if an insurance company hired or used a support organization with either actual or constructive knowledge that the support organization engaged in collection practices which did not comply with the PPSC's proposals, an individual or the FTC could sue both the insurance company and the support organization and hold them jointly liable for the support organization's actions.[28]

Property and liability companies appear to have been a special focus of PPSC insurance policy recommendation 14, which would prohibit companies from making any inquiry concerning previous adverse underwriting decisions, or whether an individual obtained insurance through the substandard insurance market, unless the reasons for such underwriting decisions also were requested.[29] In addition, companies would be prohibited from making adverse underwriting decisions "based *in whole or in part, on the mere fact of*" a previous adverse underwriting decision or an individual's having obtained insurance through the substandard (residual) market. Companies, however, could make adverse decisions based on additional information obtained from the same source.[30]

The PPSC noted that, while life insurers often use information pertaining to prior declinations or ratings to find out more about an applicant, "automobile insurers often decline applicants solely on the basis of an affirmative response to the question" (concerning prior declination or rating). The industry will bear the burden of showing that the assumption underlying this recommendation is incorrect and that the proposal is not justified. Companies also will bear the burden of proving in lawsuits that an adverse decision was not based at least "in part, on the mere fact of" prior adverse actions, if they have in their files any information pertaining to such prior actions.

Insurance policy recommendation 7, which the PPSC foresees as being implemented voluntarily, would require insurance companies to specify clearly what personal information was desired to be collected for purposes not directly related to establishing the individual's "eligibility" for an insurance benefit.[31] Despite the PPSC's suggestion that voluntary action would be adequate, companies should recognize that the proposal easily could be made mandatory by statute. Moreover, the proposal is but a modified version of a basic informational privacy concept, which holds that there should be a prohibition against the use of information for any purpose for which it was not originally collected unless the individual gives his express consent. Legislation mandating such a "consent" requirement could limit a company's ability to obtain data for marketing, research, and other legitimate purposes.

Applicants would be given a right pursuant to the FCRA to be interviewed in connection with the preparation of investigative reports if PPSC insurance policy recommendation 9 is adopted.[32] Insurance companies would be required to inform applicants or insureds that they may obtain an interview upon request and, further, would be required to institute "reasonable procedures" to ensure that such interviews, in fact, take place. If a person requesting an interview reasonably could not be contacted, the organization preparing the investigative report would be relieved of the duty to interview if it mailed a copy of the completed report, when prepared, to the individual. The Report narrative text indicates that this interview requirement would apply to underwriting investigations undertaken by insurers themselves, as well as inspection bureaus. However, the PPSC does not intend that it apply to any investigative report made in reasonable anticipation of a civil or criminal action or for use in defending or settling a claim.[33]

This provision, which would be a substantial departure from current FCRA requirements and industry practices, might cause practical implementation problems. For example, a mandatory personal interview procedure would slow down the application process in a number of cases and might result in increased costs and perhaps a loss of sales. Indeed, it is probable that many individuals simply could not be contacted. A policy question arises as to the purpose of mailing the individual a copy of the report if reasonable efforts to contact him are unsuccessful. On balance, if an individual desires disclosure of the contents of a report, it would appear far better public policy—from the viewpoint of accuracy, timeliness, completeness, and consumer understanding—for a knowledgeable official of the reporting agency or insurance company that prepared the report to explain the report to the individual, in person or by telephone.

In an attempt to curtail what the PPSC believed to be unreasonably intrusive techniques to collect information, insurance policy recommendation 2 proposes that insurance companies be prohibited by the FCRA from attempting to obtain information through "pretext interviews" or "false or misleading representations" that seek to conceal the actual purpose of the inquiry or investigator.[34] The Report narrative text states that this prohibition would apply to "all insurance inquiries—whether for underwriting or first- or third-party claims."[35] It also explains that a "pretext interview" is one in which the inquirer: (1) pretends to be someone he is not; (2) pretends to represent someone he does not; or (3) misrepresents the true purpose of the interview.[36] The text further indicates that the FTC would enforce the prohibition and that it should be a civil offense punishable by fine and/or cease and desist orders against conducting such pretext interviews or false or misleading representations. (The FTC has broad discretion in shaping its cease and desist orders.)

Because the terms "false or misleading representations" are not defined, obvious questions of interpretation arise. The industry should expect close FTC scrutiny of company and support organization collection techniques, and must recognize that the FTC would have broad latitude to label collection techniques as being "misleading." Hopefully, these terms, if embodied in statute, would be further defined, but the use of such broad statutory language, especially when used in connection with FTC regulatory authority, is not uncommon.

In addition to compliance problems, the impact of such requirements on insurance claims investigations cannot be minimized. Indirect interviews are used principally in third-party claim investigations, and usually are ordered only when a company has a suspicion that there is something irregular about a claim. Insurance companies have learned through experience that, in a third-party claim situation in which the company is dealing with an adversary claimant (as opposed to its own insured), it is not possible to develop the information needed if the interviewer discloses that insurance is involved. If the person is "speculating" on the claim, has something to cover up, or in plain and simple terms is dishonest, he will not provide the honest response necessary to evaluate his claim fairly if he knows the interview is in connection with that claim. Thus the insurance company that orders a claim report in such circumstances has a legitimate interest (for itself and for its policyholders) in securing vital information. The public obviously benefits from such investigations, since the avoidance of payment of fictitious claims works to hold down premium rates across the board.

B. Limitations on the Use of Information: The PPSC recommendations also propose a number of restrictions on the *use* of personal data after it is collected by an insurance company. For example, one such restriction was discussed previously in the context of companies being prohibited from using adverse underwriting decisions or the fact that an individual obtained insurance in the substandard market as a basis (even in part) for current adverse action, unless the current decision was based on independent information.

A similar PPSC proposal is contained in insurance policy recommendation 15, which states that no insurance company should base an adverse underwriting decision "in whole or in part" on information about an individual that it obtains from a support organization whose primary source of information is insurance institutions or insurance-support organizations; however, companies may base an adverse underwriting decision on further information obtained from the original source, which might be another insurance company.[37]

The narrative text of the Report indicates that this recommendation is based primarily upon the PPSC's finding that in life and health underwriting "there is less than perfect adherence to the industry's own rules regarding the use of information obtained from the Medical Information Bureau."[38] The PPSC suggests that, as with recommendation 14, voluntary compliance with recommendation 15 would be assisted by the exercise of the various statutory rights proposed in the Report and by actions taken by state insurance commissioners pursuant to their unfair trade practices authority.

One of the most significant PPSC proposals affecting the insurance industry is insurance policy recommendation 13,[39] which calls for the FCRA to be amended to require that, whenever the insurance company uses personal information to make an "adverse underwriting decision,"[40] such as rating or rejecting an applicant, a detailed *written disclosure* must be furnished to the consumer giving the *specific* reasons for the adverse decision and the *specific items of information* that support the decision, including the *names and addresses of institutional sources*. Medical-record information could be disclosed either directly to the individual or through a licensed medical professional designated by the individual. This written explanation of adverse action also would have to include notification of the individual's access and challenge rights proposed by the PPSC recommendations, as well as a similar notice of his rights under the FCRA. Insurance companies would have to establish "reasonable procedures" to ensure compliance with this recommendation.

The Report's narrative text explains that individuals would be able to sue companies under the FCRA for failure to perform the required duties, and the courts would order compliance. In addition, the PPSC states that plaintiffs who "substantially prevailed" could be awarded attorney's fees, and if the institution intentionally or willfully violated the individual's rights, the court could award up to $1,000 punitive damages. The narrative text suggests that repeated or systematic denials of individuals' rights could be dealt with by either the FTC or strengthened state insurance laws.[41]

Some company officials may question whether or not the PPSC

proposals for written reasons explaining adverse action are necessary or even desirable in light of current state laws and voluntary industry practices, as well as the requirements already mandated by the FCRA, not to mention the consumer's own knowledge. Even if some additional notice is deemed to be appropriate, underwriting and claims decisions can be sufficiently complex so as to make it exceedingly difficult to identify precisely the "specific reasons" and the "specific items of information" involved in adverse decisions. In any case, establishing procedures for compliance and preparing individual letters detailing this required information could involve substantial additional expense. The FTC and state regulators, of course, must be satisfied with company compliance to avoid litigation. Individual consumers, who must be advised of their rights, still will bring lawsuits, especially if the PPSC's proposal for attorney's fees and punitive damages is adopted.

As most insurance company executives are aware, questions had been raised increasingly over whether or not Congress or state legislatures should impose a "relevancy" standard on information used for underwriting decisions. The relevance issue has been debated extensively during recent attempts in Congress to amend the FCRA. Earlier drafts of the PPSC's Report proposed that there be procedures for individuals to question the relevancy of the information. However, in insurance policy recommendation 1, the final PPSC Report employs the term "propriety" of information, which could be an even more difficult standard to comply with than "relevancy."[42] The PPSC suggests that governmental mechanisms should be available for individuals to question the "propriety" of the collection and use of particular categories of information. The end result of this process, according to the PPSC, might be legislation or administrative regulations prohibiting the collection or use of certain types of information. (The supporting narrative text indicates that the PPSC used the term "propriety" instead of "relevancy" because it felt some inquiries, which "demonstrably are relevant, are objectionable on other grounds.")[43]

The text also suggests that a federal insurance administrator periodically collect the reports filed by state insurance commissioners and transmit them to Congress. Moreover, as an alternate and not mutually exclusive procedure, the federal insurance administrator, or other appropriate federal entity (presumably the FTC), could collect consumer complaints directly and file reports and recommendations with Congress.[44]

It is certain that this PPSC recommendation will be debated extensively in Congress, and it is likely that some congressmen will propose relevancy standards for the insurance industry. With such legislation, it is possible that the FTC, or the federal insurance administrator, over a period of time would be able to use this express reporting function to develop rule-making authority to control in detail what information companies may use in making underwriting, claims, and other decisions. At a minimum, the PPSC recommendation encourages far greater federal scrutiny of the insurance industry.

III. Disclosure Limitations

The final area of the PPSC's insurance recommendations pertains to procedures to ensure confidentiality of data and to limit third-party access to personal information maintained by insurance companies. The PPSC proposes, in insurance policy recommendation 17, that legislation impose a "duty of confidentiality" to prohibit insurance companies and their support organizations from disclosing identifiable personal information without the individual's *explicit authorization*.[45] This proposed new statutory duty of confidentiality would have certain limited exceptions. For example, information could be disclosed from insurance companies to a reinsurer or co-insurer, or to an agent or contractor of the company, or to any other party in interest to the insurance transaction. However, there are a number of *conditions* that must be met before this would be allowed, including that only such information be disclosed as is "necessary" for such other person to perform his function in the transaction. Consumers would have a right to sue to enforce compliance and to obtain actual damages, court costs, and reasonable attorney's fees in cases involving negligent disclosure; in addition, there would be punitive damages with a minimum of $1,000 and a maximum of $10,000 for intentional or willful disclosure. Consumers thus would have adequate incentive to challenge disclosures, even to interested parties, as being "unnecessary." (The PPSC's overall privacy proposals, if fully implemented, also could limit a company's ability to obtain necessary underwriting and claims information from institutional sources, since other PPSC recommendations apply similar duties of confidentiality to other data, such as credit and depository information.)

A related PPSC proposal in the area of disclosure would provide that "express authorization" be secured *before* information may be disclosed. Insurance policy recommendation 8 details what should be in this written authorization.[46] Among other things, it would require a written, dated authorization "in plain language," which must: specify persons to whom the consumer authorized disclosure; specify the nature of the information authorized to be disclosed; specify to the extent possible who would be authorized to make a disclosure; specify the purposes for which the information could be used at the time of disclosure and subsequently; and provide a definite expiration date for the authorization, not to exceed one year or, in the case of life insurance or noncancellable or guaranteed renewal health insurance, two years from the date of the policy.

In the PPSC's view, the requirements of this recommendation "are not as severe as they may seem."[47] The supporting narrative text proposes that recommendation 8 be implemented through the refusal of a holder of confidential information to release it unless presented with a valid authorization. In addition, the PPSC notes that it has been suggested that the National Association of Insurance Commissioners or the Commission on Uniform State Laws might well develop standard authorization forms to provide desired uniformity.[48]

While the PPSC's proposed authorization would have the greatest impact on the current practices of life and health companies, it also would require changes in property and casualty companies' procedures, since all insurance companies to some extent must secure authorizations to obtain information. The degree of burden could be increased substantially if, as is quite foreseeable, the authorization requirement is made statutory, particularly if the FTC were given authority to oversee the content of the authorization.

Insurance policy recommendation 16 calls for a federal statute to provide that no insurance institution or insurance-support organization may disclose to another insurance institution or support organization information pertaining to "an individual's medical history, diagnosis, condition, treatment, or evaluation, even with the explicit authorization of the individual, unless the information was obtained from a medical-care provider, the individual himself, his spouse, parent or guardian."[49]

The Report narrative text suggests that this recommendation is based upon not only life insurance companies' disclosures to industry data exchanges, such as MIB, but also because of property and casualty companies' reporting on claimants to the loss indexes.[50] The PPSC considers "health status information" unreliable, and notes that it "believes that the responsibility for the content of records maintained by industry data exchanges properly is placed on the reporting insurance institutions, since it is they who control the record-keeping policies of the data exchanges."[51] The text suggests that this recommendation be implemented in connection with recommendation 17's duty of confidentiality.[52]

PPSC insurance recommendation 16, as drafted, would appear to cover health information such as the fact that an individual has a cast on his arm, or, more importantly, for claims purposes, that the individual appears to function without any medical or physical impairment. The recommendation also would appear to prohibit disclosure, for example, by a support organization to the insurance company that a nonmedical source indicates that the individual uses drugs. Obviously, there are a number of types of health information that may be highly relevant and necessary for underwriting and claims purposes, and that might not be known or disclosed by a medical professional, the individual, his parent, spouse, or guardian. Yet the PPSC recommendation disregards this fact and would deny companies access to such health information.

Outlook

The PPSC is no more. Its Report is now history, and the future political process will determine whether or not and to what extent the PPSC's recommendations become law and in what form. During upcoming legislative sessions, Congress and state legislatures, after careful review of the stated views of the respective executive branches, may conclude that even more onerous controls than those urged by the PPSC are needed. On the other hand, legislators ultimately might determine that it would be inappropriate to apply most such concepts to the insurance industry by statute because they are unnecessarily burdensome or too costly.

Insurance companies would be well advised to shift their primary privacy focus from the PPSC to specific federal and state bills that incorporate informational privacy concepts, including those put forth by the PPSC. However, this does not mean that companies should not study this recent piece of history—they *must* know the Report's recommendations and their potential impact when the insurance industry is "tested" on it by legislators.

1. Privacy Protection Study Commission, *Personal Privacy in an Information Society* (Washington, D.C., U.S. Government Printing Office, 1977), p. 173.

2. Ibid., p. 37.

3. Ibid., p. xvi.

4. Ibid., p. 30.

5. Ibid., p. 8.

6. Ibid., p. 14.

7. Ibid., pp. 70-71.

8. Ibid., p. 21.

9. An insurance-support organization is defined by the PPSC as "an organization which regularly engages in whole or in part in the practice of assembling or evaluating information on individuals for the purpose of providing such information or evaluation to insurance institutions for insurance purposes." Ibid., p. 221.

10. Ibid., pp. 200-201.

11. Ibid., p. 209.

12. Ibid., p. 201.

13. Ibid., pp. 202-203.

14. Ibid., pp. 203-204.

15. Ibid., p. 202.

16. Ibid., pp. 204 and 205.

17. Ibid., p. 206.

18. The Report narrative text states that, in general, the same protection described previously in connection with recommendation 10 for claim information should apply to recommendations 11 and 12. Ibid., p. 192.

19. Ibid., p. 108.

20. Ibid., p. 192.

21. Ibid.

22. Ibid., p. 193. The narrative text expressly states that the notice as to "each area of inquiry" when information regarding character, general reputation, or mode of living is to be collected from a third party "anticipates a level of specificity finer than currently considered acceptable under the Fair Credit Reporting Act." Ibid., p. 194.

23. Ibid., p. 195.

24. Ibid., pp. 193, 195.

25. Ibid., p. 194.

26. Ibid.

27. Ibid., p. 191.

28. Ibid.

29. Ibid., pp. 211-212.

30. Ibid.

31. Ibid., pp. 195-196.

32. Ibid., p. 199.

33. Ibid.

34. Ibid., p. 190.

35. Ibid.

36. Ibid.

37. Ibid., pp. 212-213.

38. Ibid., p. 212.

39. Ibid., p. 209.

40. The Commission in the Report narrative text at p. 210 defines "adverse underwriting decision" as: "With respect to life and health insurance, a denial of requested insurance coverage (except claims) in whole or in part and/or an offer to insure at other than standard rates; and with respect to all other kinds of insurance, a denial of requested insurance coverage (except claims) in whole or in part, or a rating which is based on information which differs from that which the individual furnished; or

"—a refusal to renew coverage in whole or in part; or

"—a cancellation of any insurance coverage in whole or in part."

41. Ibid., pp. 210-211.

42. Ibid., pp. 188-189.

43. Ibid., p. 186.

44. Ibid., p. 189.

45. Ibid., pp. 215-217.

46. Ibid., pp. 196-197.

47. Ibid., p. 198.

48. Ibid.

49. Ibid., p. 214.

50. Ibid., p. 213.

51. Ibid.

52. Ibid., p. 214.

5

Privacy, the Insurance Industry, and the Consumer: A Critical View

Robert Ellis Smith

I understand that some members of the insurance industry feel that the concern about privacy is artificial, that there has been no documentation of abuses in the industry. I have abuses come to my attention regularly in the course of publishing a monthly newsletter on the right to privacy, and one of the leading areas of citizen complaints is what I shall call the insurance/health reporting/credit investigating complex. One way for me to demonstrate one consumer's experience is to talk, quite simply, about my own. This is a chronology of my experience with the Medical Information Bureau.

Medical Information Bureau

The Medical Information Bureau (MIB) stores computer records on the health history and insurance claims of 11 million Americans and makes

Robert Ellis Smith is the publisher of the *Privacy Journal* and an attorney in Washington, D.C. He has been involved in many activities surrounding the privacy issue, including serving as Associate Director, ACLU Project on Privacy and Data Collection and as Assistant Director for Public Affairs, U.S. Department of Health, Education and Welfare, Office for Civil Rights. After serving as a consultant to the National Advisory Commission on Civil Disorders on news media coverage of race riots, he became a reporter and syndicate editor for *Newsday*. He is a member of the National Association of Insurance Commissioners advisory committee on privacy. Mr. Smith received his bachelor's degree from Harvard College and his law degree from Georgetown University Law Center.

them instantly available to 700 member insurance companies in the United States and Canada. An MIB code that indicates medical or other problems is supposed to alert the insurance company to check again before accepting an individual as a risk. Testimony before the Privacy Protection Study Commission shows that the MIB scheme often does not work that way; insurance companies flatly reject applicants with particular MIB codes. The MIB says that it is not subject to the Fair Credit Reporting Act, which requires firms to tell you what is in your record, destroy adverse information after seven years, use data only for stated purposes, and reinvestigate information about you that you challenge. The MIB states that it voluntarily complies with the Act provisions with regard to individual access. Its address is P.O. Box 105, Essex Station, Boston, Massachusetts 02112 (617/426-3660).

April 1975—Robert Smith writes to MIB.

May 2, 1975—MIB responds, "In order that we may proceed further, I ask that you complete the enclosed Form D-2," which includes this statement: "I understand MIB will require reporting member companies to disclose any medical information in my MIB record to my personal physician." It further requires the requestor to sign this statement: "Except as to false information furnished with malice or willful intent to injure and except as to liability for willful noncompliance or for negligent noncompliance as in the Federal Fair Credit Reporting Act (FCRA), I release MIB and its members and any person who furnished information to MIB or its members from any claims or suits based on any information disclosed as a result of this request."

May 31, 1975—Smith returns the request, without the release.

June 11, 1975—MIB rejects the response, saying that, because consumer-reporting agencies enjoy immunity from privacy lawsuits under FCRA, MIB would be "in a legal disadvantage compared with true 'consumer reporting agencies'" if it too did not have such immunity.

June 27, 1975—Smith agrees to the release, if MIB agrees to comply with all provisions of the FCRA.

July 18, 1975—MIB's associate counsel responds, "On the behalf of this release I am instructing Mr. Jones to arrange for disclosure of your MIB record, if any." Member insurance companies may disclose if they choose to.

July 23, 1975—Robert Jones of MIB's information office writes, "Your letter of June 27 . . . indicates that you continue to object to execute the General Release. MIB cannot release medical information to your personal physician without having the protection afforded by the release."

June 18, 1976—Smith to MIB: "In a letter dated July 18, 1975, you said that Mr. Jones of MIB had been instructed to arrange for disclosure of my MIB record to me. Mr. Jones wrote to me five days later revoking that promise and to date neither I nor my physician have received anything. I want to know whether my wife has an MIB file. You provide this information promptly to third parties (according to MIB's own testimony before the Privacy Commission), and so at least you can provide the same to me. Next, I ask for a copy of any MIB information on me or my wife, disclosed either to us or to our physicians." Smith signs the "release" language again.

June 29, 1976—MIB responds, "We checked our records and found that on July 23, 1975, the MIB, coincidentally with a letter to you, wrote to your insurance company advising the medical director that he could elect to disclose. On July 28, he did write to your doctor disclosing the medical information it had reported to MIB. I can only suggest that you contact your doctor."

The Fair Credit Reporting Act requires that medical information be turned over to your physician, not to you. I think that is valid with regard to medical records in the doctor's offices or hospital offices, in which there is some sensitive information, either psychiatric or with regard to certain physical ailments that might be harmful to the individual. I do not believe that is true for MIB records. What they have, if I understand it correctly, are codes about claims I have filed and my general medical history. None of it in there is of the sensitivity that led Congress to say that medical information ought to go to a physician not to the individual.

July 1976—Smith's doctor says by telephone that he has received nothing from MIB or the insurance company.

August 1976—Smith receives new life insurance policy after deleting from application the authorization for MIB to receive medical information. (MIB had testified before the Privacy Commission on May 21, 1976 that it gets the information anyway.)

February 1977—MIB writes to *Newsweek* writer who had quoted Smith as saying that it is impossible to get access to your own file at organizations such as MIB, even though insurance companies get instant computer access. Not true, says MIB, we gave Smith his file a year ago.

February 11, 1977—Smith renews his request.

February 24, 1977—"I can only suppose something went wrong in the past," responds MIB's counsel. "I have therefore sent your doctor a copy of the insurance company medical director's letter of July 28, 1975. You might, therefore, contact him shortly." MIB insists it complied back in 1975.

May 4, 1977—"I have in my possession no evidence that the MIB sent me any information on you," writes the doctor. His office confirms this in telephone calls.

June 6, 1977—"Frankly, I cannot understand your doctor's statement," writes MIB's counsel, enclosing a copy of his original letter to the doctor and a certified receipt. "You might ask the doctor to recheck his files."

June 10, 1977—Smith's doctor reiterates his denial; Smith telephones MIB counsel William Swartz, "There can't be any sensitive medical information in your files that would hurt me if you told me directly. Can't you help me out?" Swartz' reply, "Sorry, that's our policy." There is nothing in the Fair Credit Reporting Act that prohibits a consumer-investigating company from disclosing medical information to the individual, if I am correct. That is simply a discretionary thing.

Well, that is one example. Another would be when I changed insurance policies a couple of years ago. This was right in the middle of my paper war with the MIB, and so I did not agree that my insurance company could send information about me to the MIB. I simply crossed that out of the insurance application. The insurance agent was shocked, and he did not want this hassle. He just wanted to get all the paperwork signed on the dotted line. But I think for consumers the insurance agent may be the best source of help, simply because he is anxious to sell the policy. And in the end that is what happened. I got plenty of calls from him saying, "No, the company won't accept it unless you sign that waiver," but eventually I did receive the insurance coverage without having to sign the waiver to give information to the Medical Information Bureau. Now all of that was just a paper exercise, because the Medical Information Bureau testified in answer to questions from Ron Plesser. Ron asked them a year ago at their hearings in Washington, "What happens if an individual doesn't choose to give the insurance company permission to send information to the Medical Information Bureau?" And the response was, roughly, "Well, we want them to report it anyway. We really wish they would and we expect them to."

Reading between the lines, the response was, "Whether or not we get the consent of the individual, the insurance company should report the information to the Medical Information Bureau." I do not think that is fair to the consumer. I think that the language that we all receive now in our insurance applications really does not tell the whole story. It does not tell you that you must sign a waiver, that you must take a whole lot of time out of your life to get information, and it does not say that, if you choose not to have information sent to the Medical Information Bureau, it will be sent anyway.

Equifax, Inc.

I am one of those individuals who believes that laws on the books mean what they say and are meant to be used. And so, last spring I went to the Equifax, Inc. office in McLean, Virginia to see my consumer-investigative file. And my experience was pretty good. I found no red tape, no great hassle. I just went out to McLean, Virginia and took a look at it. Equifax, as most of you know, is the dominant company in this industry, reporting on several million individuals yearly who apply for insurance coverage, insurance claims, or employment. In this work Equifax does not collect objective information about an individual's credit history and ability to pay bills (although recently it has bought up many of the companies that do that reporting—credit bureaus). Credit investigators, by contrast, report on life-styles and habits, and their main sources of information are neighbors. I was surprised, for instance, to see that Equifax used two neighbors as sources for estimating my yearly salary. I suggest that they are the worst possible sources for sensitive information of that sort. One part of the report described me as self-employed (accurate), and another part said I was not.

Consumer-investigative companies, as you know, have been required since 1971 to reveal the nature and substance of an individual's report to that individual and to reinvestigate and correct the file if necessary. Since 1976, Equifax, as a matter of company policy, has provided the individual with a copy of his file, although the law does not require this.

This process seems to work in an orderly way, if my experience is a guide. Equifax has discovered that consumers are not breaking down the doors to see their files in unmanageable numbers. What consumers want, I feel, is the assurance that they have the right to see their own record if the need arises. They want assurances that record-keeping will be improved accordingly. They do not necessarily want to see their files in every instance.

Nor will individuals want to see all of the records about them in a single organization. There have been few abuses in records about stockholders, for instance, and so you would not expect there to be a great demand in this area if federal law were to require a company to reveal to an individual any of the personal information it keeps on him. Experience under the Privacy Act of 1974, which requires individual access to federal files, has shown that citizens—not surprisingly—have concentrated their interests in three agencies: the Department of Treasury, which houses the Internal Revenue Service; the Department of Health, Education, and Welfare, which houses the Social Security Administration; and the Department of Justice, which houses the Federal Bureau of Investigation.

Companies concerned about federal privacy legislation can now draw on this experience, on the six-year experience of companies regulated by the Fair Credit Reporting Act and on the three-year experience of universities and colleges, which are subject to the so-called Buckley Amendment. These different experiences with federal privacy requirements have taken the guess-work out of assessing the cost of privacy.

I come from Washington, so I should give you a little legislative update, I guess, as to what is going on there. I do not think a whole lot is going to happen in this session, so I have not devoted most of my remarks to that. I think that there will be legislation before long bringing the Medical Information Bureau under the Fair Credit Reporting Act. I would imagine that the Act would be amended to require that the companies give a copy of the record to the individual, although Equifax's activity may well have deterred that particular move, and I would think that the taking of medical information by pretext or some other means might well be made a federal crime. I think there is a move in that direction, and the Privacy Commission has asked for reforms along those lines. I think we will see, outside of the insurance industry now, some legislation, maybe in the next year or two, that would require outsiders to go through a legal process in order to get bank records. As you may know, now, except for the Internal Revenue Service, outsiders do not have to go through any legal process to get your bank records. They can simply have a working relationship with the bank or pay the right amount or get to the right employee. And you probably are aware that federal law requires banks to copy the front and back of each one of your checks and to preserve it for five years on microfilm. So this is a vast library of information about you.

I venture to guess there is very little I could not tell about you by seeing the last five years of your checks, including your physical description, which many times is written down when you cash a check at a strange place. It is taken off your driver's license. If you are unfortunate to shop in some places, it would have your thumb print, too. And it would tell me what magazines you subscribe to, what doctors you use, what clinics you go to—perhaps from the name of the clinic I could roughly guess why you went there—and it would tell me which relatives you owe money to, which ones owe you money, and roughly what you do with your money.

It would tell me a lot of things too that are not true about you, and that is the danger. It would tell you probably that in my case I spend a lot more money in my liquor store than I really do. I use that as my bank, and many of you probably use other merchants like that, and if someone would look at my bank account and figure that the amount of money that goes through that liquor store is indicative of my consumption, I am in trouble. I say that to talk to those of you who say, "I have nothing to hide." And that is really what a lot of people say, and I do not have much to hide either. But I do not want people putting two and two together and getting five. And that is what would happen in that particular instance and in other instances; they can draw conclusions from factual information about you, and I think we have reached the point now where computer systems in different institutions can get together, put two and two together, and get five. There will be a computer decision made about an individual on perfectly factual and innocuous information that could do damage to him.

Parenthetically, I want to highly recommend an appendix to the Privacy Commission report, called "Technology and Privacy," to those of you who have responsibilities in that area. It does two things and I think awfully well, the best I have seen yet. What is the impact of all these things that I am saying—access to records, etc., correction—what is the impact of that on the design of systems? And secondly, what is the impact of the great increase in computer technology on individual privacy? It tackles both of these problems, and I think it is a very helpful document.

One of the things it says is that the finite nature of computing has really been obviated. Quoting directly, now, they say, "We assume at some point that the amount of information that computer data banks could collect would be finite. And with networking and with textual search and with some of the other technology that is coming along that is no longer true now. The capacity of computer systems to talk to each other has now led to the probability that there is no limit to the amount of information that could be accessed by one system from other systems about a particular individual."

Another trend that they mentioned is the increased use of so-called on-line systems in real time. There always has been a capacity, even in manual files, for anybody who had the wherewithal to find out what I have been doing and when I did it—for instance in American Express files. If somebody, the government or somebody else, wanted to find out from the central location of American Express what I had been doing, where I had been, they could find that out. Cumbersome, somewhat; but now, with computer technology, less cumbersome. As those systems move on-line, it would be possible for someone who wished me ill to find out where I am and what I am doing and also to stop me from doing it too if he so desired, by eating up my card at some other point. I think that is a trend to watch. In addition to all the points of individual access and correction and everything, I think that computer professionals are going to be faced with the problem of which information ought to go in the computer first of all, which information ought to go into a computer and not be on-line, and which information can be on-line and which information can be processed in real time.

One of the other problems that arises with this new demand for privacy is how to correct information. I know that I have heard from individuals who have tried to see their credit record and have disputed it, as is their right, and have put their side of the story into the record, but they are relegated to a manual file, not in the computer files. So what you in essence are creating is a three by five card file of all the trouble-makers who exercise their rights under the Act. So I think the computer systems have to be designed to accommodate that sort of updating and disposition and, in fact, a narrative account by an individual who wants to correct his own record.

Cost

A few words about cost. Three members of the Privacy Commission—a certified public accountant, a computer scientist, and the president of Aetna Life and Casualty Company—told Congress in July that the costs to implement "fair information practices" are far less than originally projected, and are hardly significant budget expenditures, especially when planned before computer information systems are designed, not afterward.

For an insurance company, the cost is well worth paying, I would think. A customer who seeks to assure the accuracy of information about himself and is concerned about disclosure of it without his consent is not a trouble-maker, but an interested customer. Companies spend millions to get customers to contact them; here is one instance in which the "privacy mandate" can be turned into a marketing asset.

I would like to raise the issue in your minds as to whether or not the cost of consumer reports is worthwhile for insurance companies. I was intrigued by testimony before the Privacy Protection Study Commission that the cost of increased losses anticipated by *not* utilizing consumer investigations does not exceed the amount now spent on them by the insurance industry. I am not an authority in the insurance industry, but as a concerned lay person I want to pose the question: Can't the industry do away with consumer reports altogether and somehow use that savings to cover possible additional risks incurred?

Equifax, after all, is the dominant company in this market, doing 80 percent or more of the business in this field. It is a company under a cloud—accused by the Federal Trade Commission of violating the Fair Credit Reporting Act, accused by the Commission of violating the anti-trust laws, accused by a subcommittee of the U.S. Senate of conducting unreliable "investigations," subjected to ridicule and anger in the national press and television news, as well as in public opinion surveys. I am curious as to why the insurance industry persists in using this company for the bulk of its reports, and why it has not questioned more closely the cost-effectiveness of these reports.

One other pet theme is the immunity provision. I want to explain it in its straightest terms from the consumer viewpoint. I use my rights under the Act to go out to McLean to see what Equifax has on me, and say I see something in there that I find very embarrassing, private, and that I think is none of their business. I sleep in the nude or take long lunch hours or let my kids run wild, something like that. I am disturbed by this, I think it is private information, I think that it is nobody's business, and I think it is irrelevant to any insurance decision. But what if it is true. I cannot sue for libel if it is true, right? I would still want to get some action. I would want to get it out of the report or I would want to make whoever gathered that information pay. And the way to do that would be with a privacy suit. I would sue for invasion of privacy, not on the grounds that the information is false, but that it is embarrassing to me and a disclosure of private facts about me. Catch 22 in the federal law is that you cannot do that. If I see information about myself in my investigative file, I am then disallowed from suing for an invasion of privacy. It was simply a quid pro quo between the Congress and the lobbyists for the industry, and translated from the Latin I think that means, "Screw the consumer." I really do. I think that a newspaper, for instance, is not immune from suit, though they do have First Amendment protection. Other industries are not immune from privacy suits for information that they gather. The industry has had seven years now to live with this sort of individual access, and I think that it makes total sense that individuals be able to sue for invasion of privacy if they find in their report information that is private and, they think, embarrassing. Now this is not going to lead to a whole lot of harassing, trivial suits as would be suspected. There is strong case law with regard to privacy and with regard to what are private facts, and so people are not going to go around suing for things that the courts through the years have not regarded as particularly sensitive. People would not be able to collect for information that, though sensitive, really did not do much harm in its disclosure.

We are all victims of information gathering, as well as practitioners of it. The credit investigator thinks that the FBI snoops too much. The law-enforcement officials blame the insurance companies. The underwriter blames government agencies. And the government bureaucrat feels that private industry is the prime invader of his privacy. The point is that we are all victims of invasions of privacy in our personal lives, as well as potential invasions in our professional lives.

So do not feel put upon. The abuses are there. They are the product of the network of information exchange now conducted between and among insurance companies, health providers, employers, investigators and reporting companies, and government agencies.

Questions and Answers

Question: *Mr. Smith, I must say, you have greatly distorted information about the MIB. It serves only as a "red flag," for one thing. Moreover, its security is second to none. It functions in the consumer's best interest. You have an incorrect perception of the MIB.*

Answer: MIB should be a red flag. That is the way it ought to work and there is an MIB rule against using it for other than that. Testimony before the Privacy Commission was otherwise, and if there was any redness in the room it was William Bailey's face. He really got flushed and mad, and he told MIB that, "Your rule about making sure that insurance companies do not deny simply on the basis of an MIB report is not being enforced. What sort of procedures do you have for enforcing it?" And he was very chagrined that was not happening. He felt that large numbers of insurers were denying simply on the basis of an MIB report and not rechecking. I agree with you how the system ought to work, and if it did work that way it would not be so bad.

Generally about MIB and with other organizations, my unwillingness to want to give my information to them is simply because I do not think it is an organization that deserves personal information about me. I am not impressed with the way they handle it. Until a couple of years ago they were not even listed in the phone book. That is not an organization that is oriented toward dealing with the consumer, as insurance people are.

You mentioned that MIB keeps the information very secure. Only a few people know the codes. That is protecting my privacy? That is protecting the security of the information. Is that protecting my right to fair information practices? It is not. Does that have anything to do with my access to the record? Does that have to do with my knowing that it is accurate and correcting it? No. You are speaking about privacy as synonymous with confidentiality, which is the traditional meaning of that word. But in the computer age, now, privacy has come to mean fair information practices. I want my insurance agent to expedite the process. I wanted to use the leverage I had, which was presumably a commission that he would get, to get him to expedite the process. I want him to do whatever has to be done so that I get my record. I am not saying that he should have access to that information.

6

Information Needs and the Insurance Industry: Where to From Here?

W. Lee Burge

The fact is that the concept of privacy protections, as it relates to the insurance industry and to other businesses that depend so much upon the free flow of information, is widely misunderstood. The words themselves have emotional connotations that can sometimes obscure their implications.

The cry for more restrictions on the free flow of information, in the name of privacy protection—and for more government machinery to enforce them—grows daily. And there can be no doubt that Americans are becoming more privacy conscious. It is essential that we recognize this fact and that we develop positive responses to the challenges it poses. It is one of today's realities, and it is likely to be with us for a long time.

But we must recognize also that, while Americans are jealously guarding their personal privacy, they are in no mood to give up any of the benefits of a free and open society. Such benefits include the privilege of asking

---

W. Lee Burge is the President and Chief Executive Officer of Equifax, Inc., whose affiliates include the world's largest consumer-reporting agency. He also serves as Chairman of the Board of Directors of Equifax's 14 affiliates and divisions. He has spent his entire business career with Equifax. A graduate of Georgia State University, Mr. Burge serves as Director and member of the Executive Committee for the First National Bank and for National Service Industries. He is a regular member of the Conference Board in New York and serves as a member of the National Chamber of Commerce's Panel on Privacy. He has testified on privacy matters numerous times before various governmental committees.

companies such as yours to risk vast sums of money to insure their lives and property.

Clearly, there is potential conflict in this. In order to qualify for the benefits they seek, people must agree to reveal sufficient personal information so that the insurer can intelligently evaluate the risk and determine how much to charge for the benefit. So the issue, it seems to me, is not absolute privacy, but the *balance* between the individual's right to be free of unwarranted intrusion into his private affairs and the businessman's right to gather and use information pertinent to a business transaction. The real concern is for *confidentiality* of such information.

Dr. Alan Westin, the eminent Columbia University law professor who was an adviser to the Privacy Protection Study Commission, said in a speech in Houston, Texas, early this year, and I quote:

> American society has never viewed privacy as an absolute,
> but always as a matter of balance in which the claim to privacy
> has to be balanced with other social interests, such as securing
> law and order, achieving social welfare programs or researching
> fundamental problems of society.

To achieve a balance between the right of privacy and the right to know requires that we implement what can rightly be called fair information practices. By this I mean information-gathering procedures that assure accuracy, and information-storage systems that assure confidentiality, *reasonable* standards of relevancy, prenotification, proper disclosure, and opportunity for consumers to put their own statements into the record. Properly formulated and conscientiously followed, none of these practices inhibits the free flow of information, and none jeopardizes the individual's right of privacy.

And, incidentally, I wish to commend the Commission for a thoughtful, sensitive, and energetic approach to a very complex subject, and for resisting the temptation to recommend omnibus privacy legislation that would be burdensome to business and costly to the consuming public. Instead, they wisely chose to make *specific* recommendations to achieve *specific* ends.

Having had the opportunity to study the Commission's report carefully, I find myself in agreement with parts of it and in strong disagreement with other parts. It is to be expected, of course, that reasonable men and women with differing perspectives will disagree on details, even when they share a common objective—which in this case is to assure that fair information practices are developed and adhered to in all sectors of public and private life in America. The highest and best purpose of the Commission's work is to provide a basis for meaningful discussions of the best ways to meet that objective.

Now that we have the Commission's report as a basis for discussion, it is essential that considerable thought be given to how the Commission's recommendations might be implemented. Certainly, if new legislation is to be passed, we must assure that proper consideration is given to the legitimate needs of the insurance industry.

Speaking for my own company, I can assure you that we certainly wish to meet the concerns of the Commission. But we know that their recommendations will have to be reconciled with the practical considerations of need, cost, and benefit.

I think it would be useful at this point for me to mention a few of the Commission's recommendations that, if translated into new legislation, could have a lasting effect on the insurance industry.

First, there is the question of what information should be collected for insurance decisions. What is relevant, and how and by whom is relevancy determined? The Commission has recommended that "governmental mechanisms" be established for individuals to question the relevancy of information collected or used.

In my judgment, insurance companies would be making a serious mistake to relinquish their right to gather certain data, and particularly if it meant delegating that right to some "government mechanism." And this is separate and apart from any consideration of whether or not the data in question are needed for decision making. It is hardly necessary to remind you that, in today's environment, certain information may be needed to prove that unfair treatment *did not* occur.

It is my contention that only the *user* of information can determine relevancy. It is not something a government agency can do; nor is it a proper function of support organizations, such as Equifax, that furnish information. In short, it is the function of risk management.

An obvious exception to this would be information on race, religion, and other areas that society, by consensus, has determined to be inappropriate for use in decision making. In all other cases, relevancy is a matter for the risk-taking insurer to determine and for its potential policyholders to accept or reject.

I think the temper of the time is such that your industry—and your individual companies—may have to communicate to the public the *reasons why* certain information is relevant. You may not agree that the public *needs* to be told, but the fact is, it is no longer sufficient simply to say what you need; you also have to say *why* you need it.

My final point on the question of who determines relevancy is that it would be an enormous task for any government agency to set and enforce relevancy standards for all industries, companies, and groups of companies that use information in their decision-making process.

Another of the Commission's recommendations that I seriously question is the one that would require insurers to use only those information-gathering agencies that comply *with the Privacy Commission's recommendations*. Let's stop for a moment to let that sink in. I think you will agree that it violates the principles of good government *and* good business. First, it gives blanket endorsement to all of the Commission's recommendations, while overlooking the fact that some of them are impractical or not needed. And, of course, recommendations have no force of law. A reporting agency would be vulnerable to all sorts of irresponsible allegations, distortions, and arbitrary decisions and could be judged guilty without ever having a chance to defend itself.

Second, this would put the government in the position of taking management prerogatives from insurance companies by dictating to them what service agencies they could use. I can foresee a time when you would have to check the government's "approved list" before ordering an underwriting report. And we know all too well how a "Good Housekeeping Seal of Approval" can be conferred and withdrawn almost on whim.

Now, I hasten to point out here that a system of government approval of reporting agencies would very likely give an advantage to my own company over some of our competitors. This is so for two reasons. First, Equifax has always complied with the letter and the spirit of the law and will continue to do so. Second, our company is larger than most other agencies and thus has the resources to cope with government paperwork and regulations.

Two of the Commission's recommendations involve suggested amendments to the Fair Credit Reporting Act and, thus, would directly affect both the insurance industry and the information-gathering industry. I would like to discuss both of these briefly.

First, the Commission would broaden the prenotification requirement of the Fair Credit Reporting Act to provide, in essence, a "Miranda-type" warning to individuals by insurers prior to information collection. It also would include a provision that insurance companies and support organizations which prepare investigative reports would be *required* to interview applicants, unless the interview is waived.

If Congress considers amending the Fair Credit Reporting Act along these lines, it should take into account the fact that the typical insurance applicant knows full well that the statements he makes on his application will be verified. The Fair Credit Reporting Act, as currently written, provides for adequate prenotification that a report on an applicant's character, general reputation, and mode of living may be made. A more elaborate prenotification statement could confuse applicants and cause them unnecessary concern. I certainly concur that an applicant should be notified that an investigation will be made, but any notification beyond that already mandated by the Fair Credit Reporting Act is purely and simply "overkill."

As to the proposed amendment that applicants must be interviewed, I can see no *practical* purpose in such a requirement. On the contrary, I can see how it would impose additional cost on the consumer and could cause unacceptable delays in issuing policies.

In making this recommendation, the Commission, understandably, was concerned that information in reports be accurate. I share this concern with the Commission, and I am sure you do also. But our experience indicates that personal interviews, while desirable in some instances, do not *necessarily* ensure accuracy. Our firm favors direct interviews, but we do not feel they are needed in every case and do not feel they should be required by law, in any case.

Another proposed amendment to the Fair Credit Reporting Act that is of concern involves the mechanics of disclosure. If the recommendations were translated into legislation, insurers and support organizations would be required to inform an individual whether it has recorded information concerning him, tell him the nature and substance of such information, and allow him to receive the information by mail, telephone, or in person, as he chooses.

As you know, the Fair Credit Reporting Act already provides for disclosure of information by reporting agencies and gives an individual the right to challenge any information in his file. These procedures work well and afford the consumer adequate protection.

Operating under this law for several years, our company has learned a great deal about disclosure. We know that disclosure in person is ideal and disclosure by telephone is second best. But we are very much against disclosure by mail. It jeopardizes confidentiality; it eliminates the opportunity for immediate clarification of questionable information and immediate correction of errors; it slows down the verification process; and it encourages court action rather than simple resolution of problems.

The Commission's recommendation does not differentiate between different types of information. As written, it applies to all recorded data. Thus insurance companies might be forced to establish disclosure systems for all information that in any way relates to an individual—including routine correspondence and billing.

I said earlier in this discussion—and I have said it many times previously—that the Privacy Protection Study Commission did its job thoroughly and well. They heard many divergent points of view, including my own, in their months of study. But I want to reiterate that the report the Commission issued in July was not the end of the dialogue on fair information practices. Instead, it was the beginning.

In the coming weeks and months, Congress, and some state legislatures, will be deliberating on proposed legislation based on the Commission's recommendations. It is my intention—both personally and through my company—to support any new legislation that I feel is in the best interests of the American people, and to vigorously oppose any that seems to be detrimental, unduly expensive, or unnecessary. I urge each of you to do likewise.

In that connection let me also point out that some time may elapse before any amendments proposed for the Fair Credit Reporting Act are legislated. The logjam of other legislation before Congress—on a wide spectrum of other important subjects—makes such delay a distinct possibility. The interim period, therefore, gives us a chance to proceed—voluntarily—to make any changes needed in our own procedures, which will more fully assure that fair information practices are a reality in our dealings with consumers.

There are at least two areas I would recommend for your consideration in this respect:

1. One concerns making sure that personnel record-keeping policies for our own employees meet the test of fair information practices in being truly equitable to the employee, to you the employer, and to the continuance of a free flow of information.

2. The other concerns setting up those *voluntary* mechanisms needed to tell a consumer *why* he has been declined or rated for an insurance benefit. Just as it is important to tell the individual why certain information is *relevant* to the transaction, so is it equally important to tell him your reason for arriving at a given decision.

I have expressed my views on several points. I do not expect total agreement with them. But I am confident that you share my main concern: that we preserve a workable balance between the free flow of business information and the protection of the individual's privacy—in short, the development of fair information practices.

Questions and Answers

Question: *I think it would be helpful for the whole group to "flush out" the mailing problem. From your experience, would you enlighten us with respect to the kinds of hard-core problems that a mailing of information can provide?*

Answer: First, we think that in the credit area particularly, just mail handling—routine, cold mail responses to the consumer—tends to confuse him more than it does to enlighten him. This is particularly true in the sector of the population that is less educated and does not really understand what the financial or the insurance mechanism is all about anyway. So we feel that personal discussion across the desk to explain things is very beneficial. We believe that personal contact is also fundamental to the correction process, because it is there that we discover some errors that we would never discover. We can determine whether or not they are sufficiently important to have affected the ultimate decision.

The alternative to the personal interview is, of course, the phone interview. As I indicated in my comments, some 70 to 80 percent of contact at the present time is by phone, and a lot of this is just sheer curiosity-type questions: "What will this do to me on future insurance applications?" "How do I go about going to another insurance company if this one has turned me down?" In other words, it is something of a counseling process. So we believe that these two things are far superior to just a mail handling.

We resort to mail handling in our company when we give a person a copy of a report after we have had a conversation with him on the telephone and he still wants a copy of the report, whether it be for consumer-credit purposes or for insurance purposes. We mail them a copy of the report after determining that it is on the right individual and that it is going to a mailing address where he can receive it confidentially, because obviously at either the home or the office there are exposures. There is a destruction of confidentiality if it arrives there without prenotification that it is going to come and how it should be addressed to be sure that it gets in his hands and not into the hands of someone else.

But that is something of a last resort. I believe that if I were designing the post-disclosure notification, in the third-party process that we are talking about here, I would do it somewhat on that same basis. In the first place, there is not always the need to disclose all of the information in all of its detail in order for the individual to be satisfied that it was right in the first instance; or, second, he is just as well satisfied for it not to be mailed to him and not to have a full copy of it. Let's take motor vehicle records as a good example. There are many instances in which the individual knows what his motor vehicle record is and its specificity. So, if you tell him that what you have is his motor vehicle record, and it shows "driving while under the influence" in December, etc., then he is sure that it is on the right person and that he is being rated for the right reason. He is not interested in his wife or his secretary finding out about that.

So on the basis of this mail disclosure, we have found that we have to really get involved in it in an infinitesimal percentage of the cases. And yet, this is on the basis of the request of the individual, as opposed to a mandatory process—a point someone made in the discussion here this morning. The same thing applies to the disclosure process as it relates to all of the detail of the information.

And, quite frequently, if he knows that he was rejected for a large life insurance application because of financial instability, he really does not want his financial statement or all the difficulties that he has had financially put into the mail again for public perusal. So I feel that if the reason for declining or rating was the consumer report, the individual should go to the consumer-reporting agency. Or, if he needs further medical information, go to his doctor, or whatever instructions you may give him to go to see if that information is correct. That might be a better process than bundling the file up and sending it to him, if in reality this is what the Privacy Protection Commission intends. So my caveat is, avoid the mail system. Put it in as a last resort from the standpoint of a workable process.

Question: *In order to ensure confidentiality, you have to make sure that you have identified the right person. And you can misidentify by telephone, by mail, or in person. Your company must have specific procedures, therefore, to verify. The Commission's report recommends* *that after verification, the insurer disclose certain information. Are you at liberty to share with us your company's procedures?*

Answer: We would be delighted to share with the industry the process we use to be sure that we are talking to the right "John Jones" and also that we have the right information on the right "John Jones," which is an equally sound problem. Somebody at lunch made reference to having the motor vehicle record on the father of the son, or the brother, or whatever, or, at least, a complication in the records. And this, of course, as you know, happens, not every day, but perhaps somewhere in the United States every day. So we do have to be sure, first, that we have the right individual, and we do go through an interview process to be sure that we do. "Mr. Jones, tell me what your address is. Tell me your date of birth." Or whatever other specific identifying information may be useful. "Where did you work last year?" if we have information on a former employer in our files. So by virtue of specifically being sure that we have the right information on the right individual, we can tell. Sometimes it is necessary that we call back to be sure again that we have the right identity. So we go through whatever mechanics are necessary to be sure that we are talking to the right individual. And, of course, some of this depends upon the sensitivity of the information involved. If you are working with a situation in which there is relatively little sensitive information, then you may not go through all the steps that you might go through under a different set of circumstances.

Question: *In giving the reason for declining or rating, how do we avoid going counter to Equifax's contract, which says that we will not reveal information in a report?*

Answer: We do not regard the giving of a reason as a violation of our contract. For example, let's assume that you have rejected an individual on the basis of a "driving-while-under-the-influence" record. I think you could very well say, "We are rejecting this application because of information with regard to past habits or driving record," and that "This information came to us as a result of an Equifax report." Or, at least, "In considering all these factors, we have obtained an Equifax report, and if you would like to discuss any information in that report with them you can go to 1600 Peachtree in Atlanta." In other words, we would suggest that you try not to divulge the detail of the report. The distinction is that the reason can be stated in a way that does not necessarily give the detail of the report but that you did make the decision on the basis of an Equifax report. They can come to us and discuss it. We do not regard that as a violation of our contract at the present time. If there is any problem with this, we will be glad to work with you individually with our representatives in the underwriting offices to be sure, and if necessary we will revamp our contract. We still feel that we are the ones that should reveal the details of investigative reports. On the other hand, you can say that information that came to you resulted in your declining him because of past habits, past health, past criminal record, past financial difficulties, or whatever. We, in turn, will take the responsibility for seeing that the information is accurate. I would have to be sure that our lawyers check out that point, but, as a "guard house lawyer," I would say that it is not in violation of the Fair Credit Reporting Act to divulge the reason that you are declining an individual, even though it is on the basis of information in a report.

Question: *Taking that hypothetical case one step further, what would the Privacy Study Commission report change in that procedure?*

Answer: My understanding of the Commission's recommendation is that as an insurer, you would sit down with your underwriting file and show the consumer the report, show him the MIB record, show him the motor vehicle record, show him any other information that you have gathered from any or all other sources, medical records, whatever else, that you are authorized to show him from a medical records standpoint, and that he in turn would have opportunity to see that. Then if he contested any piece of that—let's say he did not contest the Equifax report because of its absolute accuracy and completeness (don't anybody say this is strictly a hypothetical case), but assuming that he found that the information that you got from a third source was in error—he would leave Equifax alone and go to that other source to talk about his problem. That is the concept of the Privacy Protection Commission's process, as I understand it. And the individual has a right to copy, and he could get that disclosure by mail if he chose to do so.

Question: *Would you assume that the recommendations in the entire report, both the investigative agency and insurance-related chapters, will have a cost impact on investigative companies' service that they perform for us?*

Answer: Yes, there would be a cost impact, and obviously we cannot say whether it will be 5 percent or 50 percent or whatever at this stage of the game, because until it is written into the law we will not really know what we are required to do. There would be a cost impact. One illustration is probably the most obvious. If we were required to try to interview every person, that extra 25 or 30 percent of the people we would try to find could be more expensive than the 70 percent we now find, simply because of the complexity of that. Now the caveat to that, or the alternative, is the mailing of a copy to the individual. As I say, I would be opposed to that as a process. But if we did, that also would increase costs. And again, we would not have any basis of measuring that at this particular time, because we do not know what that would instigate in the mailing process and what action would be required after that, either in the post-investigative interview process with the people to whom we mail reports or for legal action as a result of their going to their lawyers when they got their report. We can keep that down under present circumstances because of the fact that we have an opportunity to work with them across the desk, to explain the implications and, also, to make the corrections instantaneously, if necessary. But obviously getting it cold in the mail is a different matter and may trigger a whole set of repercussions that we have no experience on at the present time, except in the consumer-credit reporting field. We do have some experience on it in that field, but that is a different field altogether.

Question: *Just one clarification on the recommendation about being interviewed. I think it is a negative option instead of a positive option. You said or inferred before, I think, that anybody can get one unless they waive it. I think the recommendation is that you are entitled to an interview only if you affirmatively ask for it. If a person does not ask for it, the investigative agency is not required to do the interview. I know that is a technical difference, but, in terms of numbers, I think that it is a considerable difference. It applies only to the people who actively check the box and say, "Yes, I want to be interviewed."*

Answer: Well that, of course, is a moderating impact, and one that would reduce the cost factor that is involved.

Question: *I would like to know what your opinion is as to the future of obtaining information. If copies of a report are required to be disclosed, it seems to me that, even though you do not have to divulge the source, many times one may be able to determine the source just from the nature of the adverse information. Aren't your sources going to dry up if copies of the report are divulged?*

Answer: This, of course, is a hazard. We have found that under the present process, where we have the interview process by phone and by personal interview, we can obviate this. We really are not overly exposed in this particular area. The one area, then, in which we do have a little more exposure than we would like is with respect to information from former employers. Nonetheless, under the present circumstances, we can keep this under control and keep a reasonable flow of information. In my text I stipulated that I felt that the basic thrust of the Privacy Protection Commission's report could be adopted and still maintain a reasonable flow of information, and I think that is right.

There are some restrictive mechanics, such as the mail process, that cause me concern about that possibility. And there may be some others that involve "overkill," as far as prenotification is concerned that might cause that, I am not sure. But, in any event, there is a sensitive area as far as medical sources are concerned in the Privacy Protection Study Commission's report that ought to be examined rather carefully by insurance underwriters, and that is where medical sources are identified. It results in an individual going to the medical source for information or questioning why it was given out, even with authorization. This could cause medical sources, who may be sensitive in the first instance, to be less cooperative in the future than at the present time. Former employers and medical sources I regard as the most sensitive two areas under the recommendations of the Privacy Commission's report.

Question: *I really did not understand your reference to "overkill." Why is there "overkill" in the prenotification process?*

Answer: As you will note, the prenotification requirement outlines all the sources, all the processes, and all the techniques that you are likely to use and the general availability of information to obtain correction. If you spell out all of the processes for the individual, it is a highly complicated explanation. And this is true especially when it pertains to notifying him as to where you may investigate and through what sources and in what ways, because there are times when we start out on what is a relatively simple, clear-cut investigation, and we would think that a generalized, safe statement would be sufficient: i.e., "We are going to check to see if you have any factors pertaining to your life insurance exposures or your automobile insurance exposures." But when we get into it, it gets more and more involved.

Let's give the illustration of what we had here this morning where, instead of investigating a man, we investigate his wife, because she is the driver and she is the one who has the morals problem or whatever. We probably would not tell the individual when we start out on an automobile insurance investigation that we are going to investigate his wife to that degree or check her police records. But that could be included in an all-inclusive document.

It is overkill if you tell them all that you may possibly do. It will scare somebody to death if, in reality, you are going to make just a very simple check of their driving record. I will cite an illustration. I was in an automobile insurance underwriter's office one day when we had just instituted the prenotification process under the Fair Credit Reporting Act, and he said, "Here's a problem I have. I have a little old lady who wears tennis shoes and drives her car to and from the supermarket on Friday afternoons. She's incensed because we're going to investigate her habits and morals." And yet the Fair Credit Reporting Act specifically says that we are going to investigate the habits and morals in the investigative process. There are a lot of people we will not investigate on their habits and morals. We will not investigate their financial situation nor their health and that kind of thing, and to tell them that we are going to investigate them is "overkill."

Question: *You just said that is already required. Our experience is that, rather than scaring them to death, the problem is in getting them to read* *and understand the notice and developing a mechanism where you know they really get it in their hand.*

Answer: I see many instances of "overkill." I agree with you that the average person neither reads it nor understands it nor is interested in it.

Question: *There is nothing in the Commission's recommendations to describe the scope of an investigation that you do not intend to carry out. What it says is, describe the scope of that investigation that you intend to carry out and then be bound by it. And if, in that process, you develop reason or need for going further, then you have a chance to provide a second notification. That is expensive, it is time consuming; but it is an option. So I think you have to keep in mind that the notification does not have to be broad. It can be as narrow or as broad or as neutral as you choose to make it.*

Answer: I would only cite a parallel. Under present-day circumstances, we have many companies that do not prenotify and ask us to get purely a consumer report, not an investigative-consumer report. We get in the field, and we find that if we had authority to have an investigative report we could clear the investigation—get more comprehensive information, perhaps give even greater protection to the customer. But we cannot see an outside source. And, therefore, we think we would have the same type of delay, and perhaps cost increase, if we circumscribe the prenotification too much at the outset under this type of an operation.

7

Insurance Executives' Thoughts on Privacy

The Conference held six workshops in which the attendees discussed general attitudes about privacy regulation, specific problems involving privacy matters, views on the implementation of Commission recommendations to specific insurance functional areas, and techniques for implementing procedures to comply with the substance, if not the letter, of the recommendations.

Company functions were grouped for the workshop as follows: (1) marketing and underwriting in life and health insurance; (2) marketing and underwriting in property and liability insurance; (3) claims administration in life and health insurance; (4) claims administration in property and liability insurance; (5) insurance operations; and (6) employment and personnel. The latter two workshops were not divided between life/property-liability lines, since it was felt that problems in these areas would be common to both major types of insurers.

Privacy is a relatively new issue for the insurance industry, and since many of those attending the Conference had not read the Privacy Protection Study Commission's Report, several individuals were asked to present brief comments in each workshop relating to privacy matters. These remarks frequently served as a springboard for workshop discussion. For our purposes, they also served to suggest the attitudes and approaches of individuals and firms that have thought through the implications of the PPSC report's recommendations. The statements of each individual should be considered his own and not necessarily those of the organization by which he is employed.

To encourage an uninhibited exchange of ideas, workshop discussions were not recorded. Many of the discussion leaders in these workshops preserved either their statements or notes, and this chapter is based primarily on those documents, supplemented by summaries provided by discussion leaders. However, the material that follows does not capture the full discussion and should be viewed in that light. Summaries of the workshop sessions on claims in life and health insurance and on employment and personnel are not included.

Because the discussion leaders' remarks ranged beyond their functional specialties to general, philosophical aspects of the privacy debate, readers will note elements of similarity—or overlap—among them. Since these presentations were written and delivered quite independently from one another, these overlapping elements were preserved, rather than edited out, both to retain the integrity of each presentation and to emphasize the remarkably common mind among industry executives as they approach privacy issues.

One dimension of this "common mind" is the conviction that little regulation—or no new regulation—of fair information practices is needed, since insurers are already highly motivated by goals for operating with the least-cost, greatest-profit methods. Inherent in these goals is operation by the least intrusive, most accurate, and least retentive information practices that can be devised. In general, insurance executives believe that regulation likely to develop from the Commission's recommendations will add significantly to cost without commensurate benefit.

A second dimension of this "common mind" is the belief that proposed limitations and prohibitions inherent in the PPSC's recommendations will benefit the dishonest few who prey on the industry and its products rather than the vast majority of consumers and claimants. Underlying this belief is the inference that the Commission either was unaware of, or disregarded, this unhappy effect of its recommendations on the insurance industry.

Property and Liability Insurance Marketing and Underwriting

Those who attended this workshop expressed concern about limitations that privacy legislation would impose on accurate underwriting. It was argued that some applicants for insurance will conceal, misrepresent, or otherwise distort information vital to an accurate classification of the risk. Moreover, there was widespread concern that, because they do not understand the underwriter's methods or goals, consumers might think information irrelevant or unimportant that underwriters consider pertinent and vital. Two possible ramifications of this misunderstanding by the general public are: (1) some types of information that underwriters need will be declared inappropriate or irrelevant because of the complaint mechanism that the PPSC recommendations propose, thereby preventing access to that kind of information; and (2) because applicants must be prenotified concerning the scope of any investigation, the possibility of uncovering evidence contradictory to that which the applicant volunteers would be foreclosed. Finally, there was general concern that implementation of these recommendations would cause massive additional bureaucracy for property and liability insurance underwriters.

James McTurnan, of MFA Mutual Insurance Company, made a presentation with which many participants seemed to agree. His presentation is reproduced here in its entirety.

Remarks of James McTurnan:

My experience has been mainly in property and casualty insurance and principally in rural areas where privacy is looked upon differently than it is in metropolitan areas. In the small community for example, a neighbor normally knows most, if not all, of the details of another neighbor's experiences and character. In a metropolitan area, the occupant of Apartment A may never see the occupant of Apartment B. Consequently, information in the smaller urban and rural areas, although applying to an individual, is in a sense public information, or at least generally known to the immediate neighborhood, whereas in a metropolitan complex such information would not only be unknown, but would be of no interest to the person next door.

If there is truth in the stories I have heard about people being attacked on the streets of our big cities, while fellow citizens passed coldly by without offering relief, it is difficult for me to think that sort of privacy is worth much.

I have served in two general areas with our company, namely the sales department and the underwriting department. A salesman learns first-hand, and quickly, the attitudes and needs of the public. An underwriter's job is to fill these needs with appropriate insurance coverage.

The purpose of underwriting is to eliminate unknowns, to identify the risks being protected, and, through the application of proper prices, to provide insurance coverage wherever the balance of price and risk will permit. If underwriters are precluded from obtaining facts, then, in my opinion, they are precluded from the acceptance of a considerable amount of business. It would not be the majority of the consumers who are benefited by limiting the underwriter's access to facts, but rather the reverse. If some applicants for insurance are permitted to withhold or misidentify the facts surrounding them or their property, and thereby avoid paying the appropriate price or secure protection on uninsurable risks, then the rest of the policyholders, or what we might call the good guys, must pay extra.

Information provided by policyholders is usually accurate, but not always. The reasons you cannot completely rely on the information are many. Some information that underwriters consider important is considered unimportant by an insured. The element of arrest, the amount of mortgage on their property, the condition of their health are all items that the insured may be reluctant to disclose. Once in a while information gets watered down or omitted by an agent because he is afraid it may spoil a sale. Finally, some applicants will deliberately limit the truth. We get hundreds of motor vehicle reports which produce additional information about applicants' driving records.

We recently paid $10,000 for a fire loss that, in retrospect, might have been anticipated. Prior to the loss we did not make any investigation of facts beyond the application. After the loss, our claim department learned that the husband had been unemployed for several months, the wife was drawing $100 a month from welfare for one daughter and $628 a month from Social Security for four other children. Also, the husband was a boozer, and the house was up for sale when it burned. The fire appeared to have started in two separate places. No one was home at the time of the fire, although the husband had returned home alone once during the day. The year before the husband had filed bankruptcy. There was a mortgage of $15,000 on this $10,000 home, and in addition, there were three other loans on the property totaling about $8,000. Payments on these were three to four months past due. Besides these debts, $3,000 was owed on a car and $4,000 on a lake lot. Some of these payments were also behind. A credit report would have alerted the underwriter to at least some of these circumstances.

I have personally talked with many policyholders about insurance pricing; some have had claims and some have not. I recall none who did not favor proportionately higher rates for those individuals who present a higher than average degree of risk. This is especially so in connection with automobile insurance where the policyholder, whether he has personally filed a claim or not, feels strongly that those persons who cause accidents and drive recklessly should be required to foot more of the cost of insurance. How would these responsible, hard-working policyholders react if they knew the cost of "fair" plans, "assigned risk" plans, and insolvency goals—AND that they were paying this subsidy.

As to privacy, there are certainly two sides to the issue. The convention that authored our country's Constitution met behind closed doors and under a bond of secrecy. That bond was never violated—I guess you could call this privacy. The Fourth Amendment to our Constitution guarantees the right of the people to be secure in their persons, houses, and effects against unreasonable searches and seizure—I guess you could call this privacy.

One of the glories of this country is our enthusiasm for independence. We were founded on it. But that same independence turns us against the man who doesn't "mind his own business." We really don't like "nibby" neighbors. It's none of my business that your home has a value of $50,000 and a mortgage for $75,000. No? Not until you ask me to insure it for $75,000, thereby including a potential $25,000 profit in your homeowners policy. It's none of my business that one of the drivers of your car is grossly irresponsible with a record of accidents and arrests. No? Not until you ask me to put a $100,000 insurance guarantee on the front bumper of your automobile. But then, as your insurance agent, it sure becomes my business. And here may be the key issue. When does personal information become business information? And who is to decide this?

There are tens of millions of private business transactions in this country every day, and every one of them relies upon facts and people to some degree. To even imagine that such magnitude in all its detail should be centrally regulated suggests a Russian-type bureaucracy—the very antithesis of what this country wants and needs. The hard working people—people who pay the bills, people who daily face up to their failures and successes and who understand that life isn't all a bed of roses—need to be left alone for awhile. Governments don't solve problems, people do.

I live on a farm and last fall we had a rash of thefts. Trucks were driving up in broad daylight and hauling off valuables, and sometimes all of a family's possessions. The sheriff tried to stop it. The state patrol tried. We already had laws and regulations about it. But it was stopped. How? By the people. They reported strange trucks in the neighborhood. They took side roads to work to look for the unusual. They had a few CB radios. The thieves disappeared.

My premise is that people do work out their problems. Not always overnight, of course, but solutions arrived at in the environment of the problem are a heck of a lot better than those—so often fanciful and speculative—conceived at an isolated distance.

I was in Russia last summer and in the evenings I saw thousands of people crowd the sidewalks of Moscow and Leningrad. We asked the Intourist guide why this was so, and she told us, "If you live in a five-room apartment and share it with four other families, you take a walk for privacy." Let's keep our system.

Insurance companies sell and are required by regulation to provide first quality products. Not only are we required to do this, but we want to. The company guarantees what it will deliver in a statement of facts called an insurance policy. The company is contractually bound by its policy. Is it then unreasonable, in return for this guarantee, to expect a full set of facts from the buyer? Is it unreasonable, in the face of known withholding of facts by some, to be allowed to verify the facts upon which the issuance of an insurance policy is based? Am I not at least to be permitted to "try on my new trousers" before I buy them? I believe vigorously in the preservation of privacy and individual freedom, but that includes the freedom to trade with openness and honesty. I am not entitled to cry if I trade knives "sight unseen" and get a broken blade. But there would be no fairness in the law which required me to make such a trade.

In our operation, we find no significant evidence that abuses of privacy exist with respect to the collection, control, and dissemination of personal information. Really, what potential for abuse there is, is largely protected already by the Fair Credit Reporting Act. If an insured asks for the information on which we based a decision, we give it to him or her. We are a mutual company—a policyholder is an owner.

Privacy regulation—and I think it only fair to observe that regulation in itself is a conflict with pure privacy—will increase the cost to the insurance-buying public. Premiums will rise, and tax money will be required for business to implement and government to enforce such regulations. A few of the extra costs to the policyholder will result from such things as:

1) Establishing the mechanical procedures necessary to implement these regulations.

2) Purging and updating files.

3) Monitoring the access to files and the dissemination of information therefrom.

4) Necessary governmental audits of company systems.

5) Physical security of file information.

Other items could be added, but you are probably already aware of them.

The following is purely a personal observation. I have a growing concern that in this land of ours we are creating a highly, if not zealously, suspicious environment.

Perhaps I have been sheltered from some of the problems that frequently find "host-plants" in our coastal areas. Perhaps I have parochial vision. But down deep I have the feeling that with all our efforts to force openness, force honesty, force privacy, force, if you will, a baring of our national soul, we are undermining our self-confidence and mutual trust of our fellow man. In all innocence we may be promoting a down-the-road disaster by the destruction of these two essentials of freedom (and indirectly privacy), by pyramiding regulation upon regulation. After too much regulation, people just give up and don't care anymore. I much prefer the risk of failure to the denial of the opportunity to succeed.

I'm not confusing honesty and privacy, but limiting reasonable access to facts through privacy regulation opens the door of temptation to withholding and concealment of facts that affect the insurance transaction. I think it much better to determine the facts before a claim occurs than to find misrepresentation that voids coverage afterwards.

Business institutions have a great deal of flexibility and can obviously operate for a while longer under the increasing burden of government regulation. However, somewhere down the road there is a breaking point. To force more and more regulations (and especially those which harass the elements of honesty, openness, and trust between buyer and seller) on business is to destroy the keystone of the private enterprise system. The result could well be the abandonment of private insurance institutions whose success in relieving hardship and guaranteeing security is unparalleled in history. If the insurance industry has one universal fault, it is in not advertising the great good it has done.

This country's great venture into governmental insurance, the social security system, is hardly a glowing success. I have personally invested hard-earned dollars in social security in the good faith that my money would be there when my time of need rolled around. The fact that my money is not there now is alarming. In Missouri, if I trust money to my banker with the understanding that I can draw it out later, and it isn't there, we call it being dishonest.

I know it is repetitious to cite the postal system, but darned if there isn't something out of whack when it costs nine cents to deliver a penny postcard. In the face of these two governmental ventures in business, it is hard to put much faith in regulations which further limit the functioning of the free enterprise system.

Could we be overinterpreting a relatively few transgressions of privacy to be a mandate for another regulatory venture which is neither needed nor wanted by the citizens? That would be the greatest of all invasions of privacy. I certainly don't oppose valid changes, even if temporarily unpopular, if the change is productive to society measured in long-term benefits. But change must be the result of real need, not speculative need.

Let not the din of a small minority, who—vested with great idleness—beat their drums ceremoniously, be mistaken for the many. Our business serves the many well. Let not those who throw mud on the wall of public opinion be thought to represent any but the mudslingers. Let not our lawmakers fall prey to the mistaken notion that it is law heaped upon law, rather than people, that ultimately solve life's major problems—I know of no greater invasion of privacy than the imposition of unneeded regulation.

Property and Liability Insurance Claims

At this workshop there was general agreement that invasions of privacy, collection of vast amounts of irrelevant information, and needless and negligent dissemination of information were not problems that currently plague the property-liability insurance industry. The general feeling was that natural competitive forces compel claim departments to gather, use, and disseminate the least amount of information possible, and then only relevant information. Hence, regulation in this area is, in their opinion, unnecessary.

Resigned to the belief that some regulation was forthcoming, the discussion centered on several of the Commission's recommendations that were most pertinent to the claims function. Attention focused first on the absolute prohibition of pretext interviews (Recommendation 2). Two types of concerns were voiced. First, it was thought that the prohibition of pretext interviews would benefit only those with fraudulent intent. It was frequently mentioned that no claimant would be hurt by information obtained in a pretext interview unless the claimant was lying or exaggerating. If the claim were legitimate, then the pretext interview would discover its legitimacy. Moreover, the economics of pretext interviews were also cited as a reason why they do not need to be prohibited entirely. As one participant noted, "They are frightfully expensive. No claim manager asks for that kind of activity unless he has strong reason to suspect that something is going on." Second, a participant noted that information that contributes to claim settlement may come from "good samaritans," or it may be developed, quite fortuitously, from another investigation quite outside the scope of the one pertaining to a particular claim. In both of these situations, claim executives were concerned that information developed in these ways might be considered developed under pretext conditions, and so it was hoped that the legislative drafting process would help to clarify the application of the prohibition against pretext interviews.

Recommendation 10 on the right of access created intense discussion. Although the recommendation does not require disclosure of claim files to third-party claimants, it does permit access to claim files by first-party claimants after the claim is settled. A consensus was that attitudes about first-party claimants are changing, and that in many cases first-party claimants are as much adversaries of the insurance company as third-party claimants. This is most clearly so in cases of suspected arson. Many claim executives agreed that if those suspicions appeared in claim files, but insufficient evidence was available to deny or prosecute, and the claimant had access to that information after settlement, this might possibly endanger the lives of people who had provided information on the suspected arson. Further, the claim executives felt that theories or other "soft" information that had been in the file would also be made available to a first-party claimant. One discussion leader suggested that the problem with this recommendation could be solved if the recommendation were changed to read "or after the claim is settled, to any record compiled in relation to a claimant." This change would delete the words, "who is not an insured or policyholder," which follow in the recommendation immediately after "claimant."

There was also considerable discussion about Recommendation 8 that deals with authorizations. Most of the concern was about the specification of an expiration date for the authorization. Most executives were worried that the expiration specified might be inadequate to encompass the full investigation of some claims. It was agreed that one approach to this problem would be to revise the recommendation so that it required the expiration of the authorization at, but not before, settlement of the claim to which the investigation applied.

Several claim executives were concerned about the impact on claim practices of limitations on operations of the Loss Index and similar efforts to identify patterns in suspected fraudulent claims. One executive asserted that the business could and must preserve the proposition that a claim, once made and paid, clearly might relate to a following claim, if only for the simplest of reasons—that the same claim should not be paid twice. Another executive noted that "the prior claim history, physical condition, injuries, and employment record often have a direct bearing on a claim under consideration." He went on to note that obtaining this information through legal discovery procedures involves additional delay and expense that might seriously diminish the value of the information sought. The group consensus sought "free dissemination of data, limited only by considerations of relevance."

Remarks of M. Croydon Johns, formerly of Johns-Eastern Company, and of Jules H. Marckmann, of Chubb and Son, Insurance, are reproduced. Also, included in this section are the prepared remarks of M.D. Knight, III, of Government Employees Insurance Company. Mr. Knight's remarks were made at the 24th Annual Workshop Meeting of the National Association of Independent Insurers on April 17, 1978. As his remarks seem to capture and enlarge on many of the points made in the claim workshop, they are included.

Finally, a brief statement by James F. Ahern, of the Insurance Crime Prevention Institute, is included. Mr. Ahern was invited to serve as a panelist at the Conference but was unable to do so. He did, however, submit prepared remarks.

Remarks of M. Croydon Johns:

For two full days I listened to speakers at this conference. Every one of them had done his homework. They all agreed. There is no substantial evidence that companies are gathering improper information. Neither is there any substantial evidence that, once gathered, information is being improperly published.

I am in the odd position of being against this proposed law (H.R. 8288) more as a private citizen than I am as a member of the insurance business. Looking at it as a member of the business, I think we can live with it, even in its present form. It is not that the law will do any good. It won't. It also won't do an immense amount of harm. The insurance camel's back is not yet at the point where this straw will break it.

The only damage that the law will do is to make gathering underwriting and claims information a little less efficient. People who have something to hide will be forewarned about what to hide and will be better able to cover their tracks. Information gatherers will have to be more defensive about the information they gather and the way they record it. They, or the companies employing them, will spend time (money) defending their investigative practices. From a claims and underwriting standpoint, a few more questionable cases will slip through. When this reflects itself in higher rates, the public will never know the difference. Maybe we in the business should not be too concerned.

Perhaps I should state my personal bias about information and privacy. I treasure relevant information. I despise misinformation. It never helps. It always hurts my client and often hurts me. Good information gathering and handling comes from good management people who want facts and scorn error. That kind of manager lines up every time with Ben Franklin, "A gentleman doesn't read another gentleman's letter to his wife." They regard information in their possession as a trust. Not every insurance employee measures up to this standard, but a lot of them must; the business has been gathering and recording an immense amount of information for a good many years, and the advocates of this legislation tell us that it has been done with almost total lack of complaint.

These men and women doing this didn't get the way they are by following a code nor a list of permitted practices. They got the way they are by being trained by people who treated information as gentlemen and ladies treat it. But let me not go overboard about how virtuous we are. We also owe the commendable record to pure money-making expediency. Bad information getting and handling wastes money and messes up sales. We are all entirely too busy to spread information around where it doesn't belong.

If ever there was a principle with two sides to it, privacy is that principle. Of course everyone wants to keep his affairs to himself. But as a tool of larceny, it can be better than a burglar's jimmy. "I just won't tell this company that I am applying to that my doctor tells me I have cancer, and I'll see to it that my doctor keeps his mouth shut. I'll threaten to sue him if he tells them." Handling conflict between desire to keep one's affairs to one's self and the legitimate "need to know" of a party at interest calls for wise, understanding men and women trained by and managed by that kind of people. If codification does it, it will upset all that thirty-five years of managing people in a personal service business has taught me. It will make management superfluous. Laudable as that might be, I doubt it will happen.

Some in our business think it important to gather sound information so that deserving policyholders can qualify for a better rate. This law may give them problems of conscience. Where it impinges on claims practices, our cynics can console themselves; if somebody collects [a claim payment] when he ought not to, it will only raise the rate a little. The rate-paying public will never know the difference. When things finally get as bad as they are in Miami in auto liability, this little step down the road will have been long forgotten.

Before getting to specifics then, as a layman, I am totally against this bill. Its proponents all but admit that it is not necessary. Its goals are already being substantially attained. If it *were* needed, that is if there *were* evidence of poor practice, law is the wrong way to accomplish its unexceptionable goals.

As a technician in the business, I have to be a realist. Sooner or later this bill will probably pass since legislators seem to feel bound to legislate. If we have to live with it, where can it be made less objectionable?

Section 671 [of H.R. 8288] deals with disclosures to first-party claimants. The concluding paragraph of that section says that requirements for disclosure do not apply to any record compiled in any reasonable anticipation of a civil or criminal action or for use in settling a claim *"while the claim remains unsettled; or after the claim is settled, to any record compiled in relation to a claimant who is not an insured or policyholder."*

As written, this requirement could be a serious stumbling block in compromising doubtful claims. Most first-party claims, whether property or life, are settled in full or denied. Nevertheless, many claims are compromised, and if this bill becomes law, only an irresponsible manager will fail to look at a potential compromise with this thought in mind: "After I settle this claim, and if the claimant's attorney comes in and exercises his right to review the file, then what seemingly harmless word or scrap of information may furnish the basis for a bad faith action?" The problem could be cured by punctuating with a period after "claimant" and cutting out the last seven words.

Section 684 deals with pretext interviews. I grant that pretext interviews, even in claims work, are exceedingly rare. I will go further and say that many probably are ordered by home office examiners who, afraid to make a decision, scratch around for something else to ask the field to do, and thus postpone that terrible moment of facing the facts. Moreover, from a practical standpoint, serious pretext interviews have a built-in self-limiting factor. They are frightfully expensive. No claims manager asks for that kind of activity unless he has strong reason to suspect that something is going on. Furthermore, pretext and undercover work are self-correcting. No claimant will be hurt by any pretext interviews or undercover investigation unless he is lying or exaggerating. If his injury is legitimate, that's what the undercover work will show. If his disability is real, a pretext interview will disclose that his disability is indeed real.

I don't like pretext work. Fundamentally, it conflicts with very important claims techniques. A good adjuster is a gentleman. An important reason for his success is that he makes claimants want to be gentlemen and ladies. His attitude encourages them to be as willing to behave reasonably as they are eager to have the carrier treat them reasonably. A pretext interview or any kind of undercover work is inconsistent with the trust that begets trustworthiness—but we live in an imperfect world.

All too often we meet another attitude: "If there is that kind of money lying around, I'm going to get mine." Where that attitude predominates, you have disaster areas like [the automobile insurance claims explosion in] Miami. And when that attitude is in full flower, sometimes the only thing to do for the beleaguered rate-payer is to try some undercover work. When one does, the chances for getting worthwhile evidence are less than even.

The whole notion that pretext or undercover work needs to be restrained is amusing to those of us familiar with claim adjusters. Adjusters don't like to investigate. Most of them have to be "beaten"—almost to a pulp— to get them to go out and do a decent job of investigation. On this subject, I am well qualified. As a field adjuster, I gave my share of ulcers to my managers. Since I became a claims manager, I have injured my share of adjusters.

The amusing aspect notwithstanding, the insurance company is a party at interest. It has a right to the truth, whether the fellow that the truth is about wants it known or not. Our duty runs considerably beyond the protection of a corporation's surplus, legitimate though that duty is. People who get away with exaggerated claims have a hand in everybody's pocket. Pretext interviews and undercover investigations have a value that extends well beyond immediate claims. The fear that he may be found out keeps many a man straight. The technique has too much to offer to the honest policyholder for us to waive even a weak tool for his defense. We owe it to him to go out and get "dirt under our fingernails," if need be, whether we like it or not.

Section 686 of H.R. 8288 deals with authorizations. The "self-destruct" feature (subsection 7)—"specific as to its expiration date . . . in the case of life insurance, two years after the date of a policy"—is unrealistic.

For the benefit of those unfamiliar with life insurance, let me explain. Life insurance policies carry what is known as an incontestability clause. This provides that if death occurs more than two years after the inception date, the claim may not be contested regardless of any misrepresentation that may have been made. The important corollary is that if death occurs within two years of the policy's inception date, it may be contested on the ground of material misrepresentation. Now consider the situation when a policyholder has been told by his doctor that he has a cancer, he applies for insurance, the examining doctor misses the cancer, the policyholder says nothing about it in his application and denies that he has a family doctor. Then he dies on the thirtieth day of the twenty-fourth month of his policy's life. In that situation, an authorization will expire the next day. It will be useless.

With respect to casualty claims, we need to seek information from so many people and so many classes of people that to avoid being obliged to go back to a claimant time and again a "blank check" authorization is the practical answer. The notion that claims people are peeping Toms or "peeping Nellies," running around for bedrooms to look into, is only amusing to those of us familiar with the claims business, the nature of adjusting, and the universal concern of the claims business with costs.

The following language would make this section much easier for claims departments to live with, whether first- or third-party departments:

> Section 686 shall not apply to any authorization taken in reasonable anticipation of a claim or of a civil or criminal action or to the use of an authorization in settling, investigating, or defending a claim while the claim remains unsettled.

From the claims standpoint, the concept of privacy affects the insurance business, and through it the rate-paying public, far more through abuse of the concept by claimants than by any alleged abuse by carriers.

In many jurisdictions we meet a complete blackout on all medical information, and the blackout is not lifted until the claimant is ready to file suit—which may be years from the date of the accident. This has an almost disastrous effect on claims departments' abilities to oppose wrongful claims. Moreover, this practice of plaintiffs' attorneys dropping the veil [after long delays] explains certain recent financial difficulties of some well-known carriers whose claims reserves were found to have been seriously inadequate.

American Jurisprudence, Volume 62, Page 700, Section 16, says: "the individual's right of privacy must in some instances yield to certain paramount rights of the public and at some point the public interest in obtaining information becomes dominant over the individual's desire for privacy . . . it is a matter of harmonizing individual right to community or social interests and it has been said that the truth may be spoken, written or printed about all matters of a public nature as well as matters of a private nature in which the public has a legitimate interest."

If the public does not have a legitimate interest in separating sound from fraudulent claims, then I have never seen a public interest. In 1905, Justice Brandeis, in a paper said to be the very foundation of the law on privacy in this country, wrote, "the right [to privacy] is not invaded by any publication made in any body, quasi-public like the large voluntary associations formed for almost every purpose of benevolence, business or other general interest. Nor would the rule prohibit any publication made by one on the discharge of some public or private duty, whether legal or moral in the conduct of one's own affairs where his own interest is concerned." If the insurance business is going to have to live with this act, it at least ought to ask for something like the following, which could be inserted as Section 685C:

> Public interest requires that insurance institutions, uninsured defendants, and insurance support organizations seek information from physicians, hospitals, employers and other persons or organizations that rendered service to, transacted business with, or recorded information about individuals making claims or from whom litigation is pending or expected. The person or organization from which such information is sought shall be immune from liability for giving or releasing information about such individuals, but the organization receiving such information shall divulge it only in accordance with the provisions of this act.

We are surrogates for the rate-paying public and, as such, we have rights. If we don't exercise and defend these rights, we let the public down. The right of a party in interest to know something that concerns his interest has never been taken away. It is violated every time a plaintiff's lawyer tells a doctor not to talk to the insurance company or he (the doctor) will face a suit for invasion of privacy. In summary then, this would be an unnecessary law, but if we have to have it, we're letting the public down if we don't ask for the indicated changes. If the law had been in effect for several years, and if there were as few complaints as our speakers told us there now are, the law would be hailed as a success. This success underlines what Judge Brandeis went on to say in his paper—there are many subjects that are better handled by social mechanisms other than law.

Remarks of Jules H. Marckmann:

The proposed (Koch/Goldwater) Bill HR 8288 to amend the Fair Credit Reporting Act dealing with insurance institutions and privacy has generated considerable interest, but only moderate consternation, as it is now interpreted to affect the handling of insurance claims. The Privacy Protection Study Commission report in Chapter 5, "The Insurance Relationship," also clearly takes a low profile in the area of claims information.

HR 8288 specifically excepts conditions pertaining to "claim settling" or "records compiled in reasonable anticipation of a civil or criminal action . . ." or "information collected respecting third or first party claims . . ." or [disclosure in] "the detection of prevention of insurance fraud in connection with loss settlements . . ." or "use of index information [being prohibited] for other than claim purposes . . . ," etc. The seventeen recommendations of the PPSC also refer only occasionally or tangentially to the area of claims (Recommendations 5, 6, 7, 9, 10, 11, 12 and 17). Some of these references will be alluded to later in these remarks.

It is clearly a matter of conjecture on my part, but when HR 8288 was introduced, the issue of claim practices, claim investigations, claim documentation, and the collection of claim data and their management and access were not foremost in the minds of the distinguished representatives sponsoring the bill. The Commission in its thorough and carefully prepared report distinguishes between first- and third-party claims, and the bill makes certain references to these distinctions, but the most important underlying concern of potential privacy invasion apparently is directed toward the use of Loss Index data banks.

If the bill becomes law, the claims function of the insurance industry must obviously carefully review its practices and its standards, but the application of new and more stringent standards proposed in the bill is not likely to have an adverse effect on the generally short-range-oriented claim investigative practices, except possibly the potential proliferation of electronically produced claim data. Especially in first-party claims, all the routines and disciplines are logically event-centered. Whatever actions the insurance carrier takes after a claim is presented depend upon the nature and class of insurance, the circumstances of the loss, and the emerging "personality" of the cast of characters involved in the claim transaction. Competitive pressures of the marketplace alone cannot help but motivate insurors to satisfy the demands and expectations of the policyholder, and there is no reason to suspect massive intrusion into personal privacy. The "service" aspect inherent in claim actions is costly, and it is simply not good business to add searching, costly, and time-consuming inquiries or the maintenance cost of an elaborate data network to the adjustment expense factor.

Admittedly, in third-party claims the rules of the game are somewhat different, but a substantial segment of the population (i.e., the policyholders themselves) has a pronounced interest in making certain that no fraudulent or illegitimate claims are readily settled. The interest of the public at large is served by those practices which identify and defeat the blatant exaggeration or out-and-out fraud when a claim is presented against an insurance carrier.

A spate of (Un)Fair Claim Settlement Practices statutes in the various states are potent enough to inhibit whatever abuses may have occurred in the area of aggressive claim resistive practices. Likewise, the various state insurance departments, through their examinations, make certain that the rights of individuals are not trampled on even if, on the surface, this would seem to bear only on the equity and amount of the claims or interpretations of the contract. Nevertheless, the normal standards and practices of claim investigation, intruding as they do and must into the area of personal facts and details of the policyholder's or claimant's life or lifestyle, are considered acceptable and necessary as responsible business practices.

Especially in the area of first-party claim frauds (i.e., arson or theft of non-existing automobiles, to say nothing of the massive fraud evidenced in the third-party claims, especially in the automobile liability field) there has been strong pressure from federal, state, and municipal government authorities for the industry to increase its effort to combat this practice, if for no other reason than that "premiums go up when losses go up. . . ." Testimony and evidence submitted [to the PPSC] by representatives of industry-supported organizations, such as the Insurance Crime Prevention Institute and the National Automobile Theft Bureau, clearly demonstrated that the public is better served by aggressively combating insurance fraud than by "throwing in the towel" and "paying off" those who prey on insurance as an opportunity for unjust enrichment.

In the area of claims inquiry and investigation, the "transactions" are generally: (a) verification of true identity of policyholder or claimant; (b) verification of policyholder's or claimant's interest in the subject of claim and the insurance policy proceeds; (c) determination and investigation of the circumstances surrounding the cause and result of the claim, and (d) determination of the true and legal valuations and extent of damages to the loss subject. Having raised the issue of potential privacy invasion in the area of claim investigation or claim transactions, we must also realize that existing legal precedent provides the right of the second party (insuror) to initiate inquiries concerning the first party (contract holder) or third party (claimant) when a claim is presented.

I suggest that we might distinguish between "defensive" and "offensive" inquiries (or possibly "sympathetic" versus "adversary"). Presupposing that not all insurance claims are going to be factually or truthfully presented, certain inquiries are unavoidable in the interest of sound and fair claim practices. The policyholder/claimant, as a member of the general public, whom Messrs. Koch and Goldwater seek to serve and protect, will tolerate and anticipate a rather searching inquiry process as a natural prerequisite to the ultimately desired result of a voluntary payment by an insuror. This is a patently different atmosphere or proposition from the inquiry process preceding the establishing of the contractual relationship in the first place, such as an application for a policy or contract renewal.

Attempting to reduce the claim data bank issue, as related to privacy protection, to clear, simple, and manageable dimensions is a little like trying to put toothpaste back into the tube after it has been squeezed out. That loss data follow the claim is as immutable as night following day and, like all unchangeable acts of the past, must and will affect acts in the future. We can and must preserve the proposition that a claim once made and paid clearly might be related to a following claim, even if only for the simplest of reasons—that the claim should not be paid two, three, or more times.

What shall be done with the information once obtained? Should the information be accessible to others? These are obvious questions. Being certain that the basic right of privacy shall be respected among individuals in the private sector is obviously as important as preserving privacy in relationships between the public and its governments. Public concern with the use of statistical claim data for actuarial purposes is far less pronounced than the use of these data, for example, in future eligibility for insurance (underwriting purposes), and this area has already been well explored and legal parameters have been set. Releasing of claim transaction information to government or law enforcement authorities is a valid issue, and one that should be carefully monitored. If taxing authorities, for instance, seek to analyze the nature of the indemnity payment as possible income by requesting legal access to loss files, they seek to exercise a privilege, rather than the legal prerogative, of placing a lien on potential proceeds.

It is, however, a sobering thought to contemplate the alarming possibility that insurance carriers might be compelled to surrender their (first-party) claim files, with all attendant reports and opinions developed during the investigation and adjustment of an insurance claim, to a policyholder or claimant or their attorneys after the claim is closed and a payment has been made. Such an implication is present in Recommendation 10 of the PPSC and, in the writer's opinion, is the single most questionable aspect of the recommended practices pertaining to claim data.

The confidentiality issue of claim data, as they exist in the form of data banks, is not nearly the same as that relating to insurance company claim file information that clearly takes on the aspect of a "work product" and, as such, is deserving of protection, lest those who attempt to resist the "forces of the dark" be inhibited and frustrated under fear of potential legal assault by opportunists or their legal counsel.

I recommend that future studies clarify the reasons for the distinction between first- and third-party claims, although there is no doubt that the Commission members seem to have accepted a distinction between "direct" and "adversary" claim relationships. The character of the business today, however, is clearly changing in the direction of hardening attitudes and adversary presumptions in the area of first-party claims as much as, if not more than, in the area of third-party claims. The conclusion of a claim, whether denied or paid, does not, in the writer's opinion, "establish a first-party claimant's right ..." of access to the file information, or at least, it should not.

The claims segment of the insurance industry obviously has considerable interest in the continuation of dialogue in this area of personal privacy in an information society. Existing industry committees and study groups should remain active and alert so that, when Bill HR 8288 becomes active in Congress again, responsible input will be provided on behalf of the insurance claims function.

Remarks of M.D. Knight, III:

Let me share with you some observations as to the probable impact of some of the recommendations of the Privacy Protection Study Commission on the operation of property and casualty claim departments. This will be a relatively narrow presentation, from my viewpoint as a professional claims man, of those recommendations most specifically affecting our claim departments. Before pursuing that rather precisely defined objective, however, I would like to make one general observation.

At several points, the Commission has suggested enforcement by way of federal regulation. There is a parable about a baby elephant that is very appropriate to any consideration of federal regulation. It seems that once upon a time, a homeowner invited a baby elephant to come into his house. At the time, the baby elephant was very helpful with household chores, and the children enjoyed having him in the house. Almost before they knew it, however, the elephant began to grow, and soon he was so big that he could not be shoved out the door. Shortly thereafter, he began to break up the furniture and take up more and more room. In the end, he made the house uninhabitable for the original owners. From this time on, whenever you think of federal regulation of the insurance industry, I hope you will remember the baby elephant.

Turning now to our primary objective of considering the probable impact of the Commission recommendations on the operation of our claim departments, let's first identify the two major functions of those claim departments. First, our claim departments are obligated to deliver appropriate benefits as expeditiously and inexpensively as possible.

Second, our claim departments are obligated to identify and resist exaggerated or fraudulent claims so that the public is not subjected to unwarranted increases in insurance costs.

The successful disposition of claims requires an investigation, analysis, and evaluation that is as expeditious and unfettered as possible. The cost to our industry is directly related to a satisfactory handling that includes both the sufficiency of the information generated as well as the time period within which it is completed. Anything that would unreasonably delay or limit that activity will be translated into dollar increases. It goes without saying that these increases must eventually be translated into increased premium charges. Thus, it is the insuring public, the very group these recommendations are designed to help, who must bear the cost of our loss payments. In this regard, the public and the insurance industry share a community of interest which I think must be kept in mind throughout this discussion.

In this context, we shall be examining six of the Commission's recommendations. The questions to be answered are whether or not these recommendations enhance the ability of our claim departments to meet our responsibilities or, in fact, create obstacles for proper disposition of claims presented to us. Specifically, we shall be considering Recommendations 2, 3, 8, 10, 16, and 17. These recommendations deal with pretext interviews, company relationships with investigative organizations, the use of authorizations, and the confidentiality of the information developed through our claim investigations.

Before getting into the specific subjects, it is necessary to keep in mind that the recommendations and the Commission's comments must be reviewed as a whole; the effect or impact of any one recommendation touches on any number of other recommendations. There is difficulty in reconciling the definitions and phrases between several recommendations. I will touch on this briefly as I discuss the specific areas that seem to me to have the greatest impact on the claims function.

Let's now look at Recommendation 2. In its entirety, it reads as follows:

> That the Federal Fair Credit Reporting Act be amended to provide that no insurance institution or insurance support organization may attempt to obtain information about an individual through pretext interviews or other false or misleading representations that seek to conceal the actual purposes of the inquiry or investigation, or the identity or representative capacity of the inquirer or investigator.

There are virtually no exceptions to this blanket prohibition.

By way of background, the Commission detailed some very questionable practices on the part of certain insurance support organizations and how they obtain information on individuals. It was the type of questionable activity that brings forth an immediate agreement in principle, but overlooks some very real problems faced by the industry.

Exaggerated or clearly fraudulent claims are a problem we face every day in the claim function. It is unrealistic to believe that the Commission meant us to be stripped of any tool with which we could fight claims where we have a real suspicion of illegality.

We also are concerned with the language in which the recommendation is couched. It speaks of false or misleading representations that seek to conceal the actual purpose or identity of the investigator. While we feel the committee was addressing itself to active misrepresentations, we would find it more comfortable to live with a clarification in this wording. Quite often a claim investigation develops information, quite fortuitously, that has a real bearing on the claim, but is wholly outside the scope of the original investigation. Also, we occasionally have a good samaritan come forward and volunteer information concerning a claim. In both these situations, we could be accused of engaging in pretext by not alerting the claimant to the possible relevance of the information revealed.

But the critical issue in considering this recommendation is whether or not the claim department will be permitted to fulfill its obligation to resist exaggerated or fraudulent claims. Remember, it is not the person with a legitimate claim who will suffer from a pretext interview. If it is verified that he is in fact disabled, his claim will be paid much more quickly and fully. If, on the other hand, the claimant is exaggerating or completely fabricating a claim for disability, in nine out of ten cases it may only be through pretext interviews that we are going to learn of this malingering.

Recommendation 3 is closely related to Recommendation 2. It reads as follows:

> That the Federal Fair Credit Reporting Act be amended to provide that each insurance institution and insurance support organization must exercise reasonable care in the selection and use of insurance support organizations, so as to assure that the collection, maintenance, use, and disclosure practices of such organizations comply with the Commission's recommendations.

Generally, we agree with the National Association of Independent Insurers' critique of the Commission's recommendations, but on this one I am inclined to support the general concept except to the extent it suggests federal enforcement. I feel that the selection of a support organization is an activity that should involve a management decision in any company. Our use and reliance on the information gathered by these organizations are critical to our operation. We would be ill-served if that information were less than the best available and were collected, maintained, and disclosed without the highest possible regard for the confidentiality involved. I do not feel that federal legislation is necessary to assure such compliance, but it is certainly in the industry's best interest to use the utmost care in the selection of their support organizations.

Recommendation 8 deals with authorizations secured by our claim departments to obtain information from someone else concerning the claimant signing the authorization. The recommendation itself is too lengthy to be quoted in its entirety. For your information, however, the Commission found that unrestricted authorizations from claimants would give rise to inquiries beyond the scope of any relevant investigation.

For that reason, real or imagined, the Commission recommended that authorization forms be tailored to the scope of the investigation necessary to develop the nature and severity of the claim being presented. Basically, the restrictions center on four areas:

1) Identification of the persons or organizations from whom data is to be solicited.

2) Identification of the nature of the data being sought.

3) Identification of the persons to whom such data may be revealed to further the investigation.

4) Limitation of authorizations to a period of one year.

The latter is probably the most objectionable from a claims standpoint, since it is often necessary, in cases involving suspected fraud or complicated or aggravated injuries, to become involved in follow-up investigations that last well beyond a year. A more realistic time frame would be in relating the duration of the authorization to the life of the claim itself.

Another area that could present problems is the requirement that the authorization be specific as to persons from whom data is to be solicited [if these persons] are known at the time the authorization is signed. It goes on to say that the authorization can be general as to others whose identity is not known at that time. We must be careful in any legislative wording of this latter portion to assure the broadest possible access to persons and data necessary to our investigation.

The nature of claims investigation is such that we are rarely given full insight into the ramifications of a claim until we have developed a good deal of the basic information. Prior inquiries and prior physical condition, as well as a claimant's employment history, often become important factors in the value of a current claim. We must be free to develop or, in some cases, rule out these factors. We must be free to pass whatever relevant data we do develop to other insurers or support organizations in order to gain access to whatever additional, relevant data they may have. Thus, while the Commission's emphasis on specific identity of sources from whom or to whom data must flow is laudable, the realities of claim investigation are such that generalities must be allowed.

Finally, the recommendations would require that the authorization include specific notice of the way in which the information may be used, "both at the time of the disclosure and at any time in the future." It seems to me this can create real problems when the claimant makes another claim several years in the future when, through the Index System, another company learns we have information in our file which would be useful to them. Can we release the information? What should we have said in the authorization to permit us to release the information? Once again, keep in mind that this restriction will work only to the advantage of those who have something to hide.

With respect to Recommendations 2, 3, and 8, there are no exemptions for claims investigations, and they apply equally to underwriting and claims. With respect to the remaining recommendations, however, the Commission did make an effort to recognize the special problems in claims work.

In many situations, the Commission specified that the recommendations did not apply to the investigation necessary for the preparation of cases for criminal prosecution or civil litigation, or for investigations conducted for the purpose of claim settlements. With respect to the exemptions for claim investigations, the Commission distinguishes between third-party claims and first-party claims. Third-party claims data generally are not covered by the recommendations, and first-party claims data are not covered by the recommendations until after the claim has been settled. The uninitiated, nonclaims person would probably conclude that these exemptions should certainly leave the claim department free to accumulate whatever information is necessary to carry out its responsibilities. Unfortunately, this is not the case.

As we shall see in discussing the remaining recommendations, there is confusion between who is a third-party claimant and who is a first-party claimant, and there would be loopholes in our ability to restrict access to our claim investigations. For example, suppose we are investigating the possibility of fraud or arson on a property loss. If we decide that prosecution is not warranted, and then settle the claim, under the Commission's recommendations the insured would then have access to our investigation. Can you imagine what would happen to people who had given us adverse information during the course of the investigation? The Commission also suggests the possibility of maintaining the anonymity of our sources, but from a practical point of view we know that isn't realistic.

Recommendation 10 provides, in part, "that the Federal Fair Credit Reporting Act be amended to provide that, upon request by an individual, an insurance institution or insurance support organization must: (1) inform the individual, after verifying his identity, whether it has any recorded information pertaining to him; and (2) permit the individual to see and copy any such recorded information, either in person or by mail." These are two limitations which are very pertinent from the point of view of the claim department. Data developed in reasonable expectation of a civil or criminal action, and data to be used to settle a claim, do not have to be revealed. However, once the claim is settled, any data in our file would have to be released to a first-party claimant.

I am sure that when the Commission exempted the preparation of criminal or civil actions, and investigations of third-party claims and first-party claims until settled, the Commission felt that it had given a property and casualty claim department all of the freedom it needed to adequately perform its responsibilities. This simply is not the case. There are very serious problems in defining first-party and third-party claims, which I touched on previously. It is specified that the sources are to remain anonymous, but in a claim investigation the very nature of the information will usually identify the source. It is not being overdramatic to say that many sources of information obtained in a claim investigation would literally find their lives in danger if we were required to reveal data through which they could be identified. The Commission states in its comments that a source who wishes to remain confidential may do so, but the very subject matter of a given piece of data will usually reveal the source regardless of his or her desire to remain anonymous. In this regard, the Commission's recommendation is unrealistic. At the risk of having been repetitious, I strongly submit, these concerns bear repeating.

If this recommendation, or several of the other recommendations, were adopted, we would have a serious problem with the distinction between third-party claimants and first-party claimants. A third-party claimant has only limited access to data in our claim files—specifically, the data used for something other than claim settlement purposes. However, first-party claimants (sometimes referred to in the recommendations as principal insureds) have full access to the data after settlement and after the discontinuance of any investigation for the purposes of preparing a criminal or civil action. What happens when an insured is a third-party claimant, a situation that frequently happens when we have losses involving more than one insured, or in cases where the insured is a passenger in his own automobile? Can he be treated as a third-party claimant after settlement? The recommendation is not clear.

There is in this recommendation an interesting suggestion on immunity. Immunity is to be granted, apparently, in situations in which adverse underwriting decisions are made on the basis of information that is false, but not furnished maliciously or willfully. If the underwriting function is to be so protected, it is even more important that the claim function have that protection, and it might be of considerable value in encouraging disclosures that could lead to a greater number of prosecutions.

Recommendation 16 concerns disclosures to industry data exchanges such as the Index System. It covers "the furnishing of medical information to insurance institutions and support organizations, including medical history, diagnosis, condition, treatment or evaluation of an individual." It prohibits dissemination of this data unless it is acquired from a primary source—the subject himself, a medical care provider, or the subject's spouse, parent, or guardian. This may or may not limit the usefulness of the original index card filing. However, the value of the Index System is in the exchange of more detailed information at a later date and may concern prior, simultaneous, or subsequent claims. This problem is closely associated with the limitations imposed by Recommendation 17.

Recommendation 17 concerns the expectation of confidentiality of acquired records and limits their subsequent dissemination. This dissemination is limited to certain parties of interest, such as independent adjusters, co-insurers, agents, or service bureaus. It also would allow dissemination to governmental bodies that have a legitimate interest in such data, such as insurance commissions and law enforcement agencies. However, when viewed in the context of the claim function, it would not allow the dissemination of data to another insurer or support organization that was investigating a different claim, whether it occurred subsequent or prior to the one which is the subject of the data acquired.

This would be a major departure from current practice, and one we find far too restrictive. The prior claim history, physical condition, injuries, and employment record often have a direct bearing on a claim under consideration. Even subsequent injuries can alter the value of a claim. It is no answer to say that this type of data could be more available through the legal procedures of discovery. The delay and additional cost would be most onerous. Free dissemination of data, limited only by its relevance to a current claim, is an operational necessity in claims handling.

In conclusion, I would like to submit the following summary with respect to the Commission recommendations that have been discussed:

Recommendation 2: Pretext interviews should be allowed in claims where there is real suspicion of fraud or exaggeration.

Recommendation 3: Claims management should be involved in the selection of support organizations.

Recommendation 8: Authorizations should remain valid during the life of the claim; and the limitations on the subject matter, persons to be contacted, and persons to whom data may be disseminated need to be only generally identified, limited only by relevancy.

Recommendation 10: A clear distinction should be made between first- and third-party claimants; sensitive data should be withheld at the discretion of the insurer; immunity should be spelled out more clearly for the claims function.

Recommendation 16: Filing of index cards should be allowed based on a first impression of the nature of the injury, even when a primary source is not available.

Recommendation 17: Dissemination of relevant data on prior or subsequent claims should be freely allowed between insurers and service bureaus.

Finally, let me remind you again of the baby elephant. Don't let him in the house, because once he gets in, we shall never get him out.

Remarks of James F. Ahern:

The Insurance Crime Prevention Institute (ICPI) is a national, non-profit organization representing over 325 mutual, stock, and independent companies writing the majority of the property and casualty insurance in the United States. The purpose of the Institute is to investigate suspected insurance frauds and to initiate prosecution of the people who plot such frauds so as to deter false claims. The Institute's primary function is to investigate fraudulent insurance claims of all kinds with the exception of accident, health and life insurance, and Workers' Compensation claims. The Institute does not in any way participate in the actual settlement of the claims investigated and does not advise members of the disposition of any claims. Member companies who ask for investigations are never asked to sign a complaint or to initiate prosecution.

As you can see from the very nature of our work, ICPI has always needed to be very concerned about the problems of privacy, confidentiality, and fair information practices. However, we have always approached these problems from the standpoint of avoidance rather than compliance. By that I do *not* mean that we attempt to circumvent the law, but rather that we purposely structure our operations so as not to be restricted by it.

The reason for this approach is obvious. As an organization that investigates criminal activity, we would be worthless if we were required to disclose our activities and records to the individuals under investigation. Unlike street crimes, such as burglary, in which the investigator already knows a crime has taken place and his primary job is to find out who did it, in the investigation of white collar crime—and in particular, insurance fraud—the investigator usually *knows who* committed the crime, and his task is to supply *evidence* connecting the criminal with the crime. If the individual under suspicion knows that he is being investigated for insurance fraud, he may very well be able to take steps to destroy evidence crucial to proving his crime, and thus frustrate any attempts to prosecute successfully.

With these factors in mind, the Insurance Crime Prevention Institute has been particularly careful to limit the scope of its investigative functions and its reporting activities. We investigate for criminal activity; we do *not* become involved in claims settlement or civil litigation. In this way, we can preserve the confidentiality of our files in the face of subpoenas from claimants who are plaintiffs in civil suits, because our files are simply not relevant. We limit our reporting activity to simple, periodic status reports concerning the stage of investigation reached and to reports of public record information regarding arrests, convictions, and so forth. By doing this—and by refusing to become involved in claims settlement—we avoid the provision of the Fair Credit Reporting Act which would otherwise require disclosure to the subject of an investigation.

Another area of concern is in the accumulation of information from insurance companies. Again, we must be able to accomplish this without a requirement that disclosure be made to the individual, or [the subject] will be alerted to the investigation. Our position on this question is that ICPI acts on behalf of the insurance companies it represents, who have a valid interest in assuring that claims filed against them are legitimate. Therefore, it does not violate a privacy right or a requirement of confidentiality when an insurance company gives us information necessary to investigate such claims.

A third way in which information may be passed is from the Institute to a law enforcement agency. Here again, our position rests on traditional legal principles that state that an individual is privileged and may reveal information when he is acting in the public interest to assist in the apprehension of criminal wrongdoers. We consider ourselves, basically, as private citizens who are coming forward with information which [it] is our duty to disclose.

One final privacy aspect of the work of ICPI operations arises in the conduct of our investigators. ICPI maintains strict controls to assure that all information received by our investigators is held confidential. Our investigators are carefully instructed in the laws of privacy, are advised on the types of information to which they are entitled, and are instructed regarding the investigative techniques that are acceptable. I personally feel that this kind of training is extremely important.

ICPI as an agency and the insurance industry in general must demonstrate concern for the privacy of those with whom we deal. We must visibly demonstrate our willingness to abide by the constraints of the laws of privacy. ICPI's interest is in swift, effective justice—NOT in defamation of character or in the invasion of the right of privacy. Consequently, all the Institute's investigations carefully protect the legal rights of suspects. Only by doing this can we establish the validity of our efforts to assure that the laws are not changed in ways that may prevent us from carrying out our activities.

Life and Health Insurance Marketing and Underwriting

Recommendations 5 and 6, which relate to delivery of a preliminary notice describing the types of information intended to be collected, the methods used to obtain it, and the intended use, worried many underwriting executives. There was general concern that the length of the documents involved would seriously interfere with the sales process. There was doubt that a document could be written that would be both simple enough to be understandable and short enough to be attractive.

Even greater concern was addressed to the authorization form, the subject of Recommendation 8. This concern was of two different types. First, if physicians, clinics, and hospitals want specific release forms for each incident of treatment, then companies and agents may have to go back to prospects "time and again" to get permission to obtain additional information as an underwriting investigation proceeds. This leads to the second concern, namely, that this procedure would appear to permit the insurance applicant to conceal any aspect of insurability he or she chooses—specifically, any aspect the individual believes might lead to higher premiums or declination. A related concern is that very long delays in completing the insuring process will develop, causing general annoyance and occasional hardship.

It was stated in the workshop that the Commission's prenotice requirement is already met by the Medical Information Bureau (MIB), and no changes would be required in their procedure if the Commission's Recommendation 5 were implemented. All agreed that if the spirit of the Commission's recommendations were to be carried out successfully, companies would have to work hard to design compact and efficient prenotice and authorization forms.

Recommendation 10 would require full file disclosure. There was some concern about what methods should be used to protect confidentiality while at the same time increasing access to the information in these files. One underwriting executive mentioned that home offices will have to begin training agents, brokers, and field office managers in the methods of protecting records in their possession. He mentioned that in many companies, particularly those operating in the brokerage market, information from a prior company's medical examination is used directly in the underwriting process, and he warned that such methods of operation must be reappraised if the Commission's recommendations are to be respected. It was noted that the MIB already has a disclosure procedure in place, and that all applicants are notified of it in the prenotice that was first installed in January 1975.

Recommendation 16 was discussed for a considerable time. This recommendation prohibits transfer of information about an individual's health unless the information was obtained either directly from the individual, or spouse, or from a medical professional. Underwriting executives believed that this would severely limit the depth of an underwriting investigation, since it would prohibit both agents and consumer reporting agencies from giving health information to the underwriter. However, one of the Commission members who was present at the discussion pointed out that the recommendation was intended to apply only to a detailed medical diagnosis or treatments, and not to general statements of appearance, function, or demeanor of the subject individual. For example, this recommendation would prevent the next door neighbor from saying that the subject individual had a heart condition, when the neighbor had no direct information that this was the case and no qualifications to obtain, process, or transmit that kind of information. The Commission member further explained that the recommendation was not intended to preclude transmittal by a neighbor of an observation that the subject individual had to stop and rest every few steps when walking, or that the individual exhibited any other behavior limitation that did not involve a specific medical diagnosis.

Prepared remarks of Robert W. Blevins, of Southland Life Insurance Company, Charles N. Walker, of New England Mutual Life Insurance Company, and Neil M. Day, of the Medical Information Bureau, are included in this section.

Remarks of Robert W. Blevins:

Privacy matters have always been a source of genuine concern in the underwriting of life and health insurance. The underwriter has long recognized the highly sensitive personal information needed for risk classification. It is significant that in the underwriting process for such coverages, involving millions of people each year, there have been only an infinitesimal number of complaints from the public we serve. Most of those complaints have been without merit. Privacy is a vital, long-time issue—not a new one. In recent years it has been in the forefront due to modern computer technology, governmental eavesdropping, and public outrage at occasional misuse of personal file information. Most of my remarks will be responsive to the final report of the Privacy Protection Study Commission, *Personal Privacy in an Information Society*.

Before looking at the recommendations that are most critical in the underwriting process, I should like to make a few comments regarding some of the distinguishing characteristics of various insurance sales. This is most important because *all* underwriting begins in the field when the sale is made. I am a firm believer that a company does at least 80 to 90% of its underwriting when it contracts and trains, or fails to train, a new field underwriter.

The *typical life insurance sale* has certain characteristics that are most important. First, there is a natural buyer reluctance for the coverage and this reluctance must be overcome by the salesperson in order to persuade the buyer that life insurance is needed. Second, the salesperson must find a way for the prospect to pay the premiums. In many instances, the buyer is planning to purchase something with more tangible and immediate value. Third, the selection process involves the evaluation of a multitude of subtle differences in health, medical history, family history, occupation, habits, hobbies, finances, and many other factors. These factors have varying severities and influences on mortality. Fourth, the coverage will be incontestable after one or two years. Fifth, extra features such as accidental death, premium waiver disability, and future insurance purchase options are frequently included in such coverage. Sixth, other than for the occasional disability claim, a claim only occurs once and that claim is at the death of the client.

The *typical health insurance sale* is different. First, often medical care coverages are sought by the applicant, although disability income coverages may or may not be sought by the applicant. Second, a high claim frequency is to be expected. This requires continuing interaction between the insured and the insurance company after the policy is issued. Third, as with life insurance, the coverage is usually incontestable after a year or two. Fourth, there are many differences in the policy structure of coverages with respect to continuation of insurance. Policies may be cancelable, renewable at the option of the company, guaranteed renewable, or noncancelable and guaranteed renewable.

The *typical casualty sale* has major differences. First, it almost always begins with an actual request from the buyer rather than a sales presentation by an agent. Second, the risks to be assumed can be defined, fully described, and replacement values can be determined. Third, policies are cancelable and premiums adjustable from time to time in the future. These distinctions are very important in the area of privacy: Such differences [are indicative of the difficulties in attempting to arrive at blanket solutions to privacy problems.]

The issues of greatest impact on the underwriting process, as detailed in the report of the President's Privacy Study Commission in the fields of life and health underwriting, have to do with basically four areas.

First, one of the most important features and one of the most critical issues is in the area of "relevancy and propriety." The recommendation is written in very general terms as follows:

> That governmental mechanisms should exist for individuals to question the propriety of information collected or used by insurance institutions, and to bring such objections to the appropriate bodies which establish public policy. Legislation specifically prohibiting the use, or collection and use, of a specific item of information may result; or an existing agency or regulatory body may be given authority, or use its currently delegated authority to make such a determination with respect to the reasonableness of future use, or collection and use, of a specific item of information.

I think it appears obvious to any seasoned underwriter that to define relevance of underwriting information for all of these different lines of insurance and variations of coverages is a most difficult assignment. There is a vast difference not only in lines of insurance but also in relevance as applied to small amounts, average amounts, large amounts, and jumbo amounts of life insurance. Many changes in the hazards of the modern world are unpredictable. After an underwriting decision has been made, it is easy to detail the relevant information.

Anticipation is far more difficult. The underwriter needs the freedom to contract or refuse to contract without such decisions being forced by legislative or regulatory fiat. I know of no parallel where a business could be forced to issue a contract involving large sums of money to someone they literally prefer not to do business with.

A quotation from the body of the Commission's report discussing intrusiveness in information practices seems especially appropriate:

From the standpoint of many applicants and insureds, the dichotomy between the individual's privacy interest and the insurer's interest in evaluating risk is probably not as great as it seems at first glance. The low-risk applicant benefits from an underwriting evaluation that results in unusual risks being eliminated or written at a higher premium because that keeps the cost of his insurance down. The Commission was continually reminded that it is in the interest of the applicant to have complete and accurate information on which this judgment can be based so that he can be insured at the proper rate; that the insurer must be able to evaluate the risk it is being asked to assume if premium charges are to bear a reasonable relationship to expected losses and expenses for all insureds within a similar classification. (Page 173)

In the Commission's quest to minimize intrusiveness, it is unfortunate that no comment was made as to the need for honest, reliable, and candid answers on applications for insurance. Complete, truthful responses produce situations that require the least possible intrusiveness from sources of information other than the applicant for insurance.

A second area has to do with items required for notice at the time of sale. I refer specifically to the elaborate requirements of prenotification and the content of the authorization or consent form to obtain medical information. These particular items are detailed in Recommendations 5, 6, 8, and 9. Both of these documents [the prenotification and the authorization form] will be of far greater length [than they are now]. The language requirement [of the recommendation] is for simplicity, but the requirements of length will seriously deter the likelihood of reading or understandability by the prospect. The authorization form is likely to be our biggest problem. It is true that our past authorization forms have been of a general nature. Physicians, clinics, and hospitals may want specific release forms for each incident of treatment. If this becomes a fact, we will have to go back time and again to our prospects to get additional forms, as we find the need to write additional physicians. If the authorization must be a specific one for each doctor, each clinic, and each hospital, and for each time of treatment, we are going to see very long delays in insuring prospects for insurance. Some practical solution must be obtained. I think it also stands to reason that the lengthy prenotification and medical authorization will likely cause us to lose some sales of life and health insurance. This will be unfortunate to the beneficiaries who will never collect from insurance that would have been placed in effect.

Another area that is of special significance in the underwriting phase has to do with the postnotification regarding information in our files and reasons for adverse underwriting decisions. These items are included in Recommendations 10, 12, 13, and 16 of the report. First, there will be some extremely sensitive cases that will produce a real test of total compliance without the sacrifice of confidentiality. These extremely sensitive areas are going to be most difficult for underwriters. We will have difficulty communicating reasons to our prospect without breaching confidentiality to his agent or someone who has no legitimate need for the information. The best means of communication may be by mail, although we do not know who might actually open a particular letter addressed to the applicant. We do not want to provide the information to our agent. The use of the telephone can be difficult because we do not know who we are talking to in many instances. I think this is an area that will have to be handled very tenderly by all underwriters.

The final area that has great impact on underwriters involves records created by agents, brokers, and field offices. We will have a vital role to play because of the necessity of training for the protection of these records. Some companies that operate only through brokers or whose agents represent many different companies may have real difficulty controlling such people, and yet there appears to be little doubt that the insurance companies will be responsible for actions of sales representatives. A truly independent agent is quick to tell you that he or she is acting entirely for his or her client, and he or she may deliberately disobey instructions and directions given to him or her by the insurance company. An area of difficulty is the use of information such as medical examination forms and attending physician reports by more than one company. It is not the case in our company, but many companies, that operate primarily in the brokerage market, not only utilize information from a prior company's medical examination but [also their forms], as two recent advertisements claim: "Other companies' medical forms accepted—a recent medical [form] along with our declaration of insurability will be accepted for underwriting purposes." Such methods of operation must be reappraised.

The Commission's report made the following comment:

> Because the chief functions of an insurer—underwriting and rating risks and paying claims—are decision-making processes that involve evaluations of people and their property, the insurance industry is among society's largest gatherers and users of information about individuals.

Any home office underwriter has great desire to obtain the best possible picture of the risk to be assumed. This is possible only with complete information about the prospect. Having such information the underwriter must make a fair decision, communicate it effectively, and protect the client's privacy rights—all of which are simply good business practices.

Remarks of Charles N. Walker:

The Commission's insurance recommendations are aimed largely at the underwriting process, which is, I think, appropriate. The two insurance functions that involve the acquisition of a considerable amount of personal information are underwriting and claims. There are a couple of important distinctions between them, however. The preponderance of claim investigations tend to be limited in scope—limited to the question of whether the claim is eligible for payment and, if so, what the extent of the company liability is. Moreover, claimants understand the need for this, understand the basics of the methods used, and accept both. The other distinction is that if the claimant disagrees with the company's claim decision, he has at least three recourses—direct protest, the state insurance department, and the courts. Any of them are likely to result in further disclosure and thus give opportunity to discover and correct inaccuracies or inadequacies.

Not so with underwriting. While an underwriting investigation may be sharply limited by the economics of policy size and competition, it can, and frequently does, range across a rather broad spectrum of subjects that are relevant to the appraisal of mortality and morbidity hazards. Moreover, it is a process that is not well understood by the preponderance of applicants. And, in the event of a disagreement with a company's underwriting decision, an applicant's ability to obtain further disclosure is more difficult than with claims. Added to this is, that even given disclosure, an applicant's lack of understanding of the underwriting process may make it difficult to understand the reason for the decision.

As for the seventeen insurance recommendations, let me make the general comment that I have no disagreement with the *intent* of most of them. This may be begging the question, since most of them merely ask us to tell our applicants more of what we know about them. Nonetheless, only six of the seventeen present serious concerns, and this is really only five, since two of them—numbers 5 and 6—really constitute a single recommendation. Let me say just a word about each.

The first recommendation asks the states to regulate relevance. I find this concept nothing short of frightening, not only because relevance is extremely difficult to define, but also because it is a dynamic thing, so that freezing it by regulatory definition is to lose the flexibility needed to meet changing circumstances. I am very pessimistic that any meaningful regulation of relevance will constrain the underwriting process and thus lead to higher prices.

Recommendations 5 and 6 would require delivery of a preliminary notice describing the types of information intended to be collected, the methods used to obtain it, and the intended use. My concern is with the method. Compliance would require a document so massive as to be counter-productive and, in fact, a serious hindrance to the sales process.

Recommendation 8 deals with the authorization. Compliance would cause a great deal of confusion and delay. The more serious concern, however, is that it would appear to permit the insurance applicant to conceal any aspect of his insurability he chooses to—specifically, any aspect he feels might lead to higher premiums or declination.

Recommendation 10 would require full file disclosure. In a very real sense, it would require the company to permit invasion of privacy, since it would give the inquirer access to information he is not entitled to have. Limitation is needed.

Recommendation 13 would require extensive explanation of every adverse underwriting decision, whether requested or not. It should be changed to require explanation only when requested, and the extent of the information required should be more carefully defined.

Recommendation 16 prohibits transfer of health information obtained from lay sources. This would seriously interfere with underwriting, since it would prohibit both agents and consumer reporting agencies from giving health information to the underwriter.

Several of the other eleven recommendations raise concerns, but they are more technical than substantive. Some appear to be unintended; others probably reflect a less than perfect understanding of the underwriting process. I am optimistic that correction can be made in any legislative or regulatory process that ensues.

Remarks of Neil M. Day:

My presentation will cover two areas. First, I will highlight privacy issues as relates to the Medical Information Bureau (MIB). Second, I will state my reaction on how to best deal with these issues.

In a nutshell, MIB is a nonprofit membership organization of 700 life [insurance] companies that operates an exchange of underwriting information in the United States and Canada. About 90% of all MIB information is medical. MIB information is sent to home office locations at member companies and is used at the home office in underwriting applications for life and health insurance and for claims on such types of personal insurance. MIB and its members represent that MIB information will be held in a confidential manner, which courts say means that MIB information must not be disclosed to unauthorized parties or to those without legitimate interest *and* that MIB has an obligation to act with integrity and to promote the trust and confidence of the individual who gave the information.

The MIB has existed for over seventy-five years and until recently had a very low profile. I am thoroughly familiar with MIB rules for the last thirty years. Those rules have historically stressed confidential treatment. In the mid 60s, the public became concerned about an individual's right to privacy or the right to be let alone. Courts have long recognized that businesses had the right to exchange information about a person who applied for insurance and that a reasonable exchange was consistent with privacy. Nevertheless, MIB operations became spotlighted by increased governmental review at the federal and state level, and this activity became intense by 1971. There have been about six major reviews of MIB activities at the federal level and each year about fifty bills that could have affected MIB have been introduced in the state legislatures.

Prior to the late 60s, MIB and its members believed that its rules and procedures were sufficient to protect privacy and confidentiality. The history of the MIB in the last seven years has been a succession of voluntary changes which reacted to expression of public concern that by and large was expressed by congressional committees and presidential-type commissions.

In the past ten years, legislators and others have considered imposing dozens of different types of requirements on MIB so as to protect better privacy and confidentiality. Time will not permit a full description of these various requirements that suggest how many interested parties would solve privacy issues suggested by MIB operations. However, I can briefly describe how some of the Privacy Commission recommendations would affect the MIB, if the recommendations became law tomorrow.

Recommendation 4 requires procedures that would assure the accuracy of MIB information, but MIB concern about accuracy has long been reflected in MIB rules.

Recommendation 5 requires that a prenotice be delivered to the applicant before information is collected and that the prenotice thoroughly describe MIB and its operation. MIB members have made such a notice a part of their application since January 1975. Many in Congress have suggested that prior express consent would be more appropriate, but MIB has argued that such express consent could allow an applicant to unreasonably withhold needed information.

Recommendation 10 would require MIB to disclose an MIB record to the subject so that the applicant could dispute accuracy where appropriate. MIB and its members implemented disclosure [provisions] and accuracy [requirements] in 1971. In 1973, congressional critics emphasized that insurance applicants had little or no knowledge of these procedures. The MIB prenotice was first included in all insurance applications in January 1975, and the notice recited the phone and mail addresses of the disclosure offices in Boston and Toronto. Since January 1975, those two offices have processed over 15,000 requests for disclosure. Only a few hundred had been handled between 1971 and January 1975.

Disclosure of medical information is made to the applicant's attending physician, and MIB has long argued with legislators that this approach should be followed in legislative recommendations. The Privacy Commission requires disclosure to the attending physician and not directly to the applicant. [Ed. Note: The PPSC would "allow" disclosure through physicians.]

Recommendation 15 would require that no MIB member could rate or decline an application on the basis of an unconfirmed MIB report. This would put a long-standing MIB rule in statutory form. MIB reports are to be used only as an alert; such use is consistent with sound underwriting practices and fair competitive practices. Moreover, such use is consistent with MIB concern about the identity and accuracy of its reports. This important MIB rule and other MIB rules have been enforced in various ways. Each year, the chief executive officer and senior underwriting officer make a written representation that all MIB rules will be followed. More recently such rules are also enforced by extensive examination of underwriting files by MIB consultants and by audits made by members. However, the Privacy Commission was skeptical about the effectiveness of self-policing by MIB and its members and, therefore, recommended that the "only as an alert" rule become law so as to create statutory rights which could be enforced by applicants and regulators. I would add that the FTC has recently issued a subpoena to MIB records of rule violations that appear related to Fair Credit Reporting Act requirements, and the MIB has negotiated a mutually agreeable response to the subpoena.

Recommendation 16 requires that reports of medical information to MIB must be based on medical sources and is consistent with an MIB rule that became effective in January 1977. At the May 1976 hearing, MIB recognized that the Privacy Commission was concerned about medical information being reported from a nonmedical source. Because of negative comment at various legislative or commission hearings, MIB deleted numerous codes in 1971, 1974, and 1977. In all, about fifteen codes were eliminated from the MIB code list and, where appropriate, were purged from the MIB data base. Most of the deleted and purged codes related to nonmedical information.

The following is my personal analysis of the best way to deal with privacy issues. If the Privacy Commission recommendations were to be made law, MIB would not have to make further changes to its rules and procedures, with a few minor exceptions. This result was achieved because MIB studied the transcript [of PPSC testimony] of May 1976 with great care and designed several additional voluntary changes that were responsive to Privacy Commission concerns.

On at least three major occasions since 1970, MIB has voluntarily made changes to its rules and procedures that are consistent with Privacy Commission recommendations. These voluntary changes may not be the best solutions, but we believe that the voluntary changes are at least reasonable and timely and go beyond the confidentiality procedures that had been historically developed by MIB. Clearly, MIB was strongly motivated by public hearings that articulated legitimate concern about MIB, by a clear desire to avoid unreasonable requirements, such as express consent, and by a membership that became increasingly concerned about the public image of MIB.

Operations

The workshop session on operations involved a discussion of what some insurers were doing on a voluntary basis to protect better the privacy of their customers and the concept that computer technology can easily be a tool for protecting better the individual's privacy.

A. Douglas Murch, of the Prudential Insurance Company of America, comments on aspects of the Privacy Commission's recommendations that affect the operations of an insurer.

Remarks of A. Douglas Murch:

Life insurance companies maintain a great variety of files of personal information. Some are manual, most are computerized; some are temporary, some are permanent; some are active and current, some are archival. Typically, many different systems—both manual and electronic—use these files to handle inquiries, and to process transactions at many different points in a company's organization.

Life insurance companies' use of personal information is a large volume operation. For example, Prudential handles 190 million transactions annually, including premium payments. Each transaction requires one or more uses of personal information. Of significance to the privacy issue is [the fact] that the great majority of personal information used in the operations area is obtained not from third parties, but directly from applicants and policyholders themselves. Effective service requires that we deal with our customers rapidly and efficiently, and without unnecessary red tape. That requires that we be able to access and use the personal information in our files rapidly and efficiently.

The legitimate concern of the Privacy Protection Study Commission, namely, that safeguards be provided to protect individual privacy, is also shared by life insurance companies. We have long recognized the private and confidential nature of the contract relationship between the company and our policyowners. In the operations area, as a rule, information concerning a life or health insurance policy is released outside the insurance organization only to the policyowner or someone specifically designated and approved by him. Necessary exceptions occur in cases such as government requests pursuant to the law or in response to a properly executed subpoena, summons, or legal process.

That our obligation to protect privacy has, in general, been effectively carried out is attested to by the very small volume of complaints as to misuse or abuse of personal information, particularly in relation to the very large volume of transactions processed. In Prudential, we track all complaints addressed to the chairman, president, any member of the executive office, any senior vice president in charge of a regional home office, any state insurance department, consumer affairs agency, or the media. The current volume of such complaints averages approximately 8,000 annually. Related to the annual base of 190 million transactions I mentioned earlier, this is a rate of one complaint per 23,000 transactions. Of the 8,000 complaints, the vast majority relate to delayed or inadequate service, outright errors in transaction processing, or misunderstandings. From a practical viewpoint, these are our principal policyholder service problems. Complaints about violating privacy or security of personal information are very rarely encountered.

Having said all this about how well we behave in the life insurance business in regard to protecting privacy, we must nevertheless acknowledge that we are not perfect, and that with such a large volume operation, individual instances of privacy problems may occur—hence our responsibility to examine constantly our practices and do what we can to strengthen our implementation of privacy protection. In that connection, I'd like to mention four specific things we in Prudential have been giving some attention recently. These are responsive to the Privacy Commission's Recommendations 4, 10, and 17.

The first is to develop a written statement of basic company policy on privacy, and to communicate that statement to all employees and agents. A number of companies have already done this. We have not yet, but we do have such a statement now in preliminary draft form. Its purpose will be not just to formalize privacy principles, but to communicate in writing to all employees the nature of the company's expectation that they, as employees, will do their part to implement that policy, and will treat the personal information they access and handle in a confidential manner.

Second, we have sharpened up, documented, and distributed procedures to be followed throughout our home office policyholder service operations in regard to releasing policy and policyowner information outside the company. The basic principles we follow are consistent with those embodied in Recommendation 17 of the Privacy Commission, namely, that no policy information is to be released by mail, over the phone, or in person to anyone other than the owner of that information, unless we have evidence that the owner has specifically authorized its release. The principal exception is when due legal process or subpoena is served, and in that case our procedures call for notifying the policyowner.

Third, we are in the process of revising and tightening up our on-line EDP data-security mechanisms. Privacy literature is full of references to the threat that computers pose to misuse of information. Not highlighted enough, however, is the fact that computers, properly used, provide an unparalleled means for tightening control, and improving security, beyond the degree of security that is attainable with manual files.

For some years we have had procedures for making certain that whenever a computer production program is run, it is the correct program, and that no unauthorized change in that program has been made. We also have procedures to make certain that when a production tape file is pulled for use by the computer, each instance is properly authorized.

With growth of on-line systems, the need has arisen for a security system to prevent the possibility of a program gaining access to on-line production data sets when that program has not been explicitly authorized to access those data sets. We are working on such a security system. It will be based upon a code that the owner of each on-line production data set will assign to his data set, which he alone should know, which he may change from time to time, and which must be input to the computer every time a program wishes to use that data set. Until we have this on-line security system implemented, we are not converting to direct access form those computer files that contain the most sensitive personal information, such as personnel and payroll files.

Fourth, and finally, we have reviewed and tightened up our procedures for access to, and use of, application files. The application file, which is manual and not computer in form, constitutes by far the largest repository of sensitive personal information in the company. It is used for many purposes and by a large number of individuals throughout the home office organization. Inasmuch as it is a manual file, it is difficult to control tightly.

It is important that, within the limits of practicality, appropriate measures be implemented to insure [the application file's] physical safety and security against loss by fire, vandalism, theft, negligence, or intentional intrusion. It is important also to restrict its access to employees with a "need to know," and to ensure that application files are handled carefully and securely when they are out of file, as well as when they are in file.

With these objectives in mind, we have developed detailed guidelines for implementation by all our regional home offices to help insure the security, privacy, and confidentiality of information in our application files. So, through steps such as these, we and other life insurance companies are taking the necessary steps to see that we remain in the forefront of those responsive to the legitimate concerns of privacy protection.

Part III

Government Perspectives

Rather than concentrating in one body the responsibility for promulgating and administering its recommendations, the Privacy Protection Study Commission (PPSC) recommended remedial action at whatever level—federal government, state government, industry association, or individual firm—and by whatever type—legislative, judicial, administrative, voluntary—most consistent with the structure of each problem addressed. Some of its recommendations, in other words, took the form of suggested amendments to the Fair Credit Reporting Act, a federal legislative remedy; other recommendations were in the form of suggestions for improving the gathering of complaints, a state governmental administrative remedy; and still others were suggestions for firms to undertake voluntarily.

Part II of this volume dealt with the non-governmental insurance-related parties affected by the Commission's recommendations. Part III deals with the governmental units affected by the recommendations. The three papers in this section sketch viewpoints of two federal governmental bodies—Congress and the Federal Trade Commission—and two state governmental bodies—the Insurance Commissioner's offices of Indiana and Illinois. The interest in this matter at various levels of government, and the willingness to act aggressively on it, should be viewed against the backdrop of a revival of interest in federal regulation of insurance, either in addition to, or in place of, state regulation.

Another set of contrasts involves the backgrounds of the regulators whose comments are presented in this part of the book. While Congressman Goldwater and Mr. Goldfarb have been immersed in privacy issues for some time, Commissioner Hudson and Director Mathias are relatively new to it. Accordingly, their reactions to the PPSC's recommendations at the Conference were more tentative than Goldwater's or Goldfarb's, but they may be more indicative of the general public's reaction to the issue at large.

The papers are not specifically related to one another, and so the order in which they appear here carries no special connotation. We begin with the state insurance commissioners—chapter 8, continue with their administrative counterparts at the federal level—the Federal Trade Commission—in chapter 9, and conclude with the U.S. Congress in Chapter 10.

8

Privacy, the Insurance Industry and the Consumer: Insurance Regulators' Views

H.P. Hudson
Richard L. Mathias

Section I: The Privacy Protection Study Commission and Insurance Regulators

by H.P. Hudson

The 654-page report filed with Congress by the Privacy Protection Study Commission promises to cause some drastic changes in the way the insurance industry has traditionally conducted certain facets of its business. The report covers 15 different issues, ranging from mailing lists to social security numbers. In the chapter devoted to "The Insurance Relationship," the introductory paragraph notes that "the insurance industry is among society's largest gatherers and users of information about individuals" because the chief functions of an insurer are decision-making processes (underwriting, rating, paying claims) that involve evaluations of people and their property.

The Commission makes 17 recommendations for the insurance industry, which stem from the Commission's following observations:

1. The problems that result from "the apparent lack of restraint exercised by insurers over organizations they use to collect information about individual applicants, insureds and claimants."

2. "Competition among insurance institutions has indicated less than adequate sensitivity to the fairness issue in record keeping."

3. "Because insurers compete against each other for the better risk they do not have much incentive to look behind some of the criteria they used to sort the good risks from the bad." (Essentially they are saying here that the industry is so steeped in tradition it is resistant to change.)

4. The "lack of attention to fairness issues in record-keeping about individuals has resulted in structuring of information flows so that neither

the insurance institution nor the individual applicant, insured, or claimant is responsible for the quality of the information used."

5. "The individual is . . . placed at a disadvantage when he is asked to sign a form authorizing the release of information . . . because he is not specifically apprised of what he is consenting to."

6. In "property and liability insurance, an adverse decision may or may not lead to the insurer divulging the reasons and supporting information to the applicant."

The Commission proceeds from those conclusions to the 17 recommendations, which it feels are designed to enhance privacy protections in the insurance process. Implementation of the recommendations is to be achieved through voluntary compliance, new state requirements, or federal legislation, depending upon the particular issue.

The recommendations fall generally into three categories: (1) intrusiveness—what and in what way should information be allowed to be collected; (2) fairness; and (3) confidentiality. The one recommendation dealing with intrusiveness provides that governmental mechanisms should exist for individuals to question the propriety of information collected or used by insurance institutions and to bring such objections to the appropriate bodies that establish public policy. Legislation specifically prohibiting the use, or collection and use, of a specific item of information may result; or an existing agency or regulatory body may be given authority, or may use its currently delegated authority, to make such a determination with respect to the reasonableness of future use, or collection and use, of a specific item of information. This particular recommendation is the one that concerns me most.

H.P. Hudson is Commissioner of Insurance for the state of Indiana. He received his bachelor's degree from the University of Minnesota, after which he managed and eventually bought an insurance agency in Indiana. He is past Chairman of the Governor's Insurance Advisory Committee. Commissioner Hudson has served as the state safety chairman, board member and vice president of the Independent Insurance Agents of Indiana, and was president-elect of that organization at the time of his appointment as Insurance Commissioner. He is President of the National Association of Insurance Commissioners.

Richard L. Mathias was Director of Insurance for the state of Illinois at the time this paper was prepared. A member of the Chicago, California, Illinois, and American Bar Associations, he received his law degree from the University of Michigan Law School. He was attorney for the State of Illinois Legislative Reference Bureau and later an associate of the Chicago law firm of Hinshaw, Culbertson, Moelman, Hoban and Fuller. He served three years as Deputy Legal Counsel to the Governor of Illinois. Prior to his appointment as Director of Insurance he was an attorney with Allstate Insurance Company.

Other recommendations would prohibit certain practices that, in my view, could result in higher insurance premiums and restructuring of classifying and rating processes and could impose potential costly compliance problems. On balance, however, one must commend the Privacy Protection Study Commission effort, inasmuch as it reflects a very diligent effort to pursue the desire to protect the rights of privacy, while allowing for information to flow to those who have need for it. Much compromise is in evidence, and that is to be applauded.

Surely, if one considers their own individual needs for privacy, no one can oppose the need to prevent unfair intrusion into the lives of all citizens. Unfair intrusion, obviously, is a very key consideration in the entire question of privacy. Unfortunately, nowhere in the report do we find any definition of "privacy." It seems to me among the best of definitions is that advanced by Dr. Alan F. Westin, who says, "Privacy is the claim of individuals, groups or institutions to determine for themselves when, how, and to what extent information about them is communicated to others." One should retain unto oneself this right of determination, but surely it cannot be construed to imply that one should have the right to withhold or otherwise secretly "cover up" information that would aid another to determine whether one is willing to engage in a relationship with another.

In considering the question of the right to privacy in transactions with the insurance industry, it seems to me that we need to keep in mind that an insurance policy is a contract, and contract right traditionally has held that, in order for a contract to be effected and binding, it must be mutually agreeable to all parties. This carries with it the clear implication that all parties should have the right to engage in a discovery process leading to a determination as to one's willingness to enter into that contractual relationship. Insurance companies are in the business of assuming risk, and insurance companies have a need to determine whether or not they are willing to assume the risk of the private citizen to the same extent that a private citizen has the right to determine whether or not he wishes his risk assumed by a given insurance company. Traditionally, insurance companies have devised rating mechanisms that reflect that to the extent one contributes greater or lesser to the likelihood of loss one should pay a greater or lesser premium for the transfer of that risk. Society traditionally has found that to be acceptable. Surely there is incentive, within that concept, for loss prevention and loss reduction, which should not be ignored. So long as that premise is held to be valid, it would appear the insurance companies have the right, indeed the need and the obligation, to determine information which might lead to the classification of risk based on insurance loss potential. However, inasmuch as the insurance company is entitled to gather certain information to make its judgments, it seems equally appropriate to me that the individual citizen should be permitted to know what information the insurance company has and the specific reason as to why a company has taken a given action—whether it be the declination of insurance, the premiums charged for insurance, or the offering of some amended insurance different from that which was applied for by the citizen. I suggest that failure to do so in the past has led to a perception that the insurance industry has something to hide and often has been perceived to have been acting in an arbitrary and suspicious fashion.

Obviously, therefore, I have no quarrel with the recommendations of the Study Commission as to these proposed provisions. This right to information by the individual is long overdue. However, I do get concerned with some of the potential cost/benefit considerations that have yet to be determined.

Within this three-tiered approach for implementation of the Commission's recommendations, certain implementation and monitoring is recommended to be accomplished at the state level. Customarily, I am a strong advocate of state rights and particularly as pertains to insurance regulation. I am firmly convinced that regulatory control can be met most responsibly at the state level, because of the many variables within the societies of the respective states and the proximity of state regulators to the people. These variations consist of political, economic, social, and litigation attitudes, desires, needs, wishes, and expectation variables that vary most extensively from one state to another.

However, as it relates to the question of privacy, I do not see the same variables from state to state. Therefore, it seems that, while certainly some of the functions recommended to be implemented by the states easily could be handled at the state level, it is questionable, in my view, as to whether or not some of these judgment values should be left to individual administrators. I am persuaded that it is more appropriate that provisions for privacy should be uniform across the nation. We are talking about basic inherent rights of citizens. Further, inasmuch as insurance companies need as much similarity as possible, I see no adverse effect to uniformity—rather there are many advantages. It leads me almost to wonder if the suggestion by the Privacy Commission that the states implement certain items is much more than just a patronizing gesture toward the states.

I find no particular quarrel with the federal regulatory control contained in the recommendations by the Study Commission. However, I do get concerned when we see the evolution of legislation, such as that which is presently pending before the Congress, which would for all practical purposes pass to the Federal Trade Commission judgment in causing compliance with all recommendations made by the Commission. There are many highly subjective terms used in the recommendations, terms such as "relevant," "necessary," "reasonable," "timely," and "constructive." I have grave reservations as to the propriety of allowing the determination of the meaning of these words to be subject to the interpretation of any individual state or federal administrator. They are highly subjective terms and will be subject to different interpretations based upon the individual administrator's own social, economic, and political attitudes and experiences. What constitutes a legitimate risk factor in the mind of one administrator might be quite different from the interpretation given it by another. It seems to me this potentially could precipitate utter chaos for insurance companies to always be subject to the changing risk selection determination process, subject only to the discretion of a given regulator or member of the Federal Trade Commission. To the extent an insurance data base can be demonstrated to show any particular factor to indicate a greater or lesser likelihood of loss, it seems very appropriate to me to allow these variables in order that those who contribute less to the likelihood of loss can benefit accordingly. To the extent that life-styles, sexual preferences, health, skills, occupations, habits, and a host of other things have been demonstrated to contribute to the greater likelihood of loss, they should be utilized. However, with a constantly evolving, more receptive attitude by society, there seems to be less indication of potential greater hazard reflected today as a result of different life-styles, sexual preferences, and so on. Many of these factors, in time gone by, were quite offensive to large segments of society and, in fact, could be demonstrated to constitute greater risk factors. With the evolution of a more "permissive" society, many previous "anti-social" behaviors are no longer looked upon with scorn. So, while they might have constituted greater risk factors in past history, it seems there are fewer such implications today. Yet, I wonder as to the propriety of a given regulator or administrator being permitted to apply his or her own judgment in determining what constitutes proper underwriting techniques and insurance selection processes. It seems to me that, if such judgments are to be made, they should be made by the legislative bodies as an expression of the wishes of society at large, rather than some individual bureaucrat, whether it be anti-social behavior rather than any demonstrated evidence that such behavior contributes to the greater or lesser likelihood of loss. Such practices should be abandoned promptly. These remedies are long overdue.

If the terms "reasonableness," "necessary," "relevant," and so on are to be used, perhaps, at a minimum, we should determine whose judgment shall be exercised in these determinations. Is the judgment to be the regulator's, the FTC administration, the insurance company; just whose wisdom is to be ultimate? Being a "state's rights advocate," idealistically, such determinations would be specified on a uniform basis by legislation at the state level. In the absence of that, I would suggest that legislation at the federal level should specify what shall be determined in interpreting these terms. Regardless of the level at which this might be accomplished legislatively, it seems that language should be designed to stipulate specifically what shall be construed to be reasonable, relevant, and so on. And perhaps a very worthy consideration in such determination would be to ask a very basic question, such as, what tangible damage would, or will, result if an informational record is collected, stored, or otherwise used in some manner other than that which might be construed to be relevant, reasonable, or necessary by a critic? With some of these judgment factors removed by statute, I would have much less concern and, in fact, probably support state implementation and monitoring through state regulators.

The whole question as to what is a proper relationship as relates to the question of privacy, contrasted with the right to know, first should be prefaced with the question as to what tangible damage would result, as opposed to being determined by the whimsical desires or experiences of an individual person. If the information gathered, stored, and used is correct and, in fact, truth, it is only a question of what judgment evolves from the knowledge of the information and whether subsequent action is justifiable. As I read the recommendations of the Study Commission, I get the feeling that perhaps the Commission is attempting to interject the question of availability of insurance and the affordability question for certain segments of society into the question of privacy. If that is the intent, I personally feel we have gone beyond the question of the rights of individuals to the detriment of the rights of insurance companies, and even the rights of other individuals who are insurance company policyholders.

Earlier I alluded to a concern with one provision of the Study Commission's report, which requires a mechanism whereby citizens can question the propriety of the usage of certain information. This recommendation (Recommendation No. 1) leaves much discretion to individual insurance commissioners in 50 states to make value judgments that potentially could distort the entire insurance mechanism. It is appropriate, in my view, to provide for some mechanism by which citizens could register their concerns or complaints about the propriety of information collected from individuals by insurance companies. But most citizens are unsophisticated as to the insurance system. Therefore, while a citizen should be allowed to register his discontent, I would be most concerned about permitting a given regulator the authority to order the insurance mechanism changed in response to consumer concerns. No one person, in my view, has such omnipotent vision. But certainly political or other potential motivation could precipitate adverse decisions.

I am further concerned about one provision of Recommendation No. 3, which speaks to the question of an insurance organization being responsible for the activities of an information-collection organization in the event it has actual or constructive knowledge of inappropriate practices by such support organizations. Certainly there can be no excuse for an insurance company continuing to do business with a support organization when it has actual knowledge that such organization has engaged in inappropriate activities. However, the word "constructive" is a highly subjective one. I wonder about the propriety of causing an insurance company to be its "brother's keeper" simply because some administrator someplace along the way decides that based on certain information, in the administrator's view, the insurance company had "constructive" notice of such inappropriate action.

My only other real concern with the recommendations is the question of Recommendation No. 11, which indicates that an insurance company, or support organization, *will* amend the information it has gathered at the request of a citizen. Such a provision conceivably could mandate that a collector of information automatically be mandated to change same, in accordance with the citizen's wishes, even though the information might be correct. It would seem appropriate to me that the provision allow for the mandatory amendment, provided the citizen could demonstrate to the satisfaction of the organization that the information they had was in error. Or, in the alternative, and perhaps additionally, simply provide that any citizen be permitted to file supplemental information and cause it to be circulated, presenting his version of the subject matter.

Even with all this possible windmilling, which surely would evolve from different value judgments, leading to possible pitfalls if the present implementation methods were used, one must conclude that the study vividly points to great need to change past practices. Society will not, and should not, tolerate the kind of questionable practices set forth in the report.

The right to see the information collected, the right to correct erroneous information, the prohibition from transferring information between organizations without the permission of the citizen, the usage only in accordance with the originally intended use, and the ultimate requirement to destroy information once it has served its purposes are to be commended. It is only when some well-intended administrator charges off on a white horse on some mission of perceived social justice, based on his subjective judgments, that I have reason for concern. To the extent citizens can use the recommendations to block access to information legitimately needed and to the extent much of the interpretation is left to the value judgments of individual people as opposed to legislative bodies, we have precipitated some potentially damaging results.

As it is with all legislative proposals, the general concept is excellent, and the general provisions are excellent. It is only when we get into the specific terminology, provisions, and implementation that the monster can take on a different complexion. The questions of the right to know, the right to avoid an appropriate intrusion, and the right to fair play are two-sided questions and must be available to, and assessed against, both the provider and the acquirer of services.

There is one thing of which we can be assured. The era of privacy concern is with us, and that concern is not going to disappear through an attempt to avoid the issue. Many individuals within the insurance system have greeted the Privacy Protection Study Commission report with alarm, anguish, condemnation, and gnashing of teeth. These attitudes will serve no positive purpose. One can find certain provisions within the report over which to be concerned, as I have in this paper. However, on balance, it is an excellent piece of work and points up very dramatically the need to change certain previous practices and procedures. If the insurance industry has performed with integrity, and if most of its past practices are defensible, as I personally believe they are, this could be a golden opportunity for that industry rather than a gross negative imposition.

The recommendations mandate certain communication. This communication can lead to better understanding. It seems to me to be a golden opportunity for the insurance industry to communicate the fact that the insurance industry is a private enterprise and that the insurance policy is a contract. While the insurance industry's purpose is to allow for transfer of risk, its objective is to make a profit. The kinds of communication mandated could, and undoubtedly will, be cause for the public to become more aware of those things that affect the cost and availability of insurance. Insurance companies, in my view, would be well advised to "get on track" with these recommendations and to cause their implementation at the earliest possible time.

Section II: Protection of Personal Privacy in Insurance: The First Step

by Richard L. Mathias

The right to privacy is one that is recognized in our Constitution and one that traditionally has been highly valued in our society. The unfortunate fact, however, is that far too often individual privacy is intruded upon by both government and nonpublic institutions. And the interesting, and perhaps frightening, point is that most people have no real idea about how much information is filed away about them.

In its report, the Privacy Protection Study Commission proposes three basic principles, which ought to serve us in considering the privacy issue as it relates to insurance. They are to: minimize intrusiveness; maximize fairness; and create reliable, legitimate mechanisms to enforce a reasonable expectation of confidentiality. I personally require little persuasion to take on the role of an advocate for these three principles as reflecting the essence of what ought to be our concern.

Increasingly, people are beginning to focus on the privacy question in the context of a technological society. Concern for privacy and confidentiality seems to cut across the broad middle ground of American political ideology, from conservative to liberal.

But our recognition of the problem and especially our ways of dealing with privacy protection seem to have been outdistanced long ago by the ability to intrude subtly upon it. The technology of information collection, retrieval, and exchange has grown geometrically, while the appreciation of its dangers has not grown nearly so rapidly.

Although the courts and legislative bodies have lengthily and controversially addressed the privacy question in terms of criminal law and, more recently, of government inquiry, relatively little attention and action have been directed toward intrusiveness by the nonpublic sector. One obvious reason, of course, is that in addition to the basically complex nature of modern privacy and technological intrusiveness, the application of Constitutional guarantees are not at all clear and, in fact, tend to cut both ways. This is not to say that there has been no action. The Fair Credit Reporting Act, despite any problems, was an important step.

The Privacy Commission and a growing public awareness and concern raise the question of what responsibility does the insurance regulator have to protect individual privacy in the conduct of the business of insurance. Again, it would be useful to refer to the Privacy Commission's three principles in dealing with the question.

The first/two, to minimize intrusiveness and maximize fairness, require answers to a broad range of questions. Those that occur most immediately are the following:

- What information by its very nature ought to be considered private?
- What information ought to be considered circumstantially private?
- What are the parameters of confidentiality? How many people can know about something or have access to something before it can no longer be considered confidential?
- To what particular uses can certain types of information be put?
- What methods of collection, maintenance, or exchange can be properly and fairly used and for what kinds of information?
- What equations or measures do we need to balance properly an insurer's legitimate need for information and a subscriber's right to privacy?
- How do we determine the balance between protecting subscribers from the fraudulent activities of other subscribers and the right to privacy of each subscriber?

These questions and many more remain to be answered. The answers certainly will not be provided by me today or tomorrow, because I think this is an evolving process. We might quite briefly, however, direct our attention to how to decide upon some mechanism for answering these questions.

The watchword in our approach to privacy protection should be "caution." We should not rush to definitions or be overly quick to designate arbiters of the public good in this matter. As I have tried to emphasize, we must first realize the utter complexity of the privacy question. The most likely development is that the Congress, the Federal Trade Commission, individual state insurance regulators and legislatures, the National Association of Insurance Commissioners, and insurers themselves will act progressively and incrementally over the next several years to deal with the whole range of issues in some suitable fashion. The critical element here, however, is that every effort be made to allow for a genuine expression of public opinion on privacy protection.

It is on this element, that of public opinion, that we in Illinois have begun to focus our attention and effort in developing appropriate mechanisms for defining and protecting privacy. It is our hope in Illinois to lay the groundwork for eventually ensuring that the insurance subscriber or applicant will be apprised, not only as to exactly what sorts of information will be collected about him and how but to what use the information will be put and with whom the information will be shared.

We consider this approach to be the essential first step for several reasons. First, it is simply too early in the game for us to believe that we can really define privacy and its limits. Second, once people know what information is to be collected, how, and for what purpose, *informed* public opinion (and I include in "public opinion" not only consumers but regulators, as well as the regulated) truly can begin to take shape. It will be on the basis of that informed opinion that those of us whose responsibility it is to take or recommend specific actions can operate. I think it is also important to realize that, in a sense, notice provisions will initiate an informal sort of public hearing on privacy (and I believe that has begun already). Third, notice requirements can bring privacy into the marketplace. The individual consumer not only will have an additional element to consider in the purchasing decision but also will be positioned on more of a par with the insurance company. In this regard, the truism that "knowledge is power" is most apt. Notice will help reduce the inequality of knowledge. Fourth, notice will bring with it the additional, but analytically separable, questions of access to files and opportunity for correction by the subject. Whether these questions should be dealt with by amendment to the Fair Credit Reporting Act, by individual state insurance regulators, or by some other method, if at all, can be answered best after we have gained some experience with notice.

Now, if we are to pursue the route of sufficient notice, what tools are available to Illinois and the other states?

● The rule-making authority of insurance regulators tends to be broad and can reasonably be believed to encompass many areas of notice and confidentiality.

● Insurance regulators can convene public hearings on notice standards and the like. This action alone can help to educate the public and the industry.

● Legislation may be desirable or necessary in some areas of notice. Recent Illinois legislation, for instance, requires specific explanation for nonrenewal or cancellation. At some point, the question of how to address explanations for declination to applicants may be addressed legislatively. This, of course, involves a more difficult balancing of burden on the industry versus the benefit to the consuming public.

● Another new Illinois law mandates an end to the insidious practice of "redlining" in the area of homeowners and fire insurance. Cancellation or nonrenewal must be explained explicitly and cannot be for reasons of geographic location, or the age, sex, occupation, race, national origin, or religion of the owner. Such notice has a definite relationship to privacy in two important respects. First, it notifies the subscriber as to what information has been collected about him. Second, it manifests the fact that, as a matter of public policy, certain characteristics or variables cannot be considered actuarially relevant to underwriting decisions.

● Another recommendation that has been made to the Illinois Department, by an independent investigator appointed by the Department, is that, as one of the recommendations of the privacy report, the underwriting files of insurers be made available to the insured. Traditionally, as you are well aware, that has not been a right of the policyholder.

- The legal authority to review policy and application forms is an important one. The forms could well be the prime vehicles for notice and consumer education in the first instance, serving to define the limits of intrusiveness.
- Departmental complaint procedures can be designed better to grapple with questions of intrusiveness and breaches of confidentiality.
- Insurance regulators can serve as models of informational propriety by maintaining their own strict standards of confidentiality in internal complaint procedures. In Illinois, complaint files are considered confidential in terms of the complainant. We receive, in the Illinois Department, 15,000 complaints a year, which we act upon and usually will contact the insurer for his comments. We are very concerned about the ability of subpoenas of various governmental agencies or courts. Previously, when faced with subpoena power, we automatically would turn over anything in the Department if we received a subpoena from either a legislative investigative commission or a court somewhere in the state or nation. We have revised that procedure in the past months, and now it is not our reaction automatically to turn over the information if we receive a subpoena. We believe that we may be violating the confidentiality or the right to privacy concerning information contained in our files.

States other than Illinois, of course, have undertaken privacy-protection efforts. Some have pursued courses which differ from that of Illinois in some respects. California, for example, has used its rule-making authority to control illicit and unfair trade practices, to hold *ad hoc* hearings, to determine what information can appropriately be collected or used in certain cases.

I think it is healthy for the time being that states be allowed to pursue a variety of approaches to privacy protection. In this way, a reservoir of experience can be developed, which will aid us over the next several years to develop a uniform, yet flexible, approach to privacy that will provide the kind of expectation of confidentiality suggested by the Study Commission.

I think this puts a tremendous burden on the states to act responsibly and to work to act with some uniformity. My reaction, if I were sitting on the other side of the table and doing business in a number of states and each state had different confidentiality or privacy requirements, would be to scream for federal preemption. I think that we in state government and state regulation have a real responsibility to act with some uniformity, but certainly with some responsibility. I also am concerned about the actions that may be taken by either the state or federal governments and the reaction that actually may occur in the marketplace.

Questions and Answers

Question: *What actual experience have you had with complaints about privacy in the life insurance field?*

Answer (Mathias): The number of complaints we have received in the life area is extremely limited. We receive 15,000 complaints (or, as many of you may prefer them to be called, inquiries) during a calendar year. We receive by far the most complaints in the property and liability area, and most of those are in the automobile area. If you go further into the category, it would be in claim settlements. The number of complaints that we have received regarding life insurers in general would probably be 1/20 of what we may receive in the property/casualty areas. Regarding the specifics of your question, we have received few complaints concerning privacy matters. However, for what limited trend there may be in the numbers, there is a trend toward more inquiries about the types of questions that are being asked by life insurers, as well as other insurers. Applicants feel they are beyond the scope of the policy they are requesting. I think this may be a result of reports, such as the Privacy Commission Report, that make people more sensitive to the questions that are being asked of them. They certainly are making the insurance departments more sensitive to the questions that we see being asked on the forms that we are asked to approve.

Answer (Hudson): I think we have a total of only 6,000 inquiries per year. Some of those are complaints, but the majority seem to be inquiries. I checked with my staff. I find no evidence of any complaint, concern, or indication of concern as to the privacy question, as such, in terms of perceived violations. The only thing that I could determine is that there are people questioning the propriety of utilizing a number of factors, primarily in the risk-selection process and the rate-determination process. We have had a few inquiries along that line, but again, it is primarily advocates of one cause or another, as opposed to "John Q. Citizen." In answer to your specific question, I see no evidence of complaints in our area.

Question: *What is your opinion of HR 8288?*

Answer (Hudson): I hope that it would not be enacted. It was one of the things I was alluding to earlier. As I understand the bill, it would pass to the Federal Trade Commission the total implementation and monitoring process of all 17 insurance recommendations—and that I am concerned with.
[*Editors' note:* HR 8288 would pass control to the Federal Trade Commission on 16 of the 17 Privacy Protection Study Commission's recommendations. Recommendation 1 is omitted from HR 8288. See Chapter 11.]

Question: *I share your concern with the inconsistency of state regulation and the need for uniformity. What could be done to improve the situation? Couldn't the NAIC [National Association of Insurance Commissioners] develop a model bill in this area?*

Answer (Hudson): If I could have some assurance that we could have a model approach at the state level in terms of implementation and monitoring, I would be totally supportive of the state approach. We took some action yesterday in the [NAIC] executive committee meeting in Madison, in an attempt to cause that to happen. It was an agenda item. There was a task force appointed for the purpose of looking into a possibility of drafting and recommending a model, to be drafted and enacted in the several states. I think we are seeing greater attempts by my counterparts across the nation to follow the enactment, or attempts to gain enactment, of these model approaches. But, ladies and gentlemen, historically we have had rather inconsistent results with model legislation. In fact, there are fewer states that follow the model approach of NAIC than states that do not. I think it is more appropriate if we can follow the model bill approach. Certainly I would like to see us retain state jurisdiction.

Answer (Mathias): I think most of us believe that regulation, if it is enlightened, should remain at the state level. With regard to privacy and the prospect of having 50 different laws that insurers, doing business in more than 1 state, have to meet, this is a problem for them. I think that we can meet the problem, but the time may be shorter here than it has been in other areas. I think you will see that the FTC would like to do something early on.

Answer (Caldwell): I agree that it should remain with the states.
[*Editors' note:* Georgia Insurance Commissioner Johnnie Caldwell served as moderator for the panel session.]

Question: *As you state, there have been few documented abuses in this area. If the insurance industry were to respond voluntarily in many of these areas—by adopting guidelines of its own for adverse decisions, and so forth—do you believe legislation would still be necessary?*

Answer (Hudson): First, I would agree with you that there has been very little documented evidence of complaint or abuse. However, the historic practice of the insurance mechanism has been to deprive or deny certain information to the public that is now going to be revealed. I wonder if, when we start sharing with the consumer the information that heretofore has been denied, we will not have more activity, more concern, more allegations of abuse, and so on. In your underwriting of health and life contracts, when you have declined the risk, you have never said, "It is for this reason." The closest we have come, as an old agent, I used to say, "It is one of these 10 reasons, Charlie. You guess." I wonder if he would have walked away as docile had he known which reason it was. In the instance of homosexuality, with a very personal high image in the community, for example, I wonder if he would have taken that and walked away. I suspect, when we start disclosing the kinds of information, the reasons for declination of coverage, the reasons for rating, and so forth, we are going to have greater concern expressed and, therefore, greater activity. This may result in an ultimate determination of what is the proper constitution of "privacy." We need some societal input on this to legislative bodies, rather than relying on the attitudes of some individuals.

Answer (Mathias): What we are concerned about today in the Illinois Department is in the area of availability and why, in property and casualty insurance, individuals are refused insurance. Many times the motor vehicle report will come back on an auto policy saying that "You have three moving violations." Once the applicant comes to us, we will respond that the insurer knows he has had three moving violations in the past year. He will say, "That's not right. Where do they get that information?" Or in homeowners, which is the hot topic in the city of Chicago, inspection reports will come back and the picture will be taken of the wrong house. When you pay $5.00 for an inspection report, you probably get about as much as you pay for. I have to agree that, in most instances, the information insurers use is pretty much "on the money." But some individuals have had bad experiences. They have complained to the Illinois Department, and we have then gone back to the insurer or the inspection company or whatever to find out that the information turns out to be incorrect. I think those are leaving a bad taste in a lot of people's mouths, as well as in the minds of the Illinois Department of Insurance. In particular, at least in my limited view in Illinois, the area in which we have more concerns is information retrieval systems, how they got information, and whether information on an individual is correct or not is related to availability.

Question: *What in your view, Director Mathias, is the best way for the insurance industry to inform the public of the information necessary for risk selection—to really get it down to a level where the public can understand it?*

Answer (Mathias): However it is being done now is not the right way.

Answer (Hudson): Dick, may I expand on that just briefly? I do not think it is a matter of how to get it to them; it is a matter of getting it to them. There are potentially, in my view, some very positive results to be had from this, simply by informing the public as to what constitutes a declination of coverage, or a rating, or so forth. I think you really have been your own worst enemy by depriving people of the knowledge of those things that lead to higher insurance costs, which lead to higher loss ratios, which lead to lack of availability, and so on. I think you will be enhanced, ultimately, by simply disclosing to people what causes these negative things that they perceive. To the extent they know about them, they can deal with them. They can respond to them. They can try to remedy them. But when you do not tell them what causes all these negative things, they have no choice but to tuck their tails between their legs and throw stones at you. And that is what has been happening.

Question: *One thing that has disturbed me is Recommendation 10, in the underwriting area, where it permits the individual to see and copy any such recorded information either in person or by mail. Quite frequently, in underwriting, we get confidential information from a doctor. Sometimes a doctor has not given all the information to his patient. We get it in our files, he comes in and sits down and says, "I want to see what you have." Do you see any conflict here?*

Answer (Hudson): I think your point is well made, and physicians are as concerned about this question as you are. The doctors that I have talked to are concerned not so much with the correctness of diagnosis and the correctness of remedies but with the mental health of the individual who may be better served by not having that information. These are some of the things that we are going to discover with this evolving process Mr. Mathias talks about. I agree with you.

Question: *I want to expand on this last point. I think the key is that we are not afraid of disclosing as long as we can disclose to a responsible person—the applicant's or the policyowner's personal physician. It is the physician's responsibility, not ours.*

We had a case, just about two weeks ago, in which a nurse had applied to us. We rated the case heavily. She did not understand why. When I talked to our medical director, I found that, in his opinion, over 50 percent of these cases with this particular disorder turn into multiple sclerosis [MS]. He said it would be absolutely ridiculous on the part of the attending physician to tell her that she has a 50 percent chance of contracting MS. So the woman has no knowledge of it, and the doctor certainly would not disclose that type of information. I think if we were providing that kind of information directly to an applicant or policyowner, we would be doing them and the medical community an injustice.

Answer (Mathias): I think that is one of the reasons, or is the reason, that I urge caution in this area. We have to be concerned with the real-world ramifications of that very theoretical and well-meaning regulation, and what you are discussing is exactly the type of real-world application that is going to be given to whatever regulation it is.

Comment (Plesser): I would just like to point out that section b of Recommendation 10 does foresee a procedure whereby insurance companies, in releasing medical information, at their own discretion, can release the information to a medical professional designated by the individual. Therefore, this was a problem that the Commission foresaw, and there is an opportunity for the insurance institution to give the information to a medical professional and not directly to the individual.

I might add that, in the medical records area of the Commission's recommendations, the Commission recommended almost an absolute right of access by patients to a doctor's record about them. I think that is important because, by giving the records to an insurance company, the doctor is not exposing himself to any greater extent than he would if he did not—for under our recommendation, the doctor would be responsible to give access in any event. By disseminating it to the insurance company, he does not create a greater disclosure in terms of access to the information.

This was a question of great concern to the Commission. An earlier version of the recommendation was that the doctor had to release information to the patient only where he was releasing it to a third party—e.g., an insurance institution. I think that would have had the pernicious result you are talking about.

Comment (Caldwell): I think what they were talking about, Mr. Plesser, was the fact that the individual would suffer from having been told that he had a likelihood of some terrible disease and that mentally this patient would be worse off.

Response (Plesser): Section b of Recommendation 10 says that disclosure may be made through a doctor.

Comment (Caldwell): But then it would be the judgment of the person handling the file as to whether this was information that the policyowner already had or did not have. How well do you think that would be managed?

Response (Plesser): There would be a professional in between, and the concern was that the insurance industry does not want to be responsible for disclosing that information directly. Recommendation 10(b) handles that.

Comment (Caldwell): As counsel for the Commission, Mr. Plesser, is it your concept, then, that when any information is asked for by a policyowner of an insurer, if these recommendations were put into effect, that rather than give the medical information directly to the individual, the insurance company simply ask for the name of the doctor that they would like to have it sent to?

Response (Plesser): That is one of the procedures that the Commission recommended for handling medical information.

Question: *I think you have a cure that is worse than the disease. If I, as an insurance company, turn you down and I further tell you, "I can't tell you the reason why—but I'll tell your doctor," then you go to your doctor and your doctor says, "I can't tell you what is wrong with your vocal chords," you are going to be even more scared than if he tells you that you have cancer. And you are going to be still more scared than if no one had ever told you anything in the first place.*

Response (Mathias): Or the reaction of the doctor may be to never give you information.

Response (Plesser): I have two responses to that. First, the individual can select another doctor, if he or she believes the first doctor is not providing the type of communication the individual desires.

Second, I would like to ask Neil Day of the MIB—which has been operating for some time now with disclosure through physicians—to comment on the results of the MIB's disclosure experience.

Response (Day—MIB): The MIB has had over 15,000 requests for disclosure, and I do not remember exactly how many actual disclosures have been made. But what Mr. Plesser suggests is accurate. Relatively few follow-up complaints from applicants to the effect that physicians refused to disclose.

Comment (from audience): The recommendation says disclosure may be made through a "medical care professional." It does not say physician or surgeon. And the definition of "medical care professional" in the Commission's report is "any person licensed or certified to provide medical services to individuals, including but not limited to, a physician, dentist, nurse, optometrist, physical or occupational therapist, psychiatric social worker, clinical dietitian, or clinical psychologist." So I can release the information through a "clinical dietitian" if I, as an insurer, so choose.

Question: *Mr. Caldwell, in your opening comments you reflected on the availability of information via data processing/computer technology. You also made comments concerning the increasing complexity of EDP. Yet some people contend that automated systems may be more secure than "paper" systems. Would you comment further on this?*

Answer (Caldwell): This might be true, to an extent. However, today on a tiny piece of tape they can have the entire record. Whereas before, if they kept accumulating information, they would not have enough warehouses to keep it. So they did not keep it for years on end. Now with the tiny amount of space that it takes on microfilm, they can keep a man's record from the time he is born until the time he dies. I think that is what this study is talking about. You can keep information for long periods of time, and you keep more of it. Also, they distribute it among themselves. Many lending institutions that belong to an association send out this information, not because another institution has asked for and needs that information about you, but they send it out anyway. That is what I gleaned from reading the study as being one of the concerns that they had. Would you gentlemen care to comment on this?

Answer (Hudson): It does not bother me so much that one collects and keeps information. It is the difference that comes about in the retrieval and usage with the advent of new technology. When you stored all this data in a warehouse, it took a little more effort to get in and use it. Perhaps it was not utilized as readily as it is today, recognizing, as you said, that on the head of a pin and a piece of silicon you can put 2,000 characters. It takes pushing a button, and the whole record spreads in front of you. The retrieval, the access, and, therefore, the possibility of considering further information is much greater today because of technology than it was back in "the warehouse era."

Answer (Mathias): I think that the whole area of insurance regulation as related to computerization of all different types of records is one of the greatest challenges that I, as a regulator, face. How do we audit computerized records that can possibly be changed overnight when they know we are coming in the next day? It is possible. It happened. Equity Funding was somewhat, although it has been overblown, that type of operation. It is the same thing with regard to claims files, financial records, premium reports—the whole idea of how do you get the information. How best to store it. Is that visual record accurate? It may not have any paper backup. If it is not accurate, who knows it is not?

I would again state that I think it is pretty early on in the privacy area. We need a lot of bright people who will address this problem and can come up with constructive solutions. We are asking for a lot of help from the industry, from academicians, and others. This is a real concern of the 1970s and 1980s. It is an issue that must be addressed and must be addressed now.

Comment (Hudson): I would hope that the insurance industry would recognize that the era of privacy concern is here. It is not going to go away. Respectfully, I would acknowledge, based on over 18 years of interacting with this industry, that typically insurance people are somewhat pessimistic—as some of the observations that have been made here illustrate. But I would suggest, perhaps, that this is one of those times when we ought not to be concerned so much with dealing with negative thoughts, but look and see if there is not some opportunity here. I firmly believe that there *is* some opportunity in this whole process for you, in terms of your accountability and improved credibility. It provides an opportunity for you to defend that which you essentially have been about. I would hope that would be your posture as we go forth and wrestle with this thing.

9

Privacy, the Insurance Industry, and the Consumer: The FTC's View

Lewis H. Goldfarb

The following are some Federal Trade Commission (FTC) staff views on the information-collection and use practices of the insurance industry and its support organizations and some comments on the Privacy Protection Study Commission recommendations, which touch on these matters. The views expressed are my own and do not necessarily represent the views of the Commission or any of its members.

I also should mention that the Privacy Commission addressed itself to certain practices that have been alleged to be violations of the Fair Credit Reporting Act and the Federal Trade Commission Act in the FTC case involving *Equifax, Inc.*, Docket 8954. The evidentiary record in that case closed in June of this year [1977]. Since that time, extensive findings of fact and supporting legal briefs have been filed with the administrative law judge by both sides. My comments today should not be interpreted as a statement on the merits of any of the issues in the *Equifax* case. They are

Lewis H. Goldfarb is Assistant Director for Credit Practices, Federal Trade Commission. Mr. Goldfarb received his bachelor's degree from New York University and his law degree from Rutgers Law School. He was a trial attorney in the Bureau on Consumer Protection of the Federal Trade Commission from 1969 to 1974 and served as Director/Counsel of the Equal Credit Opportunity Task Force at the Federal Reserve Board from 1974 to 1975. He was Assistant Director for Special Statutes in the Bureau of Consumer Protection, where he was responsible for enforcement of the Equal Credit Opportunity Act, the Fair Credit Reporting Act, the Fair Credit Billing Act, Truth in Lending, and others.

general in nature, applying broadly to the insurance industry and its various support organizations.[1]

The FTC and Privacy—An Overview

The FTC has limited jurisdiction over the insurance industry. As you know, the McCarran-Ferguson Act, 15 U.S.C. Sections 1010-1015 (1970), exempts much of the business of insurance from federal regulation, with certain exceptions. Important exceptions to this general rule are federal statutes specifically directed to the business of insurance and, from a privacy standpoint, the most important such federal legislation is the Fair Credit Reporting Act (FCRA), which at present has limited applicability to the insurance industry.

The FCRA imposes certain notice requirements on insurance companies that use consumer and investigative-consumer reports (Sections 606[a] and [b] and 615[a]) and requires that insurance companies certify that they have permissible purposes for ordering reports (Section 607[a]). In addition, insurance companies that regularly exchange information with other insurance companies concerning a consumer's general reputation, personal characteristics, or mode of living could themselves become consumer-reporting agencies unless the exchange is limited to the consumer's transactions or experiences with the company. Thus we do not claim any extensive expertise as to the information needs or record-keeping practices of the insurance industry, itself. Our familiarity with such practices is primarily related to the FTC's more general authority over the activities of consumer-reporting agencies, particularly the inspection bureaus, which provide investigative reports to the insurance industry, and to the limited-user obligations imposed by this Act.

In addition to our responsibility under the Fair Credit Reporting Act, the Federal Trade Commission also carries out a more generalized enforcement responsibility in the area of individual privacy. Thus, in a recent decision involving the misuse of tax preparation data, the Commission states:

> In light of the pervasive and specific policy of tax confidentiality, we, like the law judge, have no need to decide whether a broader consideration of personal privacy could govern this case. In declining to reach that issue, however, we do not suggest that a generalized right of personal privacy and personal control over private data is an inadequate foundation on which to ground a finding of unlawfulness under Section 5. In fact, the right of privacy has become a widely valued public policy, with Constitutional and statutory underpinning. (*CF.*, *E.G.*, *Roe v. Wade*, 410 U.S. 113, 152 [1973]; Privacy Act of

1974, 5 U.S.C. Section 522A.) Its violation in a commercial context would likely be unlawful under the Federal Trade Commission Act.[2]

The Recommendations of the
Privacy Protection Study Commission

The Privacy Commission is to be commended for its monumental report describing information-collection and use practices in various segments of our society; identifying unfair or abusive practices, which offend the concept of privacy in an open society; and making meaningful and constructive recommendations for corrective action. I would like to express our concurrence with the Privacy Commission's concern that protection of the individual's right to privacy is of paramount importance; that information be collected, stored, and disseminated fairly and only to the extent necessary; and that the consumer be an informed and effective participant in the gathering, retention, and use of such information.

There are, however, several instances in which we would question whether the Privacy Commission has recommended enforcement mechanisms strong enough to ensure that consumers actually obtain the benefits the Commission seeks to confer on them. For example, the Privacy Commission's Recommendation 17 would create a duty of confidentiality owed to any person about whom information is collected and used.[3] We agree with the concept of confidentiality of insurance data, but we are not convinced it would be implemented adequately through the Privacy Commission's recommendation, since the recommendation envisions a federal law to create a duty of confidentiality but does not designate a federal agency to enforce the proposed legislation. Enforcement is left to the aggrieved individual, who would have the right to sue to obtain actual damages for negligent disclosures and to recover within minimum and maximum limits for intentional or willful violations. As well, a defense of reasonable procedures implemented with reasonable care could be interposed successfully by the insurance company against a suit alleging negligent violation of the statute. Because there would be no federal agency to oversee compliance, and very limited rights to obtain a civil recovery, we question whether such federal legislation would be effective. While we believe that effective private enforcement is a vital component of any law that attempts to regulate consumer transactions, we also are aware of the very limited access that most consumers have to the courts and, therefore, believe that exclusive reliance on private enforcement is unwise.

My purpose today, however, is not to critique the Privacy Commission's efforts but to discuss with you the FCRA's treatment of privacy problems in the insurance industry and our position on the recommendations for new legislation to fill gaps left by the FCRA. Our past proposals in the area, of course, have been directly related to the original scope of the FCRA and do not implement the broader privacy mandate that the Privacy Commission report attempts to secure. Comparison of our recommendations with the Privacy Commission's is appropriate, however, because our past experiences are reflected in our recommendations.

The Fair Credit Reporting Act

Our enforcement experience under the Fair Credit Reporting Act since 1971 has given us a sense of the helplessness and anger felt by consumers who attempt to come to grips with a system of gathering and using personal information that often appears arbitrary and hostile. We receive complaints from many consumers who experience frustration in trying to determine why their applications were rejected, their policies rated or cancelled, or in trying to correct inaccurate, incomplete, or misleading information. This feeling is best summarized by a recent decision, which stated:

> Time and again plaintiff came to the defendant's office and went over the same credit information with defendant's employees, pointing out the errors, all to no purpose. Time and again he tried to have the defendant update and correct its report on him; he pleaded, he lost his temper, all to no avail. Like a character in Kafka he was totally powerless to move or penetrate the implacable presence brooding, like some stone moloch within the castle.[4]

In fact, some consumers have forgone the benefits and security of insurance coverage rather than repeat an unpleasant encounter with an insurance company or its support organizations. Thus one of the major problem areas, from our point of view, is the inadequacy of the Fair Credit Reporting Act to deal with the problems faced by consumers who attempt to obtain credit, seek employment, or purchase insurance.

The FTC and its staff have made repeated recommendations to Congress to strengthen the Fair Credit Reporting Act. As currently constituted, we believe the Act has not fulfilled its stated goal of meeting the needs of users of consumer information "in a manner which is fair and equitable to the consumer, with due regard to the confidentiality, accuracy, relevancy, and proper utilization of such information" (Section 602[b]).

The Privacy Commission, of course, mirrored that judgment in its report, by stating:

> Current law is neither strong enough nor specific enough to solve problems that now exist. In some cases, moreover, changes in record-keeping systems have already made even

recent legal protections obsolete. As record-keeping systems come to be used to preclude action by the individual ... it is important that the consumer be given preventive protection to supplement after the fact protections he sometimes has today.[5]

We believe that the effectiveness of the FCRA will remain, for the most part, unsatisfactory, unless the Act is strengthened in terms of its coverage, disclosure requirements, and liability. At the same time, we recognize the legitimate informational needs of the insurance and other industries and have opposed legislative proposals that we believe would interfere unnecessarily with the flow of information in these industries. Every proposed amendment to the FCRA must involve a balancing of the costs of such reform to consumer-reporting agencies and their users against the benefits to be derived by the consumer; and such balancing is by no means easy. However, the Privacy Commission, which also was aware of the need for such balancing, by and large, has made recommendations similar to ours.

Prenotification of Investigative-Consumer Reports

Section 606 of the Act provides for prenotification that an "investigative consumer report" may be ordered. Although this section has not been wholly ineffective, we believe that it is generally unsatisfactory, because it does not convey to the consumer the true significance of such a report. Moreover, we are concerned that consumers generally do not associate the notice with the investigation that follows, because they do not understand the information-gathering practices of the insurance industry or its support organizations. The effectiveness of the notice may suffer, for example, if consumers are not made aware that insurance companies hire independent investigative agencies to prepare reports, or if they are not made aware that these agencies retain file copies of reports for use with other customers. Finally, as the Privacy Commission has implicitly recognized, the FCRA's basic statutory scheme is deficient because the same investigation carried out by insurance company employees would trigger no prenotification at all as long as the company does not pass the information along to other companies.[6]

In our opinion, the approach of Section 606(b) of the FCRA for providing further information about the "nature and scope" of the investigation upon request is also deficient. Because the initial notice required by Section 606(a) must be mailed or delivered to consumers no later than three days after ordering the report, it is possible that the report itself could have been prepared and sent to the user before the consumer could request and receive further information about the investigation.

Accordingly, we have recommended to Congress that Section 606 be amended to require that an authorization be obtained from the subject. Without such an authorization, an investigative-consumer report could not be prepared. We also have recommended a requirement that a written disclosure of the methods, detail, purpose, and scope of the investigation be made before the authorization is obtained.

Although the Privacy Commission's Recommendations 5 and 6 do not require specific authorization, they do contain many of the same goals sought by the amendments we have supported for Section 606 and several other requirements, including that the consumer be informed as to:

1. The types of parties to whom, and circumstances under which, information may be disclosed without the individual's authorization and the types of information that may be disclosed.

2. The procedures whereby the individual may correct, amend, or dispute any resulting record about himself.

3. That information in any report prepared by a consumer-reporting agency may be retained by the organization and subsequently disclosed by it to others.

The Privacy Commission Recommendations 5 and 6 do not propose any amendments to the Fair Credit Reporting Act, but would be enforceable through state insurance commissioners or, with regard to Recommendation 5, may be self-enforcing through Recommendations 11 and 12, which deal with the correction of records. While the Commission's recommendations are much broader in scope than the application of Sections 606(a) and (b), we do not believe these recommendations would eliminate entirely the need for amendment to the Fair Credit Reporting Act as discussed previously. Particularly, we believe the requirement of an authorization would still be important to the consumer if an *investigative-consumer report* is to be obtained.

Reasonable Procedures to Ensure Accuracy

Another example of a recommendation of the Privacy Commission, which goes beyond our previous suggestions, is Recommendation 9, which states that the Fair Credit Reporting Act should be amended to provide that the insurance company notify any applicant or insured that he may, upon request, be interviewed in connection with the preparation of an investigative report and that, if a requested interview cannot be reasonably obtained, the institution preparing the investigative report mail a copy of the report, when prepared, to the individual. Our experience suggests that this may be an important procedure to safeguard the accuracy of investigative-type information, by giving the consumer an opportunity to confront allegations prior to being denied insurance. We are familiar with instances during which the investigator preparing the report developed damaging information of a subjective nature from neighborhood sources but made no attempt to interview the subject of the report to obtain his response or reaction to the information. While we recognize that it is not always possible to interview the applicant, the Privacy Commission's recommendation would go a long way toward making the subject an active participant in the collection process. We would urge, however, that the recommendation specifically require that any information developed during the investigation which may have an adverse bearing on the subject's application or policy be brought to the attention of the subject during the subject's interview. Although this requirement is implicit in the recommendation, it is not stated specifically.

The present FCRA adverse-action notice reveals to consumers only the sources of information that led to their denial and not the reason for the rejection. Nonetheless, upon receiving a notice of adverse action, many consumers assume they can determine the criteria for selection and the reasons for denial or rating by contacting the investigative agency rather than the insurance company. The investigative agency is required to disclose only the "nature and substance" of the information in the consumer's file and does not know the reason for the denial. Thus the agency must sometimes refer the consumer to the insurance company for answers to questions relating to specific information or the reasons for denial. In our experience, insurance companies generally are unwilling to discuss these matters with the consumer, and I believe that this inability to determine the reason for an adverse decision can contribute only to a sense of injustice and frustration on the part of the consumer.

Notices of Adverse Action—Reasons for Denial

For many years we have believed that it is important to the consumer, and necessary to the effective operation of the FCRA, for the user-disclosure obligations under Section 615 to be broadened to require the disclosure of the specific reasons for an adverse decision and the identification of the information responsible for the adverse action. Our experience with a similar requirement under the Equal Credit Opportunity Act has shown that such a provision is absolutely essential to ensuring full compliance with the FCRA and that it also ensures consumers will understand how the information reported was used. It would also avoid what consumers perceive as a bureaucratic runaround if the user is required to provide a copy of the report to the consumer upon request. The FTC has recommended amendments to the Act that would accomplish these objectives, and the Privacy Commission has made similar recommendations, but on a more comprehensive scale.

The Privacy Commission's Recommendation 13 would substantially remedy these problems through an amendment to the Fair Credit Reporting Act requiring disclosure of the specific reasons for adverse action; the specific item or items of information relied on (except medical information, which may be disclosed directly or through a licensed medical professional); the names and addresses of all institutional sources; and the individual's right to see and copy information used to make the adverse decision. Further, Recommendation 13 would permit the individual, after having received the notice of adverse action, to see and to copy all recorded information used to make the decision, except the identification of investigative sources who request to remain anonymous. The insurance company has an option of disclosing any medical information directly or through a licensed medical professional designated by the consumer.

Limitation of Liability

My strong general support of the Privacy Commission's Recommendation 13 is tempered by doubts about their recommendation that a limitation of liability similar to that now provided by Section 610(e) of the FCRA be extended to insurance institutions as well as to insurance-support organizations. This limited civil liability (which is found in other recommendations, as well) is essentially a preemption of an extensive body of state case law and statutes, which create a cause of action for defamation, invasion of privacy, or negligence in the collecting and reporting of information.

Civil Liability

The acceptability of the proposed preemption of state law, of course, is tied in to the question of how effective are the proposed civil liability provisions recommended by the Privacy Commission. We believe that the present civil liability sections of the FCRA (Section 610[e] , Section 616, and Section 617) have not been an effective deterrent to noncompliance, primarily because the chances of recovery of damages under the Act are sufficiently remote to discourage private litigants from seeking redress. While the awarding of liquidated damages in civil suits for violations of consumer-protection statutes is considered harsh by some, when such damages are available the resultant degree of compliance is enhanced measurably. An example is the Truth in Lending Act in which the minimum $100 civil liability for violations has resulted in a high degree of compliance. The FTC has recommended a similar approach to liability under the FCRA to ensure compliance in this area, although our experience under Truth in Lending suggests that such liability should be limited to "material" violations. Although they differ from our past recommendations, the Privacy Commission also has recommended more stringent civil liability provisions, including the power for the consumer to seek injunctive relief for violations of the Act.[7]

Right to Obtain a Copy of Your Consumer Report

The FTC repeatedly has advocated amendments of the FCRA Sections 609 and 610 to provide the consumer with the right to see and copy his or her file. The present statute allows almost anyone with whom the consumer does business to obtain a copy of the report, but denies the same right to the consumer. We always have considered personal inspection a necessary ingredient to any meaningful protection of privacy. Faced with the inadequacy of existing legislation, the consumer does not have a meaningful opportunity to learn of information in his or her file and to have appropriate corrections made. In my opinion, the Act's present approach is simply irrational and, more than any other failing of the FCRA, highlights the need for reform.

The FTC also has recommended the abolition of the exception found in Section 609, which results in the anonymity of investigative sources. The disclosure of these sources is necessary to afford the subject of a report containing highly personal and sensitive information a reasonable opportunity to protect himself or herself. In our view, there is no substitute for the consumer learning who is furnishing damaging information so that he or she can attempt to place the information and the source in proper context. We also have supported a compromise amendment, which would require the disclosure of investigative sources if the consumer has disputed the information removed from his file.

The Privacy Commission's Recommendation 10 would result in an amendment to the FCRA to strengthen the disclosure of information and sources along the lines I have discussed. In addition, Recommendation 10 would apply to insurance companies themselves. We also agree with and have advocated the Commission's recommendation regarding the disclosure of medical information to a licensed physician designated by the consumer. We believe that this method of disclosing medical information will provide sufficient protection against disclosure to the consumer of information which, for medical reasons, should be withheld, while providing an opportunity to have erroneous or incomplete information corrected. Finally, we agree with and have advocated the Privacy Commission's recommendation that the consumer be allowed to see and copy his or her file in person, to receive a copy by mail, or to receive disclosure of the nature and substance by telephone.

Life-Style Information

We have found that consumers complain most frequently about reports which contain allegedly inaccurate and highly inflammatory information. Of particular concern is the characterization of their habits or life-styles by neighborhood sources not in a position to have relevant facts. Feeling maligned by an unnamed source, the consumer can respond only with self-serving denials. It is common under Section 611 of the Act to place the consumer's statement or version of the facts in the file and to send a copy of it to prior and subsequent recipients if the reinvestigation does not resolve the dispute between the consumer and the reporting agency. There is serious question as to whether or not this is an effective procedure, especially in light of the fact that the inspection report is ordered by the insurance company as a check against self-serving information obtained from the applicant or the agent in the first instance.

The Privacy Commission's Recommendations 11 and 12 would be an improvement over the existing dispute and correction mechanism in the

FCRA, by requiring, among other things, that insurance companies make deletions and corrections of disputed records, and by ensuring that any deletion, correction, or statement of dispute be sent to all relevant parties, including support organizations. However, there is a question of whether or not any procedure to achieve accuracy of information relating to such matters as life-style, habits, and morals would ever achieve results satisfactory to the subject.

I believe the amendments to the FCRA that I have mentioned would create a better balance between the consumers and the insurance companies and their support organizations, while not unduly burdening the insurance industry.

Other Problems

I would like to touch on some of the other problems we see regarding the information-gathering and use practices of the insurance industry and its support organizations.

Pretext Interviews

The so-called pretext interview is used by investigative agencies, especially in connection with claims reporting. As you know, the subject of a pretext interview is led to believe the interview is for a purpose other than the investigation of a claim. His or her physical appearance is closely observed, and he or she is asked questions ranging from his or her financial status to whether or not he or she has any impairments. The pretext interview also may be used to obtain personal information from a claimant who has retained legal counsel to represent him or her against the insurance company. In our opinion, this practice subverts the individual's right to legal representation. We feel the use of this technique contravenes the principles of privacy and may well constitute an unfair and deceptive practice in violation of the Federal Trade Commission Act. We support the Privacy Commission Recommendation 2 that would amend the FCRA to proscribe the use of the pretext, or other false or misleading representations, including those relating to the identity or representative capacity of the investigator.

Reporting of Medical Information from Lay Sources

Another problem area involves the collection and dissemination of health information from neighborhood sources who are not qualified, from a medical standpoint, to give accurate or reliable information. We believe that a consumer-reporting agency's obtaining and reporting health information from a lay source—other than the physical appearance of the subject—would violate the reasonable procedures requirement of Section 607(b) of the FCRA. The Privacy Commission has recommended that the FCRA be amended specifically to prohibit this practice by an insurance company or insurance-support organization (Recommendation 16). We also concur in this recommendation.

Relevancy of Information

In the past, the Federal Trade Commission has not supported attempts to impose relevancy requirements on information contained in consumer reports. While we have been sympathetic with those who have felt that certain highly personal types of information could serve no legitimate function in a consumer report, we felt that imposing limitations on the collection of "relevant" information would be unworkable because of the disparate needs of the various users of consumer reports. However, there is an increasing body of data which indicates that the marginal underwriting relevance of certain types of information may not justify the intrusion into the personal life of the subject. Further, there is serious question as to whether or not accurate information of this nature can be developed, given the relatively modest price the insurance industry has been willing to pay for inspection reports, especially those ordered in evaluating applications for lesser amounts of insurance. We agree with the Privacy Commission's observation that the inspection bureaus are labor-intensive and that a premium is placed on the productivity of the individual investigator.[8] While strengthening the Act's disclosure and notice requirements may be a deterrent to the collection and reporting of clearly irrelevant or intrusive information, we believe that the question of the propriety of collecting certain information should be given serious ongoing evaluation. Accordingly, we support the Privacy Commission's Recommendation 1.

Accuracy

We also concur in the Privacy Commission's observation that there has been a weak economic incentive to ensure that information in inspection reports is accurate, timely, and complete. The Commission makes the point that it takes a large number of policies lost by rejection because of inaccurate inspection reports to make up for a large claim settlement that might have been avoided if the application had been rejected or cancelled on the basis of a single inspection report.[9] We are greatly concerned about the amount of pressure the insurance industry can exert on investigative agencies to produce large volumes of modestly priced reports containing details about the personal lives of insurance applicants. Further, we are mindful of the pressure insurance companies can bring to bear on their support organizations to produce information having adverse underwriting significance.

In its commentary on the question of adverse information quotas, the Privacy Commission suggested that insurance companies do not care about the percentage of reports containing adverse information, so long as the investigation is as thorough and accurate as possible.[10] We agree that insurance companies are concerned that the reports are as thorough and accurate as possible. However, it appears to us that insurance companies also are concerned about the percentage of reports that contain adverse information. We understand that the money spent by insurance companies for inspection reports is to purchase protection from risks. Accordingly, the higher the percentage of adverse information developed by a particular inspection company, the greater the volume of reports that could be justified by its insurance company customers. We ask whether insurance companies, in certain instances, place too much pressure on the inspection agencies to develop information of an adverse nature. Is the premium placed on adverse information sufficient to create a conscious or unconscious bias on the part of the investigator, especially with regard to the more subjective types of information, such as character, reputation, and life-style?

The Privacy Commission's Recommendation 4 suggests that the insurance industry establish reasonable procedures for accuracy, completeness, and timeliness of the information it collects, maintains, or discloses about an individual. This recommendation would be implemented on a voluntary basis. We believe the insurance industry may well evaluate its relationship with its investigative-support organizations to determine whether, in certain instances, it imposes unreasonable pressures on the support organizations, which may have the tendency and capacity to produce inaccurate and incomplete investigative reports.

Questions and Answers

Comment (Plesser): *I would like to make a clarification on the liquidated damages recovery point that you brought out. We suggest limited immunity, which we believe to be reasonable.*

We do suggest additional remedies for the individual who is aggrieved under the Fair Credit Reporting Act, and they are not under the existing Act. One is the right to obtain specific performance through the court issuing an injunction, with the right of attorney's fees. We do suggest $1,000 liquidated damages as provision for the successful claimant.

Comment (Goldfarb): That is for willful violations, right?

Answer (Plesser): *Right. But we do recommend liquidated damages—although not as much as you call for, and I do not think it satisfies all of your complaints. We do recommend injunctive relief. We do recommend a specific performance provision. And we recommend an attorney's fees provision.*

Comment (Goldfarb): Yes. I did not mean to suggest that the Commission's recommendation did not go beyond what already exists in FCRA, but I do want to point out that, from our experiences, we have found that civil liability really does not work, unless there is a minimum amount that can be recovered regardless of any showing of actual damages. It is extremely difficult to prove actual damages in the area of privacy.

Comment (Plesser): *The up-to-$1,000 figure is without showing damages.*

Answer (Goldfarb): Right. It is with a showing of "willful" violation, which also is extremely difficult to show, we have found. I think our experience is borne out by the number of law suits that have been filed under the Fair Credit Reporting Act.

Question: *You don't have a greater number of complaints, do you? In fact, the FCRA is working well. How do you react to that statement?*

Answer: We do not have large numbers of complaints in our files, but we are not sure at this point how representative that is of the extent of disillusion out there. There is no notice to consumers that the Federal Trade Commission enforces the Fair Credit Reporting Act or that they should write to the FTC when they have a problem. We do have some number of complaints. There is some evidence in the record on the Equifax case. That is primarily what we are relying on.

Question: *One of the reasons I was asking this question is that some months ago Senator Proxmire in a press release said that the Federal Trade Commission had some 20,000 complaints. The Associated Credit Bureaus, under the Freedom of Information Act, obtained the record of that discussion. The actual number of complaints is 6,700. That is a far cry from 20,000.*

Answer: When the request was made for the numbers, there was confusion as to whether it was numbers of written complaints submitted or both written and nonwritten complaints.

Comment (from the audience): *Some 10,000 were not written. There was no written verification.*

Question: *This morning we heard from state regulators regarding at what level–federal or state–each of the Commission's privacy recommendations should be implemented. Would you discuss your views on this?*

Answer: I cannot give a detailed discussion as to which ones should be on the state level and which ones should be on the federal level. We agree in large part with the Privacy Commission's recommendations as to the level at which they should be enforced. We believe there should be governmental enforcement to a great degree and that, if the liability provisions of the Act are enhanced somewhat, private enforcement will do a great deal toward carrying out the objective of the law.

Question: *Suggestions were made that some area of the FTC might be appropriate for oversight of privacy activities. I was curious for comments on your capability, given the experience with the Fair Credit Reporting Act. It is my understanding that the largest source of guidance for the insurance industry, in terms of its compliance with the Fair Credit Reporting Act, is the staff-drafted manual, which has never been adopted by the FTC, and that there is no action now pending to set up a codified series of rules specifically dealing with insurance company obligations. Is it true that there is still only a draft staff manual for guidance from the legal end?*

Answer: I think that is a good point. We do have a staff manual and, as you know, under the Fair Credit Reporting Act, the Commission does not have the authority to promulgate rules implementing the Act. We would welcome your support in pushing for that authority. I think the Act would be implemented more effectively if we did have rule-making authority, and that would give the industry more guidance as to the requirements of the law. I agree with your point.

Question: *Why was the Commission not given rule-making authority? Is that an expression of Congressional attitude?*

Answer: It is an expression of Congressional attitude. I know that many in the industry were opposed to the Commission having that authority at the time the Fair Credit Reporting Act was drafted.

Question: *Didn't you support, some years ago, amendments to the FCRA?*

Answer: Sure. We appeared before a few Congressional committees about two years ago when there were proposed amendments to the Fair Credit Reporting Act. We also submitted draft language to amend it. I could furnish you with copies of our testimony before these committees, which I think would be most helpful.

Question: *Just for clarification, did I hear you say that the FTC does not have rule-making authority?*

Answer: The FTC, under the Fair Credit Reporting Act, does not have regulation-writing authority to implement the Act. As under the other titles of the Consumer Credit Protection Act, the Federal Reserve Board has been given regulation-writing authority to implement those statutes. There is no comparable authority under the Fair Credit Reporting Act. The FTC has, under its enabling statute, rule-making authority. It is arguable as to whether or not it can promulgate rules having the force of law under the Fair Credit Reporting Act. That is uncertain at this point.

Question: *I'm not a lawyer, but there was a case,* Magneson-Moss, *I think. Didn't that give you rule-making authority?*

Answer: That expanded our already existing rule-making authority and delineated the rule-making procedures more clearly. There is still question as to whether we have that authority only under the FTC Act, which prohibits unfair and deceptive practices, or that we can use that authority to implement the other special statutes that we enforce—the other credit statutes. It is uncertain at this point.

Question: *Is it true that your enforcement power rests with your ability to issue cease-and-desist orders and to go to court with those who violate the order?*

Answer: Basically, that is correct.

Question: *Are you suggesting the establishment of a civil cause of action, apparently to supplement the power that the FTC itself has to implement any new regulations?*

Answer: Well, under the existing FCRA there is a provision for civil liability—for aggrieved consumers to come in and sue. But the way these provisions are now drafted, it is very difficult for a consumer to sue. So we are just recommending enhancement of the existing provision.

Question: *Are you interested in, or desirous of, a proposal to extend your own authority to enforce the Act in order to prevent widespread abuse?*

Answer: Not in what I am saying today. The Commission has the authority to seek civil penalties for violations of its orders. If we proceeded against a company and got a litigated order, we could then go into court against another company, who had notice of that order, and seek civil penalties in the first instance. So we already have substantial authority to bring about compliance. The problem I was pointing out was with the breadth and scope of the existing laws. It does not cover many of the practices that we think should be prohibited.

Question: *One of the recommendations which the FTC has made is that a investigative-consumer report could not be ordered or made without the consent of the individual. Is that correct?*

Answer: That is right.

Question: *That would be a substantial difference, as I understand it, from the Privacy Commission's recommendation. Isn't that right?*

Answer: I thought the Privacy Commission had an authorization requirement—correct me if I am wrong.

Comment (Plesser): *It is a "notification" requirement. "Notification" and "authorization" are confusing concepts. If you give notification above the signature line on an application, does it become a consent? We were more interested in making sure that the individual entering into the insurance relationship knew what information would be sought and other information practices. And whether you call that a consent or notification may be unclear.*

Comment (Goldfarb): That is probably right. That could be a condition to obtaining insurance, therefore, you are required to consent to it.

Question: *Under the FTC recommendation, if an individual, in applying for an insurance policy, refused to sign a form authorizing the insurer to order an investigative report, and if the insurer would not write the insurance because of that, would the insurer—under your proposal—incur any liability because of that refusal?*

Answer (Goldfarb): We are not recommending that insurance companies be required to issue policies without getting an investigative report.

Comment (Plesser): *And the Privacy Commission report is consistent with that.*

Question: *Could you speculate on the likelihood of federal legislation and, if so, when?*

Answer: I think there will be federal legislation. As Mr. [Robert Ellis] Smith pointed out, I do not think it will be this term, because the banking committees have a few other proposals at a higher priority—one is electronic funds legislation, another is Truth in Lending simplification and revision, and then the third I believe would be Fair Credit Reporting Act amendments. However, I think there will be changes to the Fair Credit Reporting Act.

Question: *Do the Truth in Lending changes have anything to do with the enforcement provisions that you have suggested be transferred to the FCRA?*

Answer: No. There are about seven bills that have been proposed to amend the Truth in Lending Act. It is a matter of enacting power.

Question: *What I am getting at is, as I understand the Truth in Lending changes, they would simplify what has become a burdensome amount of unnecessary detail in the Truth in Lending form, the violation of which would give rise to $100 minimum damage suits. I was wondering if any of these bills were related to $100 minimum suits that you propose be established under the FCRA?*

Answer: There are several proposals that relate to that, and one of the most significant ones, for your purposes I think, might be that they are proposing limiting the $100 liability only to certain specified significant disclosure violations, so that a creditor would not be liable across the board for every violation of Truth in Lending.

Question: *Would you be in favor of a similar kind of provision under the Fair Credit Reporting Act?*

Answer: I think we could support a similar provision, yes.

Question: *Do you conclude that there have or have not been issues within our industry in this area?*

Answer: Well, as I have said before, I can really only speak to the investigative-reporting industry, and I would say "yes" to that. The only area that I am aware of that we are looking into right now is user responsibility under Section 615 of the Fair Credit Reporting Act. We have some reason to believe that insurance companies are not providing the 615 notices where they are required under the Fair Credit Reporting Act. We now are investigating that problem.

---

1. The administrative law judge issued a 300-page initial decision in the *Equifax* case on November 11, 1977. Both sides have appealed that decision.

2. *In the Matter of Beneficial Corporation*, 86 F.T.C. 119, 172 N.9 (1975), *Modified*, 542 F.2d 611 (3d Cir. 1976). *Cert. Denied* 430 U.S. 983 (1977).

3. All references to numbered recommendations refer to recommendations in the Privacy Commission's chapter on the insurance relationship, in Privacy Protection Study Commission, *Personal Privacy in an Information Society* (Washington, D.C., U.S. Government Printing Office, 1977). (Hereinafter cited as *Report*.)

4. Nitti v. Credit Bureau, 375 N.Y.S. 2d 817 (N.Y. Sup. Ct. 1975). For a description of a similar experience with an inspection bureau, see Millstone v. O'Hanlon Reports, 383 F. Supp. 269 275-76 (E.D. Mo. 1974), *Aff'd* 528 F.2d 829 (8th Cir. 1976).

5. *Report*, p. 10.

6. Ibid., p. 208.

7. Ibid., pp. 30, 35, 217.

8. Ibid., p. 322.

9. Ibid., p. 341.

10. Ibid., p. 328.

10

Privacy, the Insurance Industry, and the Consumer: A Representative's View

Barry Goldwater, Jr.

I will discuss privacy as it pertains to the private sector and to the future liberties that we enjoy. Certainly an essential, but fragile, element of our liberty and personal freedom is this thing that we call privacy. It is an element that is riddled with paradoxes and yet, oftentimes, taken for granted; but then look at the price that mankind has paid in attempts to achieve and preserve it. It is terribly abstract, and its reality is oftentimes referred to as heaven come to earth. Nevertheless, personal privacy, your right to be left alone, your right to control your own person, is essential if a state of freedom is to exist.

The concept of privacy and individual rights is as old and as basic as our Constitution and our Bill of Rights, and yet nowhere in these two great documents do you really find the word "privacy." And yet without it, those protections guaranteed by these documents would ceast to exist. It is hard to define what privacy really is until you ask an individual what it means to him, and he can tell you what it is: the right to be left alone, the

---

Congressman Barry Goldwater, Jr. represents the 20th Congressional District of California where he was first elected in April 1969. He is a member of the Privacy Protection Study Commission and of the House Committee on Science and Technology. The Congressman has emerged as a serious, effective voice in the protection of individual rights and personal privacy and has authored several measures to protect individuals from privacy invasions. He was a principal sponsor of the Privacy Act of 1974. He is also a member of the House Committee on Public Works and Transportation.

right to be able to control your personality and extensions of that are indeed an important element in the perception of liberty.

Most Americans accept privacy as their bedrock of freedom and generally do not give it much concern, that is, until they find themselves at the end of an information-invasion situation or find out really how insidiously their privacy has been invaded. I know that some people will find it hard to believe, but current personal information practices throughout this country are causing a denuding of every person's personal privilege. We have found that both government and the private sector have been guilty from time to time. Since I first became involved in this issue back in about 1972 or 1973, my files have become full of examples of abuses, ranging from very small incidents to very traumatic incidents of human effect and involvement.

These abuses, in most instances, are really unintentional. They tend to be a result of practices that over the years have resulted in putting life, human qualities, on the back burner in the decision-making process. For some reason, our society over the years has allowed the qualities of human existence—spiritual values and ethics—to escape the importance that they should have in our lives and really in our decision-making processes. After all, our decisions affect human life. However, under the guise of expediency, of cost-effectiveness, we have moved ahead, not considering the effect that things we do have upon people—customers, employees, and others. For some reason, an atmosphere has been allowed to exist in which an individual, in exchange for a benefit or a service, is assumed to waive all rights, interest, and control over information collection, storage, and dissemination.

Too often in government, especially in government, but certainly in private practice, the importance of that individual escapes into obscurity. And we go about our way making our decisions that affect these human beings, not considering the importance of that individual and the rights that he has, not only as a human being, but certainly as a citizen of this country.

There are many areas of activity in our society that historically have played a significant and continuing role in the development of our nation. There is no doubt that the insurance industry has played a major role in fostering the development and vitality of American. Your industry has provided Americans with security. Your industry always has been ready with a helping hand in times of adversity and distress. If you did not exist, government would be filling your shoes, as it does in so many captive countries. Your industry has literally underwritten our national growth and development. Having worked for a number of years in the investment business, I am personally aware of this. The Privacy Protection Study Commission was equally aware of the importance of your industry. As a matter of fact, as you know, Bill Bailey, the President of Aetna Life and Casualty Company, was a member of the Commission.

Our Commission found that all Americans have an association with the insurance community—through individual or group health insurance, life and disability insurance, property and liability insurance. The Privacy Commission found that this deep involvement with individual citizens, while obviously generating great benefit is heavily impinging on individual personal privacy.

In most cases, the impact on personal privacy has been unintentional and without premeditation. It is regrettable, but nevertheless true, that in several significant instances the policies and activities of some companies were found to have a seriously detrimental impact on the personal privacy of Americans.

The Privacy Commission rigidly adhered to three basic precepts throughout its activities. The Commission conducted its activities without any policy or factual preconceptions. The Commission insisted on conducting as thorough an investigation as was humanly possible and in developing the facts—no matter what they were. And, when the Commission found a problem and decided that corrective action was required, we formulated our recommendations within the confines of a commitment to: (1) minimize intrusiveness; (2) maximize fairness; and (3) create a legitimate, enforceable expectation of confidentiality.

There is not, and never has been, anything punitive in the legislative proposals that I have submitted to the Congress. This is equally true with the recommendations that came from the Privacy Commission.

Rather, a serious problem exists with regard to the collection, use, and dissemination of personal information in this country. It is this problem involving personal information and your industry that I want to discuss.

Your industry obviously cannot conduct its business unless it has access to detailed personal information. As water and air are essential to human existence, personal information is to your industry. It is impossible to make a decision about whether or not to insure an individual, his property, or activities without it. It also is impossible for your industry to protect itself against fraudulent or "hyped" claims unless you have access to relevant information. And I am as aware of the growing fraudulent claims problem as anyone in the country.

So, people have said to me, what is the problem? Very simply, the problem is as follows:

1. Individuals rightly expect that their personal information, given over for a right, privilege, or benefit, will be treated confidentially.

2. Most individuals do not believe that in exchange for a right, privilege, or benefit—whether it involves monetary consideration or not—they lose all further connection to their personal information. This is true even though most citizens realize that to exist and interact in our society they must trade some of their personal privacy. It is the old barter system, and we do it willingly.

3. Individuals believe that the recipients of personal information have a responsibility to keep information accurate and up to date.

4. They believe that information given over for one purpose must not be used for another unless they are told about it and, in some cases, give their positive consent for the new use.

5. Finally, most citizens believe that these ideas are part of our English Common Law tradition, tacitly protected and assured by our Constitution and Bill of Rights, and that they are part of our statutory law as well.

What the Privacy Commission confirmed is that these expectations today have little or no basis in law and often are not consistent with practice. Nothing confirms this fact of life more than the 1976 Supreme Court decision of *United States vs. Miller*. The decision was delivered in June 1976. Basically, the Court said that banking information does not belong to the individual, that he has no control over its use or dissemination, *and* that he has no right of an expectation of privacy about his financial information.

The relationship of an individual to his financial information is almost identical to his insurance relationship. It would be easy for a bright attorney to make the same argument about your industry—despite citizen expectations and the general practices of your industry.

The problem confronting the insurance industry is further complicated by the following situations.

1. Hearsay and unverified information is included in some files.

2. Few companies have in operation consistently reliable verification and updating procedures—although over the last 18 months this situation has begun to change.

3. State law, which I would prefer to see as the controlling mechanism, has not kept up with and clarified the informational relationships and authorities you have and need. For example, with the exception of the right of discovery that lawyers have, most states have not enacted laws that give insurance companies reasonable access to relevant information when a claim is in dispute *before* court action is resorted to. The result of this circumstance has been the creation of businesses like Factual Service Bureau, Inc., which made a pretty good business out of getting personal, sensitive information without authorization.

4. Personal privacy protection—which I believe all of you subscribe to in both your personal and professional lives—is often under assault because of the adversary nature of much of the claims business. And neither your industry nor the law has moved to balance the situation acceptably.

5. Finally, much of your industry has resorted to using third-party services—such as private investigation firms, inspection bureaus, and other support organizations—and in large measure these organizations were left to their own devices regarding their information practices.

There certainly is a need for organizations such as the Medical Information Bureau, the Impairment Bureau, Loss Indexes, and so forth, and the criminal-justice system obviously has a reason to be involved in this whole process. But, as the Commission found, too often some activities violated the citizen's expectation of privacy—an expectation the industry fosters—and too often was liable to propagate "soft" or "raw" data.

It is my conviction that the protection and nurturing of personal informational privacy is essential to the continuation of our freedom, quality of life, and the goodwill that the general public should have toward its institutions, governmental as well as private. In fact, in regard to the private sector, I happen to feel that adopting basic principles and concepts of privacy is good business.

Citizens' faith and confidence in our institutions are absolutely imperative if our capitalistic, free-enterprise system is to continue to proceed. There is a direct relationship between a company's profit and loss statements and this interest of Americans. I do not believe that there is anything to be gained if, in the process of protecting personal privacy, the costs are excessive and out of proportion to the qualitative protection that results. Tying up your industry in red tape and federal bureaucrats in the name of privacy protection really will accomplish nothing, except a further destruction of our free-enterprise system.

What I have always sought is a balancing of the legitimate interests of your industry with a reasonable degree of clear-cut, understandable, enforceable personal privacy protection. I believe our quality of life, our way of life, and its institutions hang in the balance.

One final comment. I have stated repeatedly that a head-long rush by the Congress in legislation in the privacy area probably will be worse than the intended cure. The creation of the Privacy Protection Study Commission and the repeated calls by me and Representative Ed Koch to our colleagues to go slow, make sure of the facts, and legislate only when no other approach is workable have been designed to make sure that a blind legislative rush does not occur. The Congress is not rushing to legislate, although the findings and recommendations of the Privacy Commission certainly will add to the motivation of taking a hard, good look.

There is, as a result of certain banking activities today, legislation now being marked up in the Congress that incorporates the recommendations of the Privacy Commission in the area of banking, which I personally think is apropos, especially after the *Miller* decision. It is my expectation that the Congress will act eventually.

I think you have an opportunity to affect the kind of legislation that eventually might come forth. Obviously, the legislative process is a deliberative process. It is a process in which there is a lot of give and take, a lot of opportunity for input—as President Carter is finding out today. It is a "pull and a shove" proposition. It is legislation hopefully based on facts, and I think that, as your industry examines the concepts put forth by the Privacy Commission and hopefully implements this as a standard policy and procedures within the whole industry, there very well may not be a need for harsh corrective action. That remains to be seen. It depends on the commitment of the private sector in recognizing, as Bill Bailey told you, that it is not going to go away. It is here. It is an ethic that has come of age, like it or not.

With our rapidly progressing technology and advancements in science and communications, there is a need once in a while to pause and to examine where all of this is taking us and how it is affecting human beings and human life. I happen to be a great supporter of supersonic flight. I think it was, perhaps, wise that the Congress stop, as they did, to examine the effects of supersonic flight upon our environment. I think, oftentimes, in business we need to examine the policies and practices as they affect those we work for and work with.

What I want to assure you of is my commitment to see that all sides and considerations are permitted to be heard and that the Congress limits its actions to those provisions that are absolutely necessary to clarify the situation and restore the balance that should exist between our right to privacy and our society's obvious need for freedom of information.

Questions and Answers

Question: *When you introduced the sequence of ten bills in July [1977], you indicated that you intended to file an omnibus bill at a later date. Is that still your intention?*

Answer: That is my intention, but I am not really certain I can do it, because there are so many diverse areas that may not lend themselves to an omnibus package of privacy legislation. But I am going to pursue that, because I think it makes it easier to address oneself to when it is in a neat, tight package. But maybe my expectations are greater than the possiblities will allow. But I am going to continue to pursue that right now.

[*Editors' note*: An omnibus bill, H.R. 10076, was introduced.]

Question: *When would you anticipate that there will be some legislative action on the bills that have been proposed?*

Answer: That prediction I do not think I am prepared to make. Privacy concerns and privacy legislation are very elusive. The Privacy Act of 1974 went through because of the aftermath of Watergate and CIA and FBI revelations. It gave it the focus that was needed to bring it to attention, and it flew through Congress without any problems. Today we are greatly concerned with our growing shortage of energy, our floundering economy, the increasing burden on Americans of inflation, and the increasing spectacle of a government taking more and more of our hard-earned income in the form of taxes. These seem to be the paramount concerns of the Congress today. Until we resolve those issues, I do not suggest that privacy, unless it happens to fit into such as this banking bill, will be brought to the surface. So I cannot make a prediction. I do not know.

I can say that there is a comfortable and healthy awareness and concern on the part of some very key legislators in the Congress, both in the Senate and the House, so I would not say necessarily that it is shuffled under the carpet. I think it is sitting there waiting for its priority to evolve. I cannot make a prediction, but I think it is something you ought to keep your ears open to. And in the meantime, be prepared. I think your input on this is vitally important.

We tried in our deliberations with the help of Bill Bailey, Ron Plesser, and others to strike a reasonable balance and reasonable recommendations, but here again, we were only one Commission. You are millions, and I think as you evaluate these that you should let us know how they are going to fit in with the real world and give us the benefit of that. So I would not wait, is what I am saying.

Question: *Would you envision, if there is an omnibus bill, that there will be a Privacy Board with a role other than that advocated by the Privacy Commission?*

Answer: I personally would hope not. I think the last thing we need is another level of bureaucracy. But I think in the area of privacy we do need a board that would sit to be a recipient of problems, one that would sit to clarify and to explain and to help implement privacy practices within the private sector. The Privacy Commission recommended that such a board be created, without any law-enforcement privileges, to be a clearinghouse to facilitate the implementation of privacy laws. So whatever privacy laws eventually may be enacted, I am hopeful that this privacy board also would be enacted, not only for the benefit of the private sector but also for the benefit of the government itself, because the Privacy Act, which has been in existence for several years, is still having some problems as far as some of the agencies and the bureaucrats implementing the procedures prescribed. I think there needs to be some kind of body that can explain and clarify and be the recipient of comments and suggestions, as well as collecting additional research that needs to be ongoing over the years to further refine this issue, to find out more about it and its implications.

Question: *Congressman, I would like to have you comment on what your expectations are when ultimately there are hearings in Congress. What is your experience about Congress's attitude toward a Commission like this that it created? Presumably there were extensive hearings and fact finding. What would be your estimate of the kind of hearings that the bills will get in the Congress? Will they be less inclined to engage in extensive hearings, or would you say that they will treat these bills like any other bills and start all over again?*

Answer: I would predict that the Congress, when they get around to this issue, will have extensive hearings, and they will invite all interested parties to participate. I think there will be adequate time to make comments and suggestions and to present testimony. As far as being inclined to create a board of this type, I have never seen the Congress hesitate on creating another board or commission. They do it very easily and with very little consideration. I think there will be a thorough airing of these issues, especially because we are, in essence, plowing new ground. There never before has been legislation specifically addressing itself to individual, personal privacy before the Privacy Act of 1974, the so-called Buckley amendment as it applies to the admission of students or students in the schools. So this is a new area. I am going to encourage that we be deliberative in our efforts, that we be as careful as we can, and that we give it as wide and as broad an airing as conceivable, so that we understand before we jump out into thin air that we know where we are going to come down. I think it is imperative that we do that, and it is absolutely important that in this process we hear from the real world—your world.

Question: *Would you expect to see insurance regulated at the federal level as a result?*

Answer: Traditionally insurance has been a state responsibility, and I personally would like to see it that way. The legislation that we anticipate primarily goes to amending such existing acts as the federal Fair Credit Reporting Act and other existing laws on a very broad basis. And the purpose of this is to avoid some of the problems that would exist where you have various state laws applying to this question. That was one of the areas the Privacy Act required the Commission to look into, because there are all these problems that crop up in interstate commerce that do not lend themselves to individual, tailored state laws and regulations, even though we do have today in some states (California being one) some regulations coming forth. But I understand that a lot of states have been holding off, waiting for the Commission to report. I think they do recognize the precariousness of this situation. So that is why our recommendations went to acts or to laws that already exist, amending them to certain degrees, so that they affect across the board.

Question: *This is someplace between a suggestion and a plea. When legislation is enacted and you must consider enforcement, I hope that we do not get the kind of mess that we have with the ERISA and the enforcement of EEO regulations. That is one horror story, believe me. Anything you do along that line will be greatly appreciated. After hearing the spokesman from the FTC, I would say I am scared.*

Answer: Well, I can understand your anxiety because I am the recipient of those kinds of expressions on a daily basis from businesses, both large and small, who somehow run afoul of the agencies of government. Too often we see unreasonableness in the enforcement of laws. We see through administrative law the interpretation of Congressional intent that oftentimes leaves one shaking one's head. The Civil Rights Act of 1964—it was not the intentions of the Congress to require busing to ensure some racial balance, and yet we have busing, due to the interpretation of the agencies of government as well as our court system. This is the thing that we always face. Once the law is written, the interpretation of it by those enforcement agencies may take on a different tone than what was the original intent of the lawmakers passing the law. That is a failure of our system, obviously, because our lawmakers have the responsibility of oversight and of refining these laws to bring them back into perspective following the original intent. And we do see this from time to time. We just amended the Clean Air Act and the Water Pollution Act. We just refined, as you recall, the emissions standards for new automobiles, because what had happened had gotten skewed out of balance, and so the Congress, through oversight, had to come back and redo those. We should be doing that all the time. But oftentimes we have legislated so much in this country, there are so many levels of bureaucracies and agencies and commissions that are promulgating rules left and right, that it is beyond the capability of the Congress to conduct proper oversight. In no way can we really monitor these laws that are very prolific today. I am very hopeful that President Carter is successful in streamlining our government and getting rid of some of those outmoded regulations, in requiring bureaucrats to read them before they promulgate them. If he succeeds in doing that, as a Republican, I will go to the Democrat convention and nominate him myself.

11

Conclusion

Harold D. Skipper, Jr.

The purpose of this book is to facilitate discussion of privacy concepts, issues, and methods as they apply to the insurance business. Because the privacy debate is still in its early stages, the Georgia State University *Conference on Privacy and the Insurance Industry* and this book, which grew out of the Conference, represent attempts to generate meaningful discussion by providing a broad survey of how modern concepts of privacy may be applied to the insurance business. Although the book's purpose is not to suggest solutions, or to advocate viewpoints, its method is to allow others' solutions and viewpoints to delineate both the direction and the nature of the issues and solutions currently being debated.

The report of the Privacy Protection Study Commission (PPSC) has shaped the course of the privacy debate. The PPSC's report has occupied "center stage" in the drama of privacy discourse, both because it was the first comprehensive application to private business of modern concepts of privacy—fair information practices—and because it took a moderate position in proposing some changes in privacy practices and regulation. That the Commission's recommendations were moderate is attested to by the fact that some individuals have characterized them as going too far, while other equally prudent persons have said they do not go far enough.

The Commission's report is a subtle document, despite (or more likely, because of) its length. The Commission generally focused on ends, not means, and it recommended that change be implemented, where possible, at a level most consistent with existing industry and regulatory behavior. However, two significant regulatory reactions to the report—U.S. House Bill H.R.10076 [the so-called Preyer Bill], and the National Association of Insurance Commissioners' (NAIC) discussion draft *Model Privacy Legislation* [released January 1979]—show how the report's subtlety and flexibility can be altered, distorting both the sensitivity and the sense of the PPSC's recommendations. Those in agreement with the PPSC's fundamental approach clearly must be vigilant to assure that the Commission's thrust is preserved.

The issues under discussion here are difficult and complex. They involve conflicts of values as well as of ends and means. The Commission's recommended prohibition of pretext interviews exemplifies these conflicts well. The PPSC, in its investigations and hearings, discovered that certain insurance-support organizations obtained information about individuals through pretext interviews and through other false and misleading representations. The Commission found this to be an offensive practice and recommended that the Fair Credit Reporting Act (FCRA) be amended to make any such practice illegal. Many insurance claim executives believe that pretext interviews are necessary in rare instances to detect attempts to defraud insurers. This recommendation, then, involves the clash of an individual's right to be free from overly intrusive information collection practices with an insurer's obligation to protect the interests of its stockholders and policyowners and to discourage, as a matter of public policy, crimes and other acts seeking improper gain from insurance contracts. Whether the Commission's preferred resolution of this dilemma is in accord with what Congress believes the country wants is unclear.

As the fury of Watergate, of unauthorized wiretapping of the telephones of Americans, and of other intrusive events recedes, some of the intensity of the country's and the Commission's concern with privacy protection ebbs, also. In this context, the Commission included two recommendations which amount to no more than reminders to regulators and insurers to be more alert to privacy concerns in the future than has been the case in the past. Unfortunately, the purposes of these two recommendations—Number 1, calling for regulators to gather and, where necessary, act on certain Privacy complaints, and Recommendation 4, calling for insurers to have reasonable procedures to assure the accuracy, completeness, and timeliness of information they use—have been misunderstood. In the absence of a heightened private sector awareness of privacy matters, it is not unreasonable to foresee legislation to provide governmentally-mandated procedures or judicial opinions as to what procedures are "reasonable" for insurers to assure accuracy, completeness, timeliness, and, perhaps, relevance.

The PPSC Report

PPSC Inconsistencies

In an undertaking as massive as that which the PPSC faced, it is inevitable that some inconsistencies would creep into the Commission's recommendations or its discussion of them. Faced with defining principles, gathering information, and making recommendations in over a dozen disparate industries against a two-year deadline, the Commission and its staff performed remarkably well. Readers of the Commission's report are, however, under no such deadline, and they can concentrate on particular areas of the report. Accordingly, before the Commission's recommendations are acted upon, inconsistencies of logic and language should be ferreted out and rectified.

Some examples of such inconsistencies follow. These are not an exhaustive listing. First, in several recommendations, the Commission distinguishes between claimants and applicants. The fifth recommendation, for instance, dealing with notice regarding information collection, was designed to allow consumers to become more knowledgeable about the information practices of those organizations with which they deal. This recommendation is that when an insurer collects information about an individual from other than the individual himself or herself, the insurer must give the individual a notice explaining certain of the insurer's information practices. The Commission stated that the notice did not have to be given in connection with claims or marketing. In the editors' opinion, little justification exists for treating an underwriting transaction differently from a claim transaction in this case.

A second example of inconsistency involves immunity from suit in right-of-access cases. The PPSC recommended that limited immunity be extended to insurers and insurance-support organizations, but the narrative describing the recommendation states that the immunity should apply only to "adverse underwriting decisions." This, hopefully, was unintended. If immunity is to be granted for one type of insurance transaction, it seems only logical to grant it for other transactions as well.

A third example of inconsistency involves imprecision in the use of key words or phrases. The recommendation involving right of access of individuals to medical record information about them indicates that disclosure may be provided through a "medical professional," but in the editors' opinion the term in quotes is too broad for controlled disclosure. Further, the recommendation dealing with notice regarding information collection states that

> prior to collecting information about an applicant or principal
> insured from another person in connection with an insurance
> transaction, [the insurer] notify him as to . . .

Is the applicant or principal insured (or both?) to be notified? Who is a "principal insured?" The confusion should be clarified. Still further, the term "individual" has a specifically-defined meaning in the PPSC's report, but its use is not always confined to that meaning, as in the recommendation regarding authorization forms. Moreover, it is unclear as to whether the Commission intended to provide privacy protection to persons on whom information was collected and used in connection with business and professional insurance. Not to provide such protection would be inconsistent.

In an effort to provide individuals with as much control as possible over information practices affecting them, the Commission's recommendations often require the dissemination of more information at one time to individuals than they may be interested in or capable of digesting. For example, an individual who is the object of an adverse underwriting decision currently has limited opportunities to find out the reasons for the decision. To assure fairness in the decision-making process, the Commission believed the subject individual should be provided a mechanism to verify or dispute the quality of the information upon which an adverse decision was based. In the Commission's opinion, this should be accomplished by the insurer advising the individual in writing of the information upon which the decision was based and of the reasons which led the institution to render the decision.

As with the notice regarding collection, it seems unnecessary at the time the individual learns of the adverse decision to inundate the individual with the access and correction procedures. Perhaps advising the individual of the reasons for an adverse underwriting decision but not, simultaneously, of the detailed information upon which the decision was based would suffice. If the individual wanted to know upon what information the decision was based, and the access and correction procedures, the individual could request that the insurer or support organization provide the desired information and procedures. Alternatively, the insurer could decide when the information was so insensitive that if it fell into someone else's control it would not be embarrassing or humiliating to the individual and, in those cases, make the disclosure of the information.

New Privacy Problems

Some of the Commission's recommendations have, in the editors' opinion, created new privacy problems as they attempted to solve old ones. As an example, consumers do not currently have the right to see, or even learn the nature and substance of, information maintained on them by insurers or by most insurance-support organizations. (Under the FCRA, they can learn the "nature and substance" of data gathered by consumer reporting agencies.) The Commission, in recommending that individuals have a right of access to records about themselves, advocated that individuals have access to the *entire* file. In the editors' opinion, the Commission's recommendation that information about others contained in an individual's file be disclosed to the individual appears to be inconsistent with the concept of protecting privacy. At a minimum, the insurer should be able to exercise discretionary authority as to whether to disclose information on one individual which is contained in another's file. Another example of an instance in which the Commission may have created privacy problems involves its recommendations on confidentiality. Insurers and their support organizations now voluntarily assume some vague responsibility for the confidentiality of the information they maintain on individuals. However, in the Commission's judgment, the responsibility for treating information on individuals in a confidential manner should be more clearly established. Therefore, the Commission recommended that a Federal law be enacted to provide that insurers and insurance-support organizations owe a duty of confidentiality to any individual about whom it collects or receives information. By establishing that a duty of confidentiality is owed, no insurers or support organizations would disclose information about an individual without that individual's authority, except in limited circumstances.

This recommendation means that one insurer may not share with another insurer information about an individual unless the individual explicitly authorized sharing or unless the insurers were deemed to be "parties-of-interest." Insurers would be considered parties-of-interest if each had an interest in the same claim or if one acted as a reinsurer for another. Other party-in-interest exceptions would apply to certain relationships between insurers and their support organizations and between support organizations.

Problems exist with this recommendation. For example, the duty of confidentiality is owed only to "individuals." As the Commission has defined this term, numerous other parties (e.g., beneficiaries) on whom insurers had information would not be entitled to a duty of confidentiality. Moreover, the duty is owed only to the information collected in connection with an "insurance transaction." This seems unnecessarily restrictive and, indeed, would mean that information gathered for other-than-decision-making purposes need not be held in confidence.

Overregulation Problems

The PPSC's recommendations contain, in the editors' opinion, what may be characterized as occasional efforts to overregulate. Its sixteenth recommendation—that a Federal law be enacted to provide that no insurer or insurance-support organization disclose to another insurer or insurance-support organization information pertaining to an individual's health unless the information was obtained from a medical-care provider or directly from the individual—is a case in point. As originally conceived, this recommendation was to apply only to organized information data exchanges within the insurance business whose primary or sole source of information was insurers—for example, the Medical Information Bureau. As it ultimately came out, however, the recommendation applied to the transfer of information from any support organization to an insurer. This goes contrary to the PPSC's preference for regulating "ends" and leaving means to be worked out by the affected parties. In other words, the recommendation could simply say that insurers should not be allowed to use, in a manner adverse to an individual, information about the individual's health unless it was obtained directly from the individual or from a medical-care provider or it could apply only to data exchanges.

Another possible instance of overregulation in the Commission's recommendations may be its prescription for authorization forms. The Commission stated that many authorization forms now in use by insurers were " . . . so broad as to constitute an invitation to abuse." Among the problems pointed out by the Commission with such forms were that they: (1) have no stated purpose, (2) have no expiration date, (3) are not limited as to scope of investigation, and (4) are not limited as to source of information. The Commission recommended that minimum standards for authorization forms be set.

This recommendation would have relatively little impact on underwriting in property/liability insurance, although the one-year time limit on the validity of the authorization and the listing of specific individuals that are required by the recommendation could pose problems for claim departments. Perhaps the authorization should be valid during the pendency of the claim.

The recommendation will be significant to the underwriting and claims areas of life and health insurance. Administrative problems will be created because the authorization is supposed to be " . . . specific as to the individuals and institutions he [the subject individual] is authorizing to disclose information about him who are known at the time the authorization is signed, and general as to others whose specific identity is not known at the time the authorization is signed." First, the focus of the recommendation should not be on "individuals and institutions" which are known by the subject individual. To do so is to end up with the rather absurd situation where the individual "knows" of a source, does not volunteer it and, therefore, the recommendation would say, the insurer may not use the authorization because the individual was "known."

It is doubtful that a medical professional would release information—in a new era of privacy-consciousness—unless he or she were specifically named. Thus, for practical purposes, the exception to specificity allowed in part (c) of this recommendation may be useless. If someone or some organization needs information from that confidential source, the applicant or claimant likely would be asked to sign another authorization.

NAIC Privacy Task Force

The PPSC report will probably remain the standard against which proposals for changes are judged. In this connection, the NAIC discussion draft *Model Privacy Legislation* must be viewed critically. Released for comment in January 1979, the draft represented an initial attempt by the NAIC Privacy Task Force to address privacy issues. Much time and thought obviously were expended in preparing the draft for it clears many of the inconsistencies of the PPSC recommendations. In the process, however, it has created other inconsistencies. For example, it excludes privacy protections for individuals who buy insurance for business or professional reasons. Privacy protections for all claimants are almost non-existent. The duty of confidentiality the draft proposes to establish would allow a virtually free, unauthorized flow of information within the insurance business. These are but a few of the shortcomings of this draft which, hopefully, will be remedied before formal adoption by the NAIC.

The President's Privacy Initiative

Besides the NAIC Task Force, President Jimmy Carter established his own Privacy Initiative group to assist him in developing a position on privacy issues. The President's approach to promoting privacy protection involves a package of bills. Of particular interest are Title V of the "Fair Financial Information Practices Act" and, to a lesser extent, the "Privacy of Medical Information Act." The Medical Privacy Bill was submitted to Congress on April 2, 1979 and the "Fair Financial Information Practices Act" had not been submitted at this writing, but was expected soon. Title V of this bill, the "Fair Insurance Information Practices Act," was released in May 1979 for public comment before being submitted to Congress. This unusual step was taken because of the extremely delicate nature of this particular title of the package. Indeed, insurance privacy is acknowledged as *the* privacy issue for 1979-1980. To a large extent, this was true in the Privacy Commission's deliberations, and it is most assuredly true within the President's privacy package.

Generally, the President's draft bill tracks the Privacy Protection Study Commission's recommendations although it, too—like the NAIC draft—contains inconsistencies. However, the bill does not track the Privacy Commission's suggested implementation approach. The bill takes a unique approach to resolving the federal versus state question on implementation. Any attempt by the President at this time to place enforcement of and rulemaking authority for federal privacy standards as they relate to the insurance business in the hands of a federal government agency, such as the Federal Trade Commission, would be met with significant industry opposition. On the other hand, total reliance on the states to act on privacy issues is considered by many to be equally unacceptable.

The resolution to this seeming dilemma was to support a federal standards approach which relies on individual consumer action through litigation in federal courts and on enforcement and oversight by state insurance officials. In other words, state insurance commissioners could (not "must") be the enforcement vehicle if they so chose.

The Future

While the focus of the Privacy Conference and, to a large extent, this book, has revolved around insurance-related privacy issues as identified by the PPSC, one should keep in mind (1) that other PPSC-identified privacy issues are important to the insurance business (for example, the medical care relationship area, the employment and personnel area and the direct marketing area) and (2) that privacy issues other than those identified by the PPSC should not be ignored.

Whether one agrees or disagrees with the need for change, it appears that change will be forthcoming—either on a voluntary or, more likely, a compulsory basis. On balance, the editors believe the recommendations of the PPSC to be reasonable. The problems—both real and potential—identified by the PPSC justify the need for changes in insurance information practices.

The insurance business would be wise to consider the privacy issue as an opportunity to promote consumer understanding and to improve the business' public image. Openness invites this type of understanding.

Appendix A

*Excerpt from
the Report of
the Privacy Protection
Study Commission,
"Personal Privacy in
an Information Society"*

Chapter 5

The Insurance Relationship

The activities of the nation's 4,700 insurance companies touch the lives of all Americans in a variety of ways. Two out of three Americans have life insurance protection;[1] 90 percent of the civilian population under age 65 is covered by individual or group health insurance policies;[2] and 15 million are covered by the pension plans that life insurers offer.[3] It is estimated that almost 90 percent of the registered automobiles in the country are insured,[4] and few homes are without insurance coverage. In 1975, the premiums Americans paid for life, health, and pension coverage amounted to $58.6 billion[5] and property and liability insurance premiums amounted to another $50 billion.[6] The companies, for their part, paid out an estimated $75 billion in claims and policyholder benefits.[7]

The central function of insurance is to spread the economic burden of unforeseen financial losses by using the premiums paid by many insureds to pay for the losses sustained by a few. Some forms of insurance protection are mandated by law or business practice. For example, a number of States require car owners to carry auto insurance. Mortgage lenders require borrowers to carry fire insurance. Contractors are required to provide surety bonds to protect their clients against failures to perform and some fields of employment require fidelity bonds. Other forms of insurance, such as life, health, malpractice, and product and other liability coverages, are virtually mandatory in the minds of many people. Indeed, the cost and availability of insurance influence the character of society as well as the economy. It affects personal lives, life-styles, and even living standards.

Because the chief functions of an insurer—underwriting and rating risks and paying claims—are decision-making processes that involve evaluations of people and their property, the insurance industry is among

---

[1] American Council of Life Insurance, *Life Insurance Fact Book*, (New York: American Council of Life Insurance, 1976), p. 9.

[2] Health Insurance Institute, *The Source Book of Health Insurance Data 1974 - 1975*, (New York: Health Insurance Institute, 1975), p. 19.

[3] American Council of Life Insurance, *op. cit.*, p. 38.

[4] Automobile Insurance Plan Services Organization, *AIPSO Insurance Facts for 1977*, (New York: Automobile Insurance Plan Services Organization, 1977), p. 4.

[5] American Council of Life Insurance, *op. cit.*, p. 55.

[6] Insurance Information Institute, *Insurance Facts*, (New York: Insurance Information Institute, 1976), p. 12.

[7] American Council of Life Insurance, *op. cit.*, pp. 9 and 52; information obtained orally from A.M. Best and Co.

society's largest gatherers and users of information about individuals. This chapter reports the results of the Commission's inquiry into the personal-data record-keeping practices of insurance companies and the support organizations that provide them with various services, including record keeping.

The chapter begins with a short description of the industry, its sources of information about individuals, and the role that support organizations play in gathering and disseminating such information. This is followed by an examination of the way records about an individual affect his place in the insurance relationship today, and of the problems industry record-keeping practices pose from a privacy protection viewpoint. Finally, after summarizing current legal restraints on the record-keeping practices of insurance institutions and support organizations, the Commission, in the last section, presents and explains its specific recommendations for change. As in other chapters of this report the Commission's recommendations are arranged in terms of its three recommended public-policy objectives: (1) to minimize intrusiveness; (2) to maximize fairness; and (3) to create a legitimate, enforceable expectation of confidentiality.

INSURANCE INSTITUTIONS AND SUPPORT ORGANIZATIONS

There are essentially two types of insurance companies: stock companies owned by shareholders and mutual companies owned by policyholders. (Blue Cross and Blue Shield are nonprofit associations which policyholders join.) Although the largest life insurance companies are of the mutual type, the total amount of life insurance protection in force is about equally divided between stock and mutual companies. In the property and liability insurance business, the largest company is also a mutual company, but stock companies account for over 70 percent of premium volume.

Multiple-line insurance institutions are those with affiliate companies writing both life and health and property and liability coverages. The largest property and liability insurers are affiliates of multiple-line institutions, as are the largest life insurers since the expansion of some mutual companies into property and liability lines.

Companies sell insurance in four ways: by direct mail; through an exclusive agent; through an independent agent; or through a broker. While the exclusive agent represents only one company, the independent agent may have agreements with several companies, and the broker is a legal representative of his clients rather than the companies with which he places business. Agents are paid commissions or fees by companies rather than by clients. For simplicity of discussion, however, all will here be referred to as *agents*.

From a privacy protection viewpoint, insurers differ more significantly in terms of product line than they do in terms of ownership and company structure. The application form for the simpler types of life and health insurance sold by direct mail typically asks for little information. Name, address, age, sex, occupation, a statement certifying that the applicant has not had certain illnesses within a stated period of time and is currently in good health, and the beneficiary's name usually suffice. This is possible because policies sold by direct mail are relatively small ones, the population buying them is comparatively large, and they tend to be for limited coverages. Thus, the spread of risk of illness and death on which the premium rates are predicated is maintained.

In contrast, insurance sold through agents typically requires more information from and about the applicant and other insureds. Such coverages tend to be broader, more varied, and often need to be tailored to the particular needs of the applicant. Of all insurance sold through agents, the type requiring the least personal information is group insurance, which is underwritten on an aggregate rather than an individual basis, i.e., over time the premium rate is determined by the illness and death experience of the entire group.

Because the experience of large groups is statistically more reliable, the experience of many small groups may often be combined in determining premium rates. Doing so, however, demands more care in offering group insurance to smaller firms than in offering it to larger ones, lest the people in low-risk groups inadvertently subsidize those in high-risk ones. Care is also exercised in soliciting large accounts, but only as to the aggregate mix of occupations or other gross characteristics of the members of the group. Thus, while group insurance by its nature is markedly less dependent on information about the individual than on any other types of insurance, the amount of detail that can be dispensed with will depend on the size of the group involved.

As to individual life, health, and property and liability insurance that is sold through agents, the amount of information collected about individual applicants and insureds can be extensive. Moreover, the way it is collected, used, and disclosed is somewhat different in life and health underwriting than in property and liability underwriting. These differences, and the privacy protection problems they create, are principal themes of this chapter.

LIFE AND HEALTH INSURERS

Life and health insurers and their agents have different reasons for collecting and using information about individuals than property and liability insurers. In the first place, people often have to be persuaded to buy life insurance, whereas there is a ready market for property and liability coverage. Moreover, because life insurance is often sold as part of a package of financial planning services offered by agents, a life insurance prospect may be asked to divulge much information about himself even before the application is completed. For example, when insurance is used in estate building or estate conservation, the agent collects detailed information about the prospect's net worth, income, career prospects, and personal goals. When business life insurance[8] is being considered, extensive information about the financial condition of the firm or its principals is required. As a result, some life insurance agents have more comprehensive knowledge about a client's financial affairs than perhaps anyone else.

Most importantly, life insurance is a contract which binds a company to pay claims or benefits unless the policyholder fails to pay premiums when due, or unless the company can prove fraud or material misrepresentation during a limited "contestable period," generally two years after which a claim must be paid even if the application turns out to have been fraudulent. Thus, before entering into such a contract, the insurer wants an accurate health history, often supplemented by a medical examination to determine current health status, financial status information to protect against overinsurance, and enough information about personal habits to judge whether they might shorten the applicant's life. If the applicant has a significant health impairment, he is subjected to an extensive underwriting investigation to determine whether insurance can be issued to him, and if so, at what rate.

With most individual health insurance, there is less pressure to gather information about the applicant than in life insurance. Unless an individual health policy is the type that is not cancelable, the company can protect itself by increasing the price or declining to renew coverage at expiration. (Some health policies are guaranteed renewable but with the understanding that the company may increase the price at the time of renewal.) Nonetheless, detailed medical-record information is gathered in order to decide whether to accept the risk in the first instance, and how much to charge. Medical-record information is also an obvious consideration in writing disability insurance. Because these coverages are more susceptible than life insurance to abuse by insureds, companies want information concerning an applicant's character and his propensity for a disabling accident or illness. Occupation is also an important consideration—the loss of a finger is more disabling for a surgeon than a businessman—and the amount of disability income protection provided needs to be related to earned income.

The applicant and agent are the primary sources of information in underwriting life and health insurance. Because each has a financial interest in seeing the sale completed, however, investigative-reporting agencies (inspection bureaus) and other outside sources are often used to check the accuracy and completeness of the information applicants and agents provide. The types of inquiries these investigations typically involve and the manner in which inspection bureaus conduct them are described in Chapter 8. Here it is enough to point out that they can involve contacts with neighbors, employers, associates, bankers, and creditors; reviews of medical

---

[8] Business life insurance is life insurance purchased for the benefit of the business itself, e.g.: (1) to indemnify the business for the loss of a key employee; (2) as a source of funds to buy back or purchase ownership of a firm upon the death of a partner or key employee; or (3) as a source of funds in order to discharge financial responsibility pursuant to a contractual agreement.

records obtained from doctors or hospitals; and checks of public records for evidence of financial or legal difficulties.

Life and health insurers and investigative-reporting agencies acting on their behalf often contact third-party sources that have a confidential relationship with the applicant or insured, such as doctors, accountants, or lawyers, and thus an authorization is required before the information can be released. Typically, an applicant is required to sign such an authorization as a condition of having his application considered; is informed, as required by the Fair Credit Reporting Act (FCRA),[9] that an investigative report may be obtained; and is notified that information may be reported to the Medical Information Bureau (see below).

Normally, life insurance and medical expense claims are paid when a death certificate or medical bills are submitted. Claims for disability-income benefits are verified with the claimant's physician and employer and may be investigated more thoroughly if the claim appears questionable. The insurer's need for medical-record information in processing claims and the issues it raises for public policy on the confidentiality of the medical-care relationship are discussed in Chapter 7.

The Medical Information Bureau (MIB)

Like credit grantors, life and health insurers have organizations whose record-keeping services allow them to learn something about an applicant's previous contacts with other companies in the industry. The Medical Information Bureau (MIB) is an unincorporated, nonprofit trade association set up to facilitate the exchange of medical-record information among life insurers. Nearly 700 U.S. and Canadian life insurers subscribe to it and use it as an important source of information in underwriting life and health policies and in processing life and health claims.[10]

Each member company agrees to send the MIB a code anytime it develops information on an individual concerning certain medical and other conditions of some underwriting significance, except that companies are no longer supposed to report information developed in processing a claim. These codes are maintained by the MIB for seven years. Typically, a member company, on receiving an application, asks the MIB to check its files for information on the individual. If a code is found, it is sent to the inquiring company, which may then seek further details from the company that originally reported it, provided, however, that the inquiring company has first conducted its own investigation (e.g., a medical examination) to verify the reported condition. These "requests for details," which must be channeled through the MIB, are limited to 15 percent of the number of reports each company has submitted within the past year.[11] In 1975, there

---

[9] Fair Credit Reporting Act, 15 U.S.C. 1681 *et seq.*

[10] Written statement of the Medical Information Bureau (hereinafter cited as "MIB"), *Insurance Records*, Hearings before the Privacy Protection Study Commission, May 19, 1976, p. 11 (hereinafter cited as "Insurance Records Hearings").

[11] *Ibid.*, pp. 5-6.

were 75,000 of them out of a possible 300,000.[12]

The MIB does not investigate on its own, nor does it attempt to verify any information reported to it.[13] MIB Rule 9 specifies that member companies must report information regardless of the manner or form in which they acquire it.[14] Because many life insurers are also health insurers, information discovered in the course of health as well as life underwriting may thus be reported to the Bureau.

About 95 percent of the coded information contained in the MIB files is considered to be "medical." Only five percent is classified as nonmedical information, such as "reckless driving," "aviation," or "hazardous sport."[15] Currently, the MIB maintains information on 11 million individuals. Approximately three percent of all life applicants are uninsurable while six percent are "ratable."[16] In 1975, member companies submitted 2.45 million reports to the MIB,[17] and 17.5 million requests for information, while the MIB sent out 3.6 million responses.[18]

The Medical Information Bureau has been a controversial organization ever since its existence came to public attention in the mid-1960's. One of the most controversial aspects has been its use of the so-called *nonmedical* codes. In testimony before the Commission, the Bureau's Executive Director and General Counsel identified five: (1) reckless driving confirmed by the proposed insured or by official State or provincial (Canadian) motor vehicle bureau reports; (2) aviation with the proposed insured only as the source; (3) hazardous sport with the proposed insured only as the source; (4) nonmedical information where the source is *not* a consumer report (i.e., an inspection bureau report); and (5) nonmedical information received from a consumer report and not confirmed by the proposed insured.[19] He told the Commission that the fifth nonmedical code (nonmedical information received from a consumer report) could only refer to reckless driving, aviation, and hazardous sport and would not give life-style information.[20] In a letter sent to the Commission later, however, he states that "further review of MIB coding instructions shows that these nonspecific codes may also be

[12] *Ibid.*

[13] According to the report of a 1975 interview with then MIB Executive Director, Joseph C. Wilberding, the information companies were reporting to the Bureau came from the following sources: 33 percent from physicians, hospitals, or medical organizations; 15 percent from inspection bureau reports; and 53 percent from insurance forms filled out by the applicant himself or by the insurance agent, or from medical exams required by the companies. Mark Reutter, "Private Medical Records Aren't So Secret," *Baltimore Sun*, July 13, 1975, "Trend" Section, pp. 1-4.

[14] MIB, "General Rules," *Handbook and Directory*, 1971, Rule 9. Since the Privacy Protection Study Commission hearings, the MIB has changed its rules. Rule 9 has been replaced by Rule D.2, which states that: "Underwriting information involving any impairments listed in the MIB Code Book and received by members from original medical or other sources, from official medical records, or from the applicant during the course of an application for personal life or health insurance must be reported to MIB regardless of the underwriting decision."

[15] Written statement of the MIB, Insurance Records Hearings, May 19, 1976, p. 10.

[16] *Ibid.*, p. 3.

[17] *Ibid.*, p. 4.

[18] *Ibid.*, p. 5.

[19] Testimony of the MIB, Insurance Records Hearings, May 19, 1976, pp. 236 - 38.

[20] *Ibid.*, p. 240.

used to report other types of nonmedical information, such as 'age,' 'environment,' 'foreign residence or travel,' 'occupation,' and 'finances.'"[21]

Another object of controversy has been a code for reporting information about an individual's health, which, because of source, does not conform to the definition of medical-record information in the Fair Credit Reporting Act, i.e., information obtained from licensed physicians or medical practitioners, hospitals, clinics, or other medical or medically related facilities. *[15 U.S.C. 1681a(i)]* Such information could be reported in one of two ways. First, it could be reported by noting the specific code for the condition involved together with an additional symbol indicating that the information does not come within the FCRA definition.[22] Or second, as indicated in Executive Director Day's letter, it could be reported by using a code for "medical information received from a consumer report, not confirmed by the proposed insured or medical facility . . . ."[23]

On October 28, 1976, some months after the discussion of these matters in the Commission's hearings, the MIB informed the Commission that it was proposing the following changes to its code list. First, it was deleting three codes: (1) nonmedical information where the source is *not* a consumer report; (2) nonmedical information received from a consumer report not confirmed by the proposed insured; and (3) medical information received from a consumer report not confirmed by the proposed insured or a medical facility. The MIB assured the Commission that in the future "medical impairments may be reported only if information or records are received from the applicant or from licensed physicians, hospitals, clinics, or other medical or medically related facilities." It further stated that the three eliminated codes "will no longer be transmitted to member companies and will be purged or subjected to a 'no report order.'"[24]

Second, the remaining nonmedical codes (reckless driving, aviation, and hazardous sport confirmed by the proposed insured) may now only be reported to the MIB if such activity has occurred within the three years preceding the application at hand.[25] This was in response to the complaint that very old information could get into MIB files; that the practice of purging information *reported* more than seven years ago does not mean that all events or conditions coded in MIB records *occurred* within the previous seven years. For example, a reckless driving conviction that occurred 20 years ago could be noted in MIB records if a company reported it within the previous seven years.

Finally, the MIB also proposed to change the code which reports medical information obtained from a Federal agency to read "medical information obtained from a Federal medical source."[26]

A further source of controversy has been that codes dropped in the

[21] Letter from Neil M. Day, Executive Director and General Counsel, MIB, to the Privacy Protection Study Commission , September 30, 1976.

[22] Testimony of the MIB, Insurance Records Hearings, May 19, 1976, p. 279; Letter from Neil M. Day, MIB, to the Privacy Commission, September 30, 1976, p. 4.

[23] Letter from Neil M. Day, MIB, to the Privacy Commission, September 30, 1976, p. 4.

[24] Letter from Neil M. Day, MIB, to the Privacy Commission, October 28, 1976, p. 4.

[25] *Ibid.*

[26] *Ibid.*

past, as far as reporting requirements were concerned, are nonetheless still in the MIB file and thus can still be reported to MIB members. In reaction to this criticism, the MIB informed the Commission that the following discontinued codes will be purged or subjected to a "no report order": "'information obtained through a disability or health claim,' 'nonconformity,' 'age,' 'environment,' 'foreign residence or travel,' 'occupation,' 'insurance hazard,' and 'finances,'" and, of course, the three nonmedical codes mentioned above.[27]

Finally, the entire MIB system is predicated on the rule that the receiving company may not base an adverse underwriting decision on the information received from the MIB, but must make its own independent investigation.[28] Rule 14 reads:

> The information received through the Bureau shall not be used in whole or in part for the purpose of serving as a factor in establishing an applicant's eligibility for insurance.

> The application of this rule means that: (a) an application for insurance shall never be denied nor shall any charge therefore be increased wholly or partly because of information received through the Bureau and (b) all information received through the Bureau shall only be used as an alert signal.[29]

MIB's Executive Director told the Commission that ". . . Rule 14 is strictly adhered to by members who are regularly visited under the Company Visit Program."[30] When questioned, however, he agreed that the requirement to conduct an independent investigation may mean simply going to an investigative agency and getting old information that was once before the basis for an MIB report.[31] (Presumably this problem will be alleviated by the proposed elimination of inspection bureaus as authorized sources of certain types of information.) As to the Company Visit Program, moreover, it became apparent that Rule 14 may not be as strictly observed as the MIB would like to believe.

From time to time MIB staff members visit member companies to make certain that underwriters understand the Bureau's rules and to check on compliance with them.[32] A typical visit includes a check and review of the member's security arrangements and an "audit" of 20 randomly selected files.[33] Two major kinds of violations are looked for: (1) requests for details on MIB codes that have been submitted without first conducting the

---

[27] *Ibid.*, p. 5.

[28] Written Statement of the MIB, Insurance Records Hearings, May 19, 1976, p. 5.

[29] MIB, "General Rules," *Handbook and Directory*, 1971, Rule 14. This is now Rule D.4, which reads: "Underwriting information received from MIB shall be used to alert members of the need for further investigation of the applicants insurability. In the interest of sound underwriting and to avoid unfair competitive practices in the underwriting of risks, MIB record information shall not be used as the basis for establishing an applicant's eligibility for insurance." MIB, "General Rules," 1977, Rule D.4.

[30] Written statement of the MIB, Insurance Records Hearings, May 19, 1976, p. 13.

[31] Testimony of the MIB, Insurance Records Hearings, May 19, 1976, p. 250.

[32] Written statement of the MIB, Insurance Records Hearings, May 19, 1976, p.7.

[33] *Ibid.*, p. 16.

required independent investigation; and (2) adverse underwriting decisions that have been made solely on the basis of an MIB code (i.e., violations of Rule 14).[34] In a letter following his hearing testimony, the Executive Director told the Commission that in 1975, "161 member companies were visited and 3,200 underwriting files were examined . . .," but that "in fact only fifteen violations [of Rule 14]" were discovered.[35] Since the MIB sends out 3.5 million positive responses to company queries each year this means, if the sampling procedures permit such extrapolation, that overall there were approximately 15,000 violations of Rule 14 in 1975.

The efficacy of the investigation procedure was also questioned by the Commission. Each year the Company Visit Program looks at about 3,000 files (three companies per week, 150 companies per year, 20 files per company).[36] Because companies may have several regional offices, however, and because at the rate of 150 companies per year it would take five years to cover all the members, a considerable amount of slippage could go undetected.

Thus, in response to the Commission's expression of concern, the MIB has proposed the following changes. Each MIB member will now be required to adopt formal procedures to protect the confidentiality of MIB information. In addition, starting in 1977, each member must conduct at least annually "a self-audit program to determine whether it has complied with MIB's constitution and rules and whether its internal procedures have protected the . . . confidentiality of MIB information." In addition, the MIB investigation program, "will be expanded during the course of 1977 to include review of the results of members' self-audits." Such a review will include an on-premise inspection of internal procedures instituted by companies to implement certain aspects of MIB policy.[37]

Whether this voluntary program will be effective remains to be seen. The Commission, however, took the proposed changes into account in making its recommendations regarding insurance institutions and support organizations and believes that it has also found several ways of reinforcing the MIB initiative.

The Impairment Bureau

The Impairment Bureau, a service of the National Insurance Association, is another support organization that exists solely to facilitate communication among life and health insurers. The Impairment Bureau, however, differs from the Medical Information Bureau in several important respects.

In the first place, the Impairment Bureau's membership is much smaller and while all of its member companies may forward information to it, only five do so on a regular basis. Second, information about an individual is only sent to the Impairment Bureau when his application has been declined. Third, each member regularly receives a report on every

---

[34] Testimony of the MIB, Insurance Records Hearings, May 19, 1976, p. 235.

[35] Letter from Neil M. Day, MIB, to the Privacy Commission, September 30, 1976, pp. 2, 5.

[36] Testimony of the MIB, Insurance Records Hearings, May 19, 1976, pp. 245-47.

[37] Letter from Neil M. Day, MIB, to the Privacy Commission, October 28, 1976, pp. 1-3.

declination reported to the Bureau without having to ask for information on any particular individual. The Bureau compiles the information it receives on sheets which contain approximately 60 entries per page. Each entry contains the name of the applicant, his date and place of birth, the date of the rejection, a coded entry representing the cause of the declination, a coded entry representing the name of the reporting company, and the city and State where the applicant resides. This information, on approximately 2,000 declined applicants a year, is sent every other month to all member companies.

Like MIB records, Impairment Bureau records contain some information on conditions other than medical ones. Unlike the MIB, however, the Impairment Bureau does not have any specific rules to govern the use of the information it disseminates to member companies or the functioning of the Impairment Bureau itself. Each company may use the declination information as it sees fit and could, for instance, decline an applicant on the basis of the previous declination alone. On the other hand, the Impairment Bureau does not retain copies of the information submitted to it and has not done so since 1964. It merely compiles and distributes information to its members on the basis of the reports it gets from them. Once it has performed this function, the incoming reports are destroyed.[38]

PROPERTY AND LIABILITY INSURERS

In contrast to most life insurers, a property and liability insurance company has a ready market among people concerned about the replacement cost of tangible assets or about protecting themselves against liability claims brought by others. A property and liability company, moreover, can increase the price charged a policyholder or effectively cancel the risk by declining to renew coverage at the expiration of each contract period. Yet, as in the case of life and health insurance, detailed information is needed to decide whether to accept the risk in the first instance and how much to charge.

With property insurance, the items to be insured need to be identified accurately and valued, and the degree of care taken to protect them against fire, theft, or loss established. Since these coverages are also susceptible to abuse and fraud, the company wants to know enough about an applicant to make a reasonably confident estimate of his probable loss characteristics. Because liability insurance protects a policyholder against legal damages he may incur through negligence, underwriters consider it important to know, in the case of homeowners coverage, whether his home is well maintained and reasonably free of hazards, or to know, in the case of automobile insurance, whether he and others regularly using the car are responsible drivers. Although the applicant and agent are again primary sources of such

---

[38] This description of the Impairment Bureau is based on a letter from Charles A. Davis, Executive Director, National Insurance Association, to the Privacy Commission, May 17, 1976; and a Privacy Commission staff interview with Clarise Hall, National Insurance Association, August 27, 1976.

information, a company often checks the information they provide through an inspection bureau report or other sources considered more impartial.

The types of information needed to underwrite automobile insurance include name, address, date of birth, marital status, sex, occupation, driver's license number, use of vehicle, any physical impairments, how long licensed (if less than three years), and information regarding any accident or moving traffic violations in the past three years. State motor vehicle department records are often checked to verify the driving record of the applicant and members of his family. Some companies also require a physician's statement for elderly or physically impaired drivers. Finally, automobile underwriters sometimes order an investigative report on an applicant to find out whether his character, mode of living, and reputation in the community, may, in the judgment of the underwriter, influence the frequency of claims or the applicant's "defendability" in court. In other words, these reports are used by an auto insurer to determine whether the premium at which a policy may be issued is the correct one, but also, if highly derogatory information is uncovered, whether the policy should be issued, or if it has already been issued, whether it should be renewed.

For underwriting other forms of personal property and liability insurance, such as homeowners' policies, personal property floaters, fire policies, and boat policies, information requirements vary widely. To prepare and issue homeowners and fire policies, for example, the information required would include type of construction, age of dwelling, and distance to the nearest fire hydrant and fire department. For certain properties, an appraisal of their value may be required.

Information is, of course, also sought in the settlement of property and liability claims. Usually, this involves no other contact beyond the insured, the police or fire authorities, and the repair concerns involved in placing the property back in its original condition. Where the policy covers bodily injuries, however, contact may be made with the attending physician, the hospital, or other providers of medical services regarding the nature and extent of the injuries and the reasonableness of fees charged for services. In those few situations involving suspected fraud, the investigative activity may involve more extensive interviewing which can include witnesses, discussions with local law enforcement officials, and securing other background information that may be necessary to prepare for an effective defense if the claim is denied.

The investigation of claims or losses to determine the policyholder's liability to others (i.e., "third-party claims") will generally result in greater information gathering. A very detailed and complete investigation will frequently be made to determine the insured's responsibility for injury or damage and the degree or extent of such injury or damage. The role of inspection bureaus and private investigative agencies in the settlement of property and liability claims is briefly described in Chapter 8.

THE LOSS INDEXES

In the processing of claims, the indexes of the American Insurance

Association (AIA) may be checked to determine whether the claimant has had a series of prior losses or is submitting claims for the same loss to other companies. These indexes cover fire, burglary and theft, and fine arts losses, as well as third-party personal or bodily injury claims arising under automobile, homeowners, malpractice, and worker's compensation policies.[39] Many property and liability companies in the industry subscribe to the loss indexes. When a claim is filed, the insurer reports basic information on the claim to the proper index and, in return, receives from the index a copy of any previously filed reports on the claimant. In addition, the insurer, on the basis of such a report, can go to the company that filed it for further information.

The Fire Marshal Reporting Service

The Fire Marshal Reporting Service (FMRS) reports to fire marshals in 27 States on fire claims its members have paid. In addition, the FMRS maintains an index on reported fire losses in every State which any member can use to determine the prior loss record of a claimant as a check, for example, on arson. Membership in the Service is available to all interested insurance companies in the United States. At present 189 belong.[40]

Unlike reports made to the other indexes, reports made to the Fire Marshal Reporting Service are made after the claim has been paid. Reports are mandatory in those 27 States where the Fire Marshal must be notified of all losses above a minimum amount ranging from $10 to $250. Otherwise, the Service accepts reports of losses in amounts of $250 or more. Currently, there are 1,067,000 loss reports on file, all of them generated within the previous six years.[41]

Like Index System records (see below), Fire Marshal Reporting Service records are obtainable solely for the purpose of processing claims. "For a subscriber's authorized reporting office to initiate a search, the office must be handling and report a claim under the lines of coverage serviced . . . ."[42] The requirement that records be used only for claims purposes is enforced by requiring an index card from the inquiring subscriber before making any search or giving out any information.

The Burglary and Theft Loss Index

The Burglary and Theft Loss Index is maintained separately from the Fire Marshal Reporting Service, but membership in the FMRS entitles a company to receive reports from both systems. By using the Burglary and Theft Index, a member may detect simultaneous claims on the same item or a claim on a loss for which the claimant has previously been reimbursed. Part of the Burglary and Theft Loss Index is the Fine Arts Loss Index whose

[39] Testimony of the American Insurance Association (hereinafter cited as "AIA"), Insurance Records Hearings, May 21, 1976, pp. 755, 764 - 66.

[40] *Ibid.*, pp. 764 - 65.

[41] *Ibid.*, p. 765.

[42] *Ibid.*

function is to expose fraudulent claims involving art objects and to help locate missing ones that have been the subject of prior claims.[43]

The National Automobile Theft Bureau

The National Automobile Theft Bureau is a service organization sponsored, operated, and supported by approximately 500 insurance companies writing automobile, fire and theft insurance. The primary objectives of the Bureau are to assist in the recovery of stolen automobiles, to investigate automobile fire and theft losses which may be fraudulent, and to promote programs designed to prevent or reduce such losses. The Bureau operates as a national clearinghouse for stolen car information. Member companies report automobile thefts to the Bureau and the Bureau notifies member companies of recoveries, which are made primarily from police tow-away pounds.

According to its operations manual, the Bureau maintains the following record systems:

- *National Stolen Vehicle File.* This contains all Bureau members' reports on stolen vehicles and is used to detect fraudulent theft claims when several companies provide theft coverage on the same vehicle. Subfiles include information on impounded vehicles and stolen parts.
- *National Salvage File.* Records in this system indicate the disposition of all late model vehicles sold for salvage by member companies. Each entry of a salvage record creates an automatic inquiry against the master file by vehicle identification number, State license number, named insured, and salvage purchaser. Inquiries to the system may detect dual insurance coverage, multiple losses by a named insured, fraudulent claims based on the use of salvage documents or counterfeit documents on nonexistent vehicles.
- *Manufacturers' Production Records.* These are used in verifying that a vehicle was actually produced, and may also be used to find the dealer to whom a particular vehicle was originally sold. Each of the major U.S. manufacturers provides them to the Theft Bureau on microfilm.

The Index System

The Index System accumulates and makes available to its subscribers records concerning third-party personal and bodily injury claims. The Index System is maintained solely for use in claims processing. Ten branch offices serve all 50 States, the District of Columbia, the Commonwealth of Puerto Rico, and the Virgin Islands.[44] Subscribers report claims to the office servicing the territory where the incident occurred. Receipt of a properly

---

[43] *Ibid.*, p. 766.
[44] *Ibid.*, p. 756.

completed index card from a subscriber triggers a search of the Index. If the search turns up prior submissions on the claimant, the subscriber will be sent a photocopy of all of them.

The Index System is decentralized. Searches are normally limited to the records of the receiving branch office. Where the submitted index card shows that the claimant lives or once lived in the geographic area of another office, however, the inquiry is automatically referred to that other office for further checking and disclosure directly to the inquiring company of any record found.[45] The Index System "Instructions for Subscribers" says that "each subscriber is expected to cooperate by furnishing information contained in its claims files to other subscribers . . .,"[46] and also permit the insurer who has been asked for information to ask, in turn, for information from the inquirer. This allows two insurers who are in the act of settling claims by the same individual to communicate with each other.

There are two limits to these exchanges of claims information directly between insurers. First, "the exchange of information on [auto-related] medical payment, death and disability claims is at the discretion of the subscriber."[47] Second, "the Inquiry Form is to be used only in cases where *substantial claims* are involved to relieve subscribers of unnecessary work in procuring and examining closed files."[48] (Italics in the original.)

Reports to the Index System must be limited to claims of the following types: automobile liability (including uninsured motorists); automobile accident reparation (or personal injury protection); liability other than automobile, including liability claims under homeowners, commercial, multiple peril, yacht, pleasure craft, and aircraft policies; claims based on false arrest, assault and battery; malpractice claims; and worker's compensation claims. Worker's compensation claims are supposed to be reported only when they involve: (1) disability due to amputation, back injury, disfigurement, dislocation, eye injury, fracture, head injury, hernia, loss of hearing; (2) injuries with possible lost time payments of $500; (3) occupational diseases with possible medical and lost time payments of $1,000; (4) lost time claims by longshoremen and construction workers; or (5) a suspicion of fraud. A report *must* be made on any claim falling in these areas, except that reports on auto-related medical, death and disability claims are discretionary.[49]

Subscription to the Index System is open to "all insurance companies writing bodily injury liability coverages without regard to membership in the American Insurance Association."[50] To belong to the System, one must either be a liability insurer where liability claims are made against an

[45] American Insurance Association, "The Index System: Instructions for Subscribers," May, 1974, p. 2; Testimony of AIA, Insurance Records Hearings, May 21, 1976, p. 757.
[46] AIA, "Instructions for Subscribers," p. 3.
[47] *Ibid.*, p. 3.
[48] *Ibid.*
[49] *Ibid.*, p. 1.
[50] Testimony of AIA, Insurance Records Hearings, May 21, 1976, p. 755.

insured, or a self-insurer (such as an employer) which may have liability claims made directly against it.[51] About 26 percent of the Index System subscribers are self-insurers, but they represent a very small percentage of those that report.[52] In total, the Index System currently has 1,183 subscribing insurers and self-insurers and maintains records on approximately 28 million bodily injury claims reported during the System's six-year report retention period.[53]

A witness from the Index System offered some anecdotal evidence of its efficacy in uncovering fraud. One story tells of an elderly woman who constantly sustained minor injury to her mouth because of glass in a sandwich.

> In appearance, she resembled the classical image of . . . [a] grandmother—unassuming, nondemanding, doing a public service by calling attention to a deficiency in an insured's kitchen with no intent of making a fuss. From the viewpoint of the insurance carrier, liability was there; the demand was modest. The settlement was simple and uncomplicated. In fact . . . the insurance company almost had to force payment upon the claimant to accept any compensation for her inconvenience and minor injury.
>
> The sad truth was that "grandma" was a professional claimant. In her purse, she carried glass fragments which she would place in her mouth to cause a laceration. She would, then, call the waiter, display the physical evidence of the glass bit and the bloody napkin. Her manner would be mild and full of concern for other diners who might not be so fortunate in sustaining only a minor injury. She was literally in the claim business.
>
> Fortunately, in her travels, she did establish a pattern of reports involving subscribers [to the Index System] which led to an investigation of her activities and . . . agreement to divert her activities to more constructive lines.[54]

INFORMATION FLOWS FROM INSURANCE INSTITUTIONS

Both life and health and property and liability insurers routinely disclose information about an applicant or insured to the agent, to the extent necessary to service the policy; to reinsurers (when a company underwriting a large policy wants to reduce its exposure to loss); to an insured's physician; to inspection bureaus to facilitate the preparation of an investigative report; and to other types of investigators asked to prepare such reports. Because insurance is often required to buy a house, operate a car, pursue a career, or conduct a business, they may also disclose information about an individual to loan institutions and employers.

Further, life and health insurers, as indicated in the preceding sections, also disclose information to the Medical Information Bureau or the

---

[51] *Ibid.*, p. 769.
[52] *Ibid.*, p. 773.
[53] *Ibid.*, p. 756.
[54] *Ibid.*, pp. 760 - 61.

Impairment Bureau, and may provide details to another member insurer when requested to do so. Property and liability insurers, for their part, routinely notify the loss indexes of certain claims, and, in some cases, may notify the Insurance Crime Prevention Institute (see below).

Some potential insureds are judged to be so likely to produce adverse claim experience that they cannot obtain insurance in the normal manner. The driver with a poor record poses two problems. The first is meeting his own acute need for financial protection and perhaps his ability to qualify legally as a registered vehicle owner. The second is protecting society from the harm which an unsafe driver is likely to inflict on others. State "assigned-risk" insurance plans were formed to provide coverage to a driver whom companies consider an unacceptable risk and thus can require information about him to be disclosed to the administrators of the plan as well as to the insurance company to which his application is assigned.

Both life and health and property and liability insurers may release information about individuals to State insurance department officials in response to inquiries or complaints, and in the course of periodic examinations of company underwriting practices and procedures by such officials. Independent auditors employed by an insurance company make similar checks for the same purpose. In addition, because insurance companies are repositories of detailed information about individuals, their records are often requested by Federal as well as State government agencies and law enforcement authorities.

Finally, to make it possible for residents and property owners in high risk locations to purchase insurance against losses due to crime, civil disorders, and floods, partnerships have been formed between insurers and government agencies which make it necessary for insurers to disclose information about individuals to the agencies participating in such programs.

Information Flows From Support Organizations

The extensive flow of information about individuals into and out of organizations that conduct underwriting and claims investigations for insurers is described in Chapter 8. Medical Information Bureau rules, however, require a court order before information about an individual may be disclosed to anyone other than a member insurance company and while the property and liability loss indexes will be satisfied with a subpoena, rather than a court order,[55] they normally disclose information in their records only to a subscribing insurer submitting a properly prepared index card in connection with a current claim. The exceptions to this policy are the disclosures the Index System makes to the Marine Index Bureau and the disclosures any of the indexes may make to the Insurance Crime Prevention Institute (ICPI).

As indicated earlier, subscribers to the Index System are told to report

---

[55] A witness told the Commission that the loss indexes receive about 100 subpoenas a year from government agencies and that while for many they have no information to disclose, when they do have information they comply. *Ibid.*, p. 776.

lost-time claims filed by longshoremen. One reason for this is to make such information available to the Marine Index Bureau, whose subscribers are vessel owners. The owner of a vessel is responsible for its seaworthiness, which includes the quality of the crew.[56]

In addition, an index may disclose information about an individual to the Insurance Crime Prevention Institute. As one witness from the indexes told the Commission: "We are an indicator. If the reports from the index system discern a pattern that might be of interest to the carrier or the ICPI . . . it is referred to them."[57] According to the testimony, however, an index would not send unsolicited reports to the ICPI unless it receives "four within a relatively short period of time of the same nature," or unless, in a two-claim situation, "the accident occurred on the same date with different insurers or at a different place with the same injury." Alternatively, the ICPI may come to an index and ask for a search, in which case it is treated in the same manner as any subscriber.[58]

The Insurance Crime Prevention Institute

The Insurance Crime Prevention Institute is a nonprofit corporation which operates as a trade association to uncover insurance fraud for property and liability insurers. The ICPI has its headquarters in Westport, Connecticut, maintains regional offices in New York City, Chicago, and Los Angeles, and has investigators stationed in major cities throughout the country.[59] Membership is open to property and liability insurance companies licensed in any of the 50 States.[60] Currently its membership is made up of 312 companies that underwrite 70 percent of the casualty and property insurance business.[61]

ICPI's purpose is to prevent and detect fraudulent insurance claims. Its focus is solely on criminal fraud, and the Institute's bylaws specifically prohibit it from assisting companies in claims settlement or civil actions incident to settlements.[62] Typically, an Institute investigation begins when a member sends information on a claim which the company suspects may involve criminal fraud. Other investigations are initiated by the ICPI based on information it receives from various sources, such as law enforcement agencies, "inside tipsters,"[63] or the loss indexes. In either case, however, the ICPI has complete control over its investigative activities, and may decline or initiate investigations as it sees fit.

If an ICPI investigation produces reasonable evidence of fraud, the

---

[56] *Ibid.*, p. 769.

[57] *Ibid.*, p. 768.

[58] *Ibid.*, p. 772.

[59] Statement of the Insurance Crime Prevention Institute (hereinafter cited as "ICPI"), Insurance Records Hearings, May 21, 1976, p. 1.

[60] ICPI, "By-Laws," Art. III, § 1.

[61] Written statement of ICPI, Insurance Records Hearings, May 21, 1976, p. 1; Testimony of ICPI, Insurance Records Hearings, May 21, 1976, p. 776.

[62] Written statement of ICPI, Insurance Records Hearings, May 21, 1976, p. 1; ICPI, "ICPI 1975," p. 2; ICPI, "By-Laws," Art. I.

[63] Written statement of ICPI, Insurance Records Hearings, May 21, 1976, p. 1

matter will be "reported to a public law enforcement agency for whatever action it deems to be appropriate."[64] The ICPI investigator may go to insurance companies or an index for information. Going to an index will, of course, lead the investigator back to the insurers that have had claims filed by the individual under investigation. The investigation may consist of interviewing the claimant, verifying medical statements, verifying lost-wage statements, or searching police or court records.[65]

The Director of the ICPI testified that the Institute

> exercises extreme care in referring its investigative findings to law enforcement agencies . . . . Each case is checked for completeness of investigation and sufficiency of evidence before the investigator is authorized to present his report to a law enforcement agency. Aside from considerations of fairness to the subject of the investigation, civil tort law provides adequate incentive for caution.[66]

Where there is evidence of professional misconduct, such as where a physician inflates a bodily injury insurance claim, the ICPI can also make its file available to licensing authorities.[67]

ICPI characterized its relationship with the law enforcement community in its testimony as that of a "citizen coming forward with evidence of a crime."[68] The Institute will sign criminal complaints to initiate prosecution in instances where an insurance company has been the victim of a fraud and, when it does so, will voluntarily give a copy of its file to law enforcement officials. As the ICPI Director testified:

> It is a generally recognized exception to the principle of confidentiality that an insurance company, finding itself to be the victim of a fraudulent claim, may voluntarily release the pertinent records of that transaction to the police to obtain criminal justice . . . . The Institute, in effect, does no more than to perform this task for the insurance company.[69]

Occasionally, law enforcement officials will come to the ICPI for information:

> If there is a large arson in the Bronx on Sunday night, on Monday morning we are going to get a call to ask if we have a file on the owner . . . . If it is a legal and valid investigation, we will assist them in getting the information.[70]

The ICPI employs approximately 70 full-time investigators, most with

---

[64] *Ibid.*

[65] Testimony of ICPI, Insurance Records Hearings, May 21, 1976, pp. 776 - 77; ICPI, "ICPI - 1975."

[66] Written statement of ICPI, Insurance Records Hearings, May 21, 1976, p. 2.

[67] ICPI, "A Prosecutor's Introduction to ICPI," p. 4.

[68] Written statement of ICPI, Insurance Records Hearings, May 21, 1976, p. 2.

[69] *Ibid.*, citing *Burrows v. Superior Court*, 13 Cal. 3d. 238, 245 (1975) as by analogy providing an exception from the rule of confidentiality.

[70] Testimony of ICPI, Insurance Records Hearings, May 21, 1976, pp. 784 - 85.

law enforcement backgrounds, and is licensed as a private detective agency in those jurisdictions which require licensing.[71] It investigates about 6,000 cases each year. In 1976, this resulted in the indictment of about 600 people. According to the testimony, it concentrates on two main areas of criminal fraud. The first is the ambulance-chasing attorney or the doctor who exaggerates claims, and the second is organized crime.[72]

THE INDIVIDUAL IN THE INSURANCE RELATIONSHIP

As is evident from the preceding sections, the insurance industry is highly dependent upon recorded information about individuals. This dependence creates a number of privacy protection problems, some of which are inherent in the insurance system, but can be controlled, and some of which present real or potential abuses that need to be eliminated.

THE INTRUSIVENESS OF CERTAIN COLLECTION PRACTICES

Insurance underwriting involves two separate decisions: (1) whether the insurer wants to insure the applicant at all (selection); and if so, (2) at what price and terms (classification). The need to make these two judgments dictates the kind and quality of information an insurance institution collects and maintains about an individual applicant or policyholder.

In making these two types of decisions insurers look to physical hazards—medical hazards in life and health underwriting and in property and liability underwriting, the condition of the property, its use, and its surroundings. Underwriters also look to what is termed moral hazard. Evaluation of moral hazard is made by examining attributes of the applicant which suggest a greater than average likelihood of a loss occurring or the potential for unusual severity of loss—either an absence of a desire on the part of the individual to safeguard himself or his property from loss or a positive willingness to create a loss or to deliberately inflate a claim.

Thus, it is not surprising that the evaluation of moral hazards, particularly in property and liability underwriting, is the area where the greatest number of objections to insurers' information collection practices have been raised. An inquiry may cover drinking habits, drug use, personal and business associates, reputation in the community, credit worthiness, occupational stability, deportment, housekeeping practices, criminal history, and activities that deviate from conventional standards of morality, such as living arrangements and sexual habits and preferences. Because the relevance of many of these particulars can be hard to demonstrate, and because the judgment as to their relevance is often left to the underwriter handling a particular case, their propriety has become subject to question.

From the standpoint of many applicants and insureds, the dichotomy between the individual's privacy interest and the insurer's interest in evaluating risk is probably not as great as it seems at first glance. The low-

---

71 *Ibid.*, p. 778; Written statement of ICPI, Insurance Records Hearings, May 21, 1976, p. 1; ICPI, "ICPI-1975," p. 9.

72 Testimony of ICPI, Insurance Records Hearings, May 21, 1976, pp. 786-87.

risk applicant benefits from an underwriting evaluation that results in unusual risks being eliminated or written at a higher premium because that keeps the cost of his insurance down. The Commission was continually reminded that it is in the interest of the applicant to have complete and accurate information on which this judgment can be based so that he can be insured at the proper rate; that the insurer must be able to evaluate the risk it is being asked to assume if premium charges are to bear a reasonable relationship to expected losses and expenses for all insureds within a similar classification.

Economic forces may, however, work against a given individual. Because insurers compete against each other for the better risks, they do not have much incentive to look behind some of the criteria they use to sort the good risks from the bad. If their experience suggests, for example, that slovenly housekeepers make poor automobile insurance risks, they tend to be wary of all slovenly housekeepers. The problem, in other words, is not that the category of information lacks predictive value in all instances, but rather that it is applied too broadly.

Another source of concern in the area of intrusive collection practices stems from the use of so-called pretext interviews and other false or misleading information-gathering techniques. This concern was brought into sharp focus by recent publicity concerning Factual Service Bureau, Inc. (now Inner-Facts, Inc.), an investigative-support organization whose services were used by insurers in a number of cities throughout the country. Factual Service Bureau employees regularly misrepresented their identity and purpose in order to obtain medical-record information from hospitals and other medical-care providers without authorization. The insurers that used Factual Service Bureau should have known that it employed such intrusive techniques and generally engaged in questionable methods of information collection. Factual Service Bureau openly advertised its ability to procure confidential information about an individual without his authorization.[73] Thus, even the insurers who had no actual knowledge of the techniques being used by Factual Service Bureau on their behalf may be said to have condoned its activities by their silence or failure to investigate more fully the practices and techniques used.

The Factual Service Bureau case also illustrates a broader problem which results from the apparent lack of restraint exercised by insurers over the support organizations they use to collect information about individual applicants, insureds, and claimants. In the claims area particularly, where a great deal of money may be at stake or where the suspicion of fraud may be high, many insurance companies have tended to look the other way while hiring support organizations that use questionable information collection practices and techniques.

---

[73] A Factual Service Bureau advertising flyer asks, "Have you been denied medical authorization by a claimant? Does the claimant's attorney withhold medical information from you, or submit only 'partial' medical records? If either of the above is true, let Factual Service develop the true medical picture. We have specialized in background medical investigations for over two decades."

Unfair Collection, Use, and Disclosure Practices

Because of their acknowledged dependence upon information about individuals, insurance institutions are reluctant to deprive themselves of inexpensive access to it. There are few restrictions within the industry on the sharing of personally identifiable information or on obtaining it from sources outside the industry. This is true of insurance institutions and support organizations alike, and can lead to some highly questionable collection, use, and disclosure practices.

As indicated earlier, the Medical Information Bureau, until recently, retained claims information even though it no longer allowed it to be reported, and inserted a "failure to find impairment previously reported" code rather than deleting the impairment reference. To maximize the utility of information already collected, insurance institutions also piggyback on the information collection and use practices of other insurance institutions and support organizations. This dependence adds to the widespread exchange of information throughout the industry, not only by organizations like the Medical Information Bureau and the Impairment Bureau but by investigative-reporting agencies (inspection bureaus) and other insurance-support organizations that save and reuse the information they collect. Thus, once a mistake enters the system, its adverse effects are likely to proliferate, resulting in repeated unfairness to the individual.

The competition among insurance institutions has generally militated against adequate sensitivity to the fairness issue in record keeping. To be sure, this situation has been changing as particular companies have promulgated privacy protection principles to be followed in the conduct of their business. Except for the support organizations subject to the Fair Credit Reporting Act, however, record-keeping practices still remain by and large discretionary within the industry.

Insurance institutions and their support organizations have been concerned about certain types of disclosures to third parties and about data security problems. The admitted purpose of these safeguards, however, is to protect the business privilege as a limited defense to common law actions of defamation. Thus, they do little to constrain exchanges of information about individuals within the industry or to control the quality of the information used.

The lack of attention to fairness issues in record keeping about individuals has resulted in the structuring of information flows and uses so that *neither the insurance institution nor the individual applicant, insured, or claimant is responsible for the quality of the information used.* The individual is at a disadvantage because record-keeping practices within the industry are opaque from his point of view. He currently enters into an insurance transaction without being aware of the relationship's implications for his personal privacy because he does not understand how extensive or intrusive information gathering may be. Nor does he know the consequences of the notices on his application—for example, that the Medical Information Bureau notice means information about him may be reported to the Bureau not only from the application itself, but also as a consequence of the underwriting investigation the insurer may conduct. Because he lacks adequate knowledge of the practices followed, the individual cannot make the forces of the marketplace work for him. He is not given an opportunity to weigh the relative benefits which might be obtained through the insurance transaction against the personal cost of revealing and having others reveal information about him.

Nor does the individual always know why the insurer is collecting information about him, or when it is being collected for purposes unrelated to establishing his eligibility for an insurance benefit or service. Insurers frequently collect marketing and actuarial information through the application. When a claim is filed, they may collect information for the purpose of reviewing the propriety of a treating doctor's fees or procedures as well as the eligibility of the particular claimant or the particulars of the specific claim. They may collect additional information to determine the advisability of continuing to market a particular kind of insurance. Yet, they do not normally advise the individual that this is being done.

The individual is also placed at a disadvantage when he is asked to sign a form authorizing the release of recorded information about himself, because he is not specifically apprised of what he is consenting to. The commonly used blanket authorization form, in essence, authorizes the release of all information about the individual in the hands of anyone. Moreover, the type of authorization form currently used by insurance institutions typically has no stated purpose or expiration date, and may not be limited either as to the scope of the investigation or as to the sources of information. This again reflects the natural reluctance of insurance institutions to deprive themselves of easy access to any potentially useful information, or to decide in advance what information is needed for what purpose.

As far as fair use is concerned, the relationship between the individual and an insurer is often unnecessarily and undesirably attenuated. Information he provides about himself is only partly the basis for the decision made about him, and the decision is made by someone he does not know and with whom he normally has no direct interaction. In addition, records maintained by a variety of institutions within and without the industry may be brought to bear on the decision about him, while he believes he is only dealing with one such institution. That one institution, moreover, assumes no obligation to give him access to the information compiled about him or to afford him the opportunity to correct or amend information he believes to be inaccurate.

Under the existing system, the individual cannot adequately protect himself against the use of poor quality information in making underwriting decisions about him. Frequently, the individual is not told the reason for an adverse insurance decision. The insurance laws and regulations of many States require insurers to disclose to the individual (in some cases, only on request) the general reasons for *cancelling* or *refusing to renew* a personal automobile insurance policy. Few States, however, require insurance institutions to give individuals the reasons for a *declination* or a *rating*.[74] If the reason and supporting information for an adverse underwriting or rating decision do not arise out of a report prepared by a support organization subject to the disclosure provisions of the Fair Credit Reporting Act, the individual may be unable to find out why the decision was made, or whether inaccurate or incomplete information was at fault.

Life and health insurance institutions generally advise an applicant of the information that led to an adverse underwriting or rating decision only if they consider the information harmless (e.g., hazardous occupation, obvious health impairment). Typically, however, the specific items of information and their source are not revealed unless they came from a support organization subject to the Fair Credit Reporting Act, or from the applicant himself. When an individual requests a specific explanation for an adverse decision and the basis was medical-record information, most life insurers will divulge the information, but only to the applicant's personal physician. However, they virtually never tell the individual the specific reasons and supporting information for an adverse decision when the information concerns his character, morals, or life-style.

In property and liability insurance, an adverse decision may or may not lead to the insurer divulging the reasons and supporting information to the applicant. As in the life and health area, whether the *insurer* considers the information to be harmless will be a factor. With the exception of the State automobile insurance laws and regulations mentioned above, however, the consumer has no legal right to be told the reasons or information supporting an adverse insurance decision.

When an individual contacts the Medical Information Bureau, he or his physician, in the case of medical-record information, only learns the summary data that has been reported about him.[75] He does not learn how the reporting insurance company translated the underlying information into a code, and while he is told where the underlying information is, he, unlike another insurer, cannot get it automatically from the reporting company.

If the adverse decision was based on information in a report prepared by an inspection bureau, the Fair Credit Reporting Act only requires the insurer to tell the individual the organization's name and address. *[15 U.S.C. 1681m]* The individual has the right to learn the "nature and substance" of the information about him in the inspection bureau's files, but this is no assurance that he will be able to identify the reason for the adverse decision or the particular items of information on which it was based. To go to the inspection bureau is time-consuming for the individual and may effectively prevent him from getting on firm enough ground to ask for reconsideration of the decision if it turns out that there was erroneous information in the

---

[74] William J. Giacofci and John A. Andryszak, "Summary of State Insurance Laws and Regulations Serving to Protect the Individual's Right to Privacy," Maryland Casualty Company, July 1976.

[75] Testimony of the MIB, Insurance Records Hearings, May 19, 1976, pp. 265-67. The Federal Trade Commission believes that the MIB is subject to the Fair Credit Reporting Act and thus must give access. While the MIB denies this, it nonetheless grants access and thus the issue has not been brought to a head.

report. *To have a real voice in the quality of information on which decisions are based, the individual needs to know the reasons for the adverse action and the specific items of information that support the reasons.*

The Commission is also concerned that the mere fact of a previous adverse underwriting decision may unfairly stigmatize an individual who applies later for comparable insurance. Without knowing the reasons for it, some insurers use the mere fact of a previous declination or other adverse decision by another insurer as the basis for rejecting an applicant.[76] Yet a previous declination may have nothing to do with the individual's qualifications where, for instance, the insurer that declined him did so only because it had decided to restrict its underwriting in a certain area. Thus, when an insurer acts on the fact of a previous adverse decision alone, it may reject an individual whom it would otherwise have accepted if accurate and complete information were developed. Stigma may also result when an individual has previously purchased insurance from a "substandard" insurer or through an "assigned-risk" plan, even though the reasons for such previous action may not involve the individual or his eligibility directly.[77]

The Commission has not found that this problem exists in life and health insurance underwriting to the degree that it clearly does in personal property and liability insurance. Property and liability insurance applications often ask the individual whether he has previously been declined or rated, but rarely ask the reason for the rejection, presumably because, under the current system, the applicant will seldom know. A high percentage of the reasons may, in fact, relate to adverse characteristics possessed by the individual applicant or insured, as opposed to a general market condition unrelated to the individual's characteristics. Present practice, however, fails to distinguish between the two types of rejections.

Accepting from lay sources information that only a professional is competent to report is another questionable practice that stems from an insurer's reluctance to deprive itself of any information that may turn out to be useful. Medical-record information is crucial to life and health insurance underwriting and to claims processing. Collection of such technical information from anyone other than the individual himself, a medical source, or a close family member invites inaccuracies. Nevertheless, some insurers not only seek information concerning an individual's health from agents, or from the individual's neighbors, friends, and associates, but also use it as the basis for declining his application. Such information may also be communicated to other insurers. Until recently, the Medical Information

---

[76] Written statement of Federal Insurance Administration, Department of Housing and Urban Development, Insurance Records Hearings, May 20, 1976, pp. 6 - 11; Department of Transportation Study, "Motor Vehicle Crash Losses and Their Compensation in the United States;" Testimony of Benjamin Lipson, Insurance Records Hearings, May 20, 1976, pp. 407-09.

[77] Written statement of Federal Insurance Admininstration, Department of Housing and Urban Development, Insurance Records Hearings, May 20, 1976, p. 9; Department of Transportation Study, "Motor Vehicle Crash Losses: Their Compensation in the United States." p. 68.

Bureau accepted medical information obtained from lay sources, and the Impairment Bureau and the property and casualty loss indexes still do.[78]
Although support organizations such as the Medical Information Bureau have rules with respect to the type and quality of information reported to them, the rules are difficult to implement and enforce. The MIB, for example, has no way of knowing, except through periodic audits of member companies, whether medical or other information reported to it has come orginally from an authorized source. Thus, it cannot effectively control the quality of information in its files. Nor does the Bureau keep a complete accounting of all the disclosures,[79] the result being that it cannot always propagate corrections when inaccuracies are discovered. The property and liability loss indexes also have no way of knowing whether a subscriber has falsely filed an index card without having a real claim, or whether, once received by an insurance institution, the index information is used for other purposes, such as underwriting, or making a personnel decision.[80]
Perhaps the best example of the inability of support organizations to regulate the use of the information they provide is the Medical Information Bureau's rule which prohibits the use of a Bureau report, intended only as an alert, as the basis for declining an applicant.[81] Compliance with this rule has not been carefully audited in the past, and testimony before the Commission by the MIB indicates that as a result of the MIB's own audits there is evidence that some life insurers do render adverse decisions based solely on Medical Information Bureau codes.[82] Furthermore, the reinvestigation requirement the MIB imposes on its members can be satisfied by going to an inspection bureau and getting information on file there—the same information which another insurer may have used to decline the applicant.
To some extent these problems are endemic to data exchanges, like the MIB, that are controlled by their users. Being wholly dependent, they cannot be expected to enforce their rules against those who sustain them. The end result, however, is that poor quality information can, in a variety of ways, cause an individual to be denied an insurance benefit or privilege for which he would otherwise be eligible. The insurer may lose too, by forfeiting a customer or by having its relationship with an existing policyholder deteriorate. Obsolete, inaccurate, or incomplete information serves no one.

THE ABSENCE OF A STRICT DUTY OF CONFIDENTIALITY

There is an understandable public concern about the confidentiality of records about individuals that insurance institutions and their support

---

[78] Testimony of the MIB, Insurance Records Hearings, May 19, 1976, p. 263.
[79] *Ibid.*, pp. 235-36; 244-58.
[80] Testimony of the AIA, Insurance Records Hearings, May 21, 1976, p. 771.
[81] MIB, "General Rules," *Handbook and Directory*, Rule 14. Rule 14 is now Rule D.4.
[82] Testimony of the MIB, Insurance Records Hearings, May 19, 1976, pp. 234-36; 244-58. The Commission has no testimony from the Impairment Bureau on this issue, but problems no doubt exist with its subscribers as well. This would seem especially true since the Impairment Bureau lacks even those safeguards and rules under which the Medical Information Bureau operates.

organizations maintain. As previously noted, the collection of information about an individual without his full knowledge of the scope of the inquiry and its consequences may weaken the relationship between the insurer and the individual. The individual may be deterred from applying or may mistrust the insurer when he does apply. The Commission heard testimony that some people do not buy insurance for fear that the resulting information flow will come back to haunt them, either in a subsequent insurance decision or through disclosure to their employer.[83] Others do not use their benefits—for instance, psychiatric coverage—for fear claims information will not be held in strictest confidence.[84] In addition, the individual may be more likely to lie about information which he feels may go beyond the insurer. Confidentiality has become such a concern that some who maintain records about individuals, such as doctors and psychologists, are increasingly reluctant or unwilling to disclose the information in them, even when authorized to do so by the individual.[85] Other sources, such as neighbors and associates, may also refuse to provide information or may provide inaccurate information.

Although insurance institutions and support organizations now assume some responsibility for the confidentiality of the information they collect and maintain on individuals, earlier parts of this chapter show the extent to which personally identifiable information is disclosed by numerous insurance industry organizations. Within the industry, information sharing occurs on a routine basis. Moreover, information may be disclosed to those outside the industry without the individual's knowledge.[86] The Commission believes that the key to solving this important problem is to create an enforceable expectation of confidentiality which clearly delineates the circumstances under which an insurance institution or support organization may disclose information about an individual without his authorization.

CURRENT LEGAL RESTRAINTS ON RECORD-KEEPING PRACTICES

STATE INSURANCE REGULATION

The primary regulatory mechanisms for overseeing the activities of insurance institutions are at the State level. State regulation has developed around two basic aims: (1) maintaining the solvency of individual insurance companies; and, (2) assuring fair business practices and pricing. Although interest in the record-keeping practices of insurance institutions has increased in the last few years, few States have focused significant attention on the privacy protection problems the Commission has identified. No

---

[83] Written statement of Benjamin Lipson, Insurance Records Hearings, May 20, 1976, p. 7.

[84] *Ibid.*, p. 8; Testimony of Jerome S. Beigler, American Psychiatric Association, Insurance Records Hearings, May 20, 1976, pp. 358-360.

[85] Testimony of Jerome S. Beigler, American Psychiatric Association, Insurance Records Hearings, May 20, 1976, pp. 370-73.

[86] Testimony of the Index System, Insurance Records Hearings, May 21, 1976, p. 769; Testimony of Jerome S. Beigler, Insurance Records Hearings, pp. 361, 372; Written statement of the Blue Cross Organizations, Insurance Records Hearings, May 20, 1976, p. 5.

State, to the Commission's knowledge, has enacted privacy protection legislation which would affect insurance record-keeping practices. Moreover, regulation of insurance record-keeping practices at the State level is limited because State Insurance Departments do not have regulatory authority over most insurance-support organizations.

There are, however, existing regulatory mechanisms at the State level which could be used to implement some of the Commission's insurance recommendations. These include the unfair trade practices provisions of State insurance laws, and the authority State Insurance Commissioners have been given over the contents of those application forms which are considered part of the policy.

Most States have passed a version of the Model Unfair Trade Practices Act.[87] These laws are applicable to all types of insurance and are designed to protect the insurance consumer by prohibiting insurance institutions from engaging in a wide range of practices specifically defined by the Act to be unfair. The Act includes prohibitions against false advertising, defamation of competitors, boycotts, fraudulent financial statements, rebates, and unfair discrimination. Many States have added to this statute an Unfair Claims Practices Act which protects claimants by forbidding unreasonable claim settlement practices, including misrepresentation, delays in claim payments, and claim settlement offers which are so low as to compel claimants to institute litigation to collect their claims.

The Model Act provides the State Insurance Commissioner with several mechanisms to enforce the prohibition against defined unfair trade practices. The Commissioner has the authority to promulgate regulations identifying the methods of competition or practices which come under the specific prohibitions enumerated in the Act. In addition, the Commissioner may hold a hearing and issue a cease and desist order whenever he believes an insurer is engaging in one of the unfair practices. Monetary penalties or suspension or revocation of a company's license may also be imposed for a violation of the defined unfair trade practices where the insurer knew or should have known that it was in violation of the Act.

In addition to the Commissioner's powers to enforce defined unfair trade practices, the Model Act also provides that he may hold hearings on any act or practice which he believes is unfair, even though the practice is not specifically defined in the Act. If, after a hearing, an undefined act or practice is found to be unfair, the Commissioner may issue a cease and desist order. The Model Act, however, does not empower the Commissioner to add by regulation new acts to the defined unfair trade practices, or to impose monetary penalties for engaging in undefined unfair trade practices.

Some States already make use of the Unfair Trade Practices Act prohibition against unfair discrimination to regulate record-keeping practices. The regulations, however, are limited in scope and, in almost all instances, are concerned with the use of information in the underwriting process rather than its actual collection. For instance, the Privacy Commission heard testimony on the regulation of the relevance of information used

---

[87] Note: *e.g.*, Cal. Ins. Code §§ 790.01, *et seq.* ; Mass. Gen. Laws Ann., ch. 93a; Vt. Stat. Ann. tit. 63, § 2451; Ill. Rev. Stat., ch. 121 1/2, § 261.

in the underwriting process from a representative of the California Insurance Department. California has used its regulatory authority under its unfair trade practices laws to prohibit unfairly discriminatory practices on account of sex, marital status, unconventional life-styles, and sexual orientations differing from the norm. The California Department normally does not attempt to prohibit collection; rather, it acts on an *ad hoc* basis to prohibit the *use* of certain criteria in underwriting decisions upon the receipt of complaints from insurance consumers.[88]

Because the Model Unfair Trade Practices Act is applicable to all lines of insurance and contains strong enforcement provisions, it can serve as an appropriate regulatory mechanism for several of the Commission's recommendations. It will, however, be necessary to amend the Act to define certain unfair record-keeping practices as unfair trade practices. These unfair practices would then be subject to the full range of regulatory and enforcement authority granted Insurance Commissioners under the Model Act, including the power to hold hearings and issue cease and desist orders, and to impose monetary penalties.

Many State Insurance Commissioners have an additional power which could assist in the implementation of certain of the Commission's recommendations. In many States, Commissioners have the authority to approve policy forms. In the case of life and health policies, application forms are considered a part of the policy, so they would be subject to the Commissioner's approval. Thus, Insurance Commissioners in a number of States would be in a position to monitor and enforce the Commission's notification, authorization, and previous adverse decision recommendations insofar as life and health insurance are concerned.

FEDERAL REGULATION

The Federal government has only one law which affects the record-keeping practices of the insurance industry—the Fair Credit Reporting Act. The FCRA governs the use of inspection bureau reports prepared by support organizations in connection with underwriting decisions by insurers, and thus its effect on insurance institutions is limited to their role as users of such reports. There are also a few State fair credit reporting statutes similar to the Federal one. The Commission believes that amending the Fair Credit Reporting Act is a good mechanism to implement many of its recommendations that are beyond the scope of the present Act, including some of its insurance recommendations. The scope of the Act could be broadened, and its title and enforcement framework could be altered to reflect the new scope presented by some of the Commission's recommendations. In addition, the oversight functions presently given to the Federal Trade Commission could be expanded, thus avoiding the necessity of creating a new Federal agency to oversee implementation of those Commission recommendations which are proposed for adoption by amendment of the FCRA.

[88] Testimony of the California Department of Insurance, Insurance Records Hearings, May 20, 1976, pp. 496-98.

THE COMMON LAW

The final constraint upon record-keeping practices in the insurance industry is provided by the common law actions of defamation and privacy. Defamation provides liability for damage to reputation caused by the publication of untrue information about an individual. The tort of invasion of privacy provides liability under certain circumstances for, among other things, public airing of private information about an individual. Insurance institutions and support organizations may be able to raise a qualified privilege in defense of such actions.

In recognition of the need for a free flow of information in commercial transactions, most States have recognized a qualified business privilege which provides a defense for otherwise defamatory statements when made to the proper parties, in a proper manner, and for a valid business purpose, except if the statement is false and made with malicious intent to injure the individual to whom it refers. Similarly, there is a qualified privilege for invasion of privacy actions. These limits on common law actions enable insurance institutions and support organizations to exchange information for legitimate purposes relatively free of legal restraints. As noted earlier, however, the privilege is available only when information is disclosed to someone deemed to have an interest in it. It is for this reason that insurance institutions and their support organizations are careful to guard against the disclosure of information to anyone outside of the industry.

RECOMMENDATIONS

The Commission's approach to the problems described in this chapter has been to focus on strengthening and balancing the relationship between the individual insurance applicant, policyholder, or claimant and the insurance institution with whom he deals. As indicated at the outset, the Commission's recommendations have three objectives:

(1)   to create a proper balance between what an individual is expected to divulge about himself to a record-keeping organization and what he seeks in return (to minimize intrusiveness);

(2)   to open up record-keeping operations in ways that will minimize the extent to which recorded information about an individual is itself a source of unfairness in any decision about him made on the basis of such information (to maximize fairness); and

(3)   to create and define obligations with respect to the uses and disclosures that will be made of recorded personal information (to create a legitimate, enforceable expectation of confidentiality.)

In the insurance area, as in others it has studied, the Commission also believes that giving an individual certain rights without placing corresponding obligations on the institution with whom he has the primary record-keeping relationship is not likely to bring about adequate remedial action. Thus, the Commission believes that insurance institutions and insurance-support organizations must assume greater responsibility for their personal-data record-keeping practices. In some cases, this can be accomplished by bringing the forces of the marketplace to bear on record-keeping policy and practice, through voluntary adoption of standards set forth in this report, or through court action by individuals to enforce their rights. In others, government agencies should also be called upon to play monitoring and corrective roles. The Commission believes that both parties will benefit from this approach. The individual's position with respect to the records the insurance relationship generates about him will be strengthened, while insurers and insurance-support organizations will be assured of obtaining the kind of information that promotes fair and efficient operations. Greater confidence in insurance institutions and their role in society should result from opening up the process in this way.

One of the major reasons legislation is needed is that the individual is currently at a disadvantage in the insurance relationship. Some of the Commission's recommendations have attempted to protect the applicant, policyholder, or claimant by placing certain restraints on the insurer—limiting certain collection techniques, creating standards for the authorization forms used, and requiring reasonable procedures in the collection, use, and disclosure of information about an individual. The Commission's aim, however, is not so much to constrain insurance institutions and support organizations as it is to enhance the position of the individual so that he can protect his own privacy interests. To this end, the Commission has concluded that the insurer should inform the individual of the scope of its underwriting inquiry by a clear notice and an adequate authorization form; that the subject of an investigative report should be interviewed if he so desires; and that a mechanism should be created whereby the individual can question the propriety of a specific type of inquiry made in connection with an insurance decision about him. These recommendations are designed to give the individual a central role in the record-keeping practices (including information collection) of the insurance industry.

The ability of the individual to protect himself depends upon the knowledge he has of the records that are made about him. Thus, an individual should have access to a record about himself and a mechanism should exist whereby disputes concerning the accuracy of such a record can be settled. Access and correction rights are also needed to enable the individual to protect himself from investigations which exceed the scope of the notice he is given at the time he seeks to establish a relationship with an insurer, and to assure that the records maintained about him are accurate, timely, and complete. In addition, the individual should be informed of the reasons for an adverse decision about him and the specific information which supports those reasons, so that he can protect himself from unfair treatment resulting from the use of inaccurate, obsolete, or incomplete information.

This approach is not simply intended to be a procedural one. Rather, it is intended that the dynamics of the relationship between the insurer and the individual, rather than action by a legislature or regulator, will create certain standards governing the collection, maintenance, use, and disclosure of information by insurance institutions and support organizations. The Commission believes that notice, access, dispute, and an enforceable expectation of confidentiality are the tools an individual must have if he is to play an effective role in preventing the record-keeping practices of insurance institutions and support organizations from trespassing on his privacy interests. Armed with them, he can exert constructive pressure upon an insurer or agent. Even where the abuse concerns an insurance-support organization, pressure will be most effective on the insurer or agent, because the individual has a direct relationship with them, and because the prospect of adverse publicity that could affect the insurer's position in the market-place provides the insurer with more incentive to be responsive than the support organization.

Overall, the Commission believes that the strategy it proposes for implementing these recommendations is a reasonable and practical one in that it:

- uses existing regulatory and legislative mechanisms to the maximum extent possible;
- keeps the cost of administration and compliance at acceptable levels;
- provides inducements to comply willingly so that disputes over compliance can be kept to a minimum; and
- provides reasonable protection against liability for unintentional failure to comply, coupled with appropriate penalties for willful failure to comply.

As previously noted, because insurance is regulated primarily by State Insurance Departments, the Commission believes that the responsibility for implementing some of its recommendations should be properly lodged at the State level. In addition, the personal-data record-keeping practices of insurance institutions are also regulated to some extent by the Federal Fair Credit Reporting Act which the Commission believes is the proper vehicle for implementing recommendations that aim to strengthen the insurance relationship by eliminating artificial distinctions between the record-keeping practices of insurance institutions and the record-keeping practices of their support organizations. Finally, for reasons that are fully elaborated in Chapter 9 on government access to records about individuals maintained by organizations in the private sector, the Commission has concluded that the enforceable expectation of confidentiality it recommends must be implemented by Federal statute.

It should be noted, moreover, that the recommendations to be implemented by Federal statute, including those that would be implemented by amending the Fair Credit Reporting Act, give the individual actionable rights against insurance institutions and support organizations. The Commission has explicitly rejected the establishment of a Federal regulatory structure that could be quite costly both to the taxpayer and to the insurance industry. Instead, by making those who do not comply civilly liable for their failure to do so, and by making it comparatively easy for such actions to be brought, the Commission believes that a strong incentive for systemic reform will be created without subjecting those who favor reform to unnecessarily costly government regulation. The burden will fall on those who by their actions willfully and repeatedly disregard their responsibilities rather than on those who make a good faith effort to comply fully. In short, the implementation of the Commission's recommendations is designed to place an increasing financial burden on those companies who encourage costly disputes by resisting openness, or who fail to adopt reasonable procedures to control the collection, use, or disclosure of records about individuals.

Finally, insurance institutions should not be unduly exposed to liability which arises only because of the openness of the process. The objective of the Commission's recommendations is to cleanse the system of decisions based on inaccurate or incomplete information; not to create windfall recoveries for bad information or practices of the past.

Definitions for some of the terms used in the recommendations and discussion which follow may be found in the glossary at the end of this chapter.

Intrusiveness

The Commission's first three recommendations address the scope and character of the inquiry to which an insurer may require an individual to submit as a condition of establishing or maintaining an insurance relationship. Because insurance is concerned with the protection of individuals or personal property, the process of granting insurance coverage necessarily involves intrusions on personal privacy. The question is simply (or perhaps not so simply) how much of an intrusion and by what methods.

GOVERNMENTAL MECHANISMS

For some years now, controversies over the propriety of asking certain kinds of questions of an individual have generally centered on the relevance of the information sought to the decision to be made. For example, the Privacy Act of 1974 requires each Federal agency to limit its collection, maintenance, use and dissemination of information about individuals to that which "is relevant and necessary" to a purpose the agency is required to perform by statute or Executive Order.[89] The California Insurance Department, relying on its authority to prevent unfairly discriminatory practices, investigates the relevance of certain items of information used by insurers doing business in the State and may prohibit the use of any item whose relevance to underwriting decisions or pricing cannot be demonstrated to the Department's satisfaction.

A related, and in many respects more difficult, question concerns inquiries which, while demonstrably relevant, are objectionable on other grounds. Legislatures may prohibit, and have prohibited, the use of certain

---

[89] 5 U.S.C. 552a(e)(1).

items of information on fairness grounds. Race, for example, has been excluded as an eligibility or rating criterion for life underwriting even though its relevance to life expectancy can be demonstrated.[90] On the other hand, the Privacy Act of 1974 strives, not very successfully, to ban the collection and use of information pertaining to an individual's exercise of his First Amendment rights on the grounds that such inquiries by government agencies constitute an unwarranted invasion of personal privacy, i.e., that they fail the test not of relevance or fairness, but of propriety.[91]

Thus far, there have been few ins ances in which items of personal information have been proscribed on grounds of impropriety, i.e., unwarranted intrusiveness. In the insurance area, California has come close in proscribing the collection and use of information concerning "moral life-style."[92] The California approach is almost unique among State insurance regulatory authorities and all the California Department's other investigations, except for "moral life-style," have turned on other issues, such as fairness. In some cases regulation has not been necessary because the impropriety of certain types of inquiries is universally recognized. An example would be collection of information about an individual from his priest, minister, or rabbi.

It should be noted, moreover, that fairness and propriety issues usually cannot be dealt with in the same way. As briefly discussed in Chapter 2, when fairness is the overriding concern, such as in the Equal Credit Opportunity Act as amended, *[15 U.S.C. 1691 et seq.]*, continued collection of certain information may be necessary to demonstrate that it is no longer being used to make decisions about individuals. For example, one cannot show that sex and race are not being systematically used to make credit decisions unless one can show that credit has been extended to women and minorities in proportion to their relative numbers in the credit grantor's market. And the most practical way to do that may well be to have the credit grantor record the sex and race of all applicants. This, however, is much different from situations where impropriety is the reason for proscribing information. There, the first act must be to prohibit collection, since the problem lies primarily in the asking of the question. Use may also be prohibited in such a situation but only to make sure that the information is totally excluded from the decision-making process.

The Commission believes that, in the future, society may have to cope with objections to the collection of certain information about an individual on the grounds that it is "nobody's business but his own." In some cases, these propriety issues may be resolved by prohibiting an inquiry on the grounds that it is irrelevant, but in others, where relevance can be

---

[90] See, for example, *Vital Statistics of the United States, 1972, Vol. II—Morality, Part A*. Table 5-3, Expectation of Life at Single Years of Age by Color and Sex, United States, 1972 (pp. 5-8), published by U.S. Department of Health, Education and Welfare, Public Health Service, Health Resources Administration, National Center for Health Statistics, Rockville, Maryland: 1976.

[91] 5 U.S.C. 552a(e)(7).

[92] Testimony of the California Department of Insurance, Insurance Records Hearings, May 20, 1976, p. 497; Letter from Angele Khachadour, California Department of Insurance, to the Privacy Commission, July 30, 1976. California Department of Insurance, Ruling No. 204.

demonstrated, proscription may be necessary on propriety grounds alone. In the Commission's view, questions of this nature are best resolved on a case-by-case basis. One must be concerned about undue government interference in such controversies. The Commission believes, moreover, that all such determinations must be prospective, so as to avoid retroactive punishment for behavior which at the time was wholly consistent with prevailing societal expectations and norms. However, the Commission also believes that institutional mechanisms are needed so that such questions can be raised and resolved.

Insurers have historically enjoyed considerable latitude in determining what information is and is not necessary to a given decision about an individual. Underwriting is far from an exact science. Moreover, industry spokesmen argue that the cost of collecting information is a powerful enough incentive to collect only relevant information. Yet others claim that insurance institutions collect a great deal of information whose relevance is questionable. Indeed, the industry has been criticized for *not* taking advantage of its actuarial and computer expertise to refine its relevance criteria.

To a large extent, the relevance-propriety issue in insurance stems from some insurers' belief that they should insure only those of "high moral character," and should shun those whose mode of living differs from what society considers normal. In a society as diverse as ours, however, determining what "society considers normal" is no easy task, and relying on the independent judgment of underwriters to make this determination has led to considerable difficulties.

The Commission is mindful of the complexities that lie beneath the surface of the relevance-propriety issue in the insurance area. It is aware that a few States have taken an interest in certain insurance-related inquiries. Most, however, have not. The Commission, moreover, is not fully persuaded that the problem can be handled exclusively through market mechanisms. Although *Recommendation (5)* (see below) seeks to set corrective market forces in motion, the necessity of insurance in today's society may make it difficult for individuals to make their objections felt. Furthermore, should there be sentiment in favor of banning a particular category of inquiry, irrespective of its relevance, some way will have to be found for society to estimate and consider the cost involved in such an action and the way in which the cost will be distributed. Thus, in light of all these considerations, and out of its desire to eliminate unreasonable invasions of personal privacy, the Commission recommends:

Recommendation (1):

That governmental mechanisms should exist for individuals to question the propriety of information collected or used by insurance institutions, and to bring such objections to the appropriate bodies which establish public policy. Legislation specifically prohibiting the use, or collection and use, of a specific item of information may result; or an existing agency or regulatory body may be given authority, or

use its currently delegated authority, to make such a determination with respect to the reasonableness of future use, or collection and use, of a specific item of information.

To implement this proposal, the Commission recommends that each State Insurance Commissioner collect individuals' complaints and questions concerning the propriety of particular types of inquiries, prepare periodic summary reports on the number of questions and complaints by category, and make them available to legislative bodies. If already authorized by the legislature, the Commissioner may take action. In California, for example, the legislature empowered the Commissioner to promulgate rules and regulations under the unfair trade practices article of the State insurance laws and the Commissioner then used that authority to declare discrimination based on sex, marital status, or sexual orientation a prohibited practice.[93] *[§790.03 and 790.10 of the California Insurance Code]*. The rules the Commissioner adopts may prohibit the use of certain information in one line of insurance but not in another. Furthermore, within a given line of insurance, the Commissioner might allow certain information to be used as the basis for rating or determining risk, but not unless it has an impact on one or the other. For example, inquiry into the fact of cohabitation might be relevant in determining *use of a vehicle,* a valid rating criterion, but the mere fact of cohabitation, unrelated to vehicle use, could not be the basis of an underwriting or rating decision.

Currently, most Insurance Commissioners could address the use of irrelevant information under their general authority to hold hearings and issue cease and desist orders in connection with undefined unfair trade practices. The Commission believes, however, that the rule-making technique is fairer and more effective than looking one at a time at possible violations of a general prohibition against unfair trade practices. Not only will more insurers than the one offender have a say in the wisdom of the Commissioner's proposed prohibition, but the Commissioner's decision will only be subject to the narrow judicial review generally applied to rule-making decisions. The Federal Insurance Administrator could also collect the reports compiled by the State Insurance Commissioners and periodically report on them to the Congress.

An alternate and not mutually exclusive suggestion is that the Federal Insurance Administrator, or another appropriate Federal entity, collect complaints concerning the propriety of insurance inquiries directly from individual consumers and from time to time report and make recommendations on them to the Congress. It is not recommended, however, that the Federal Insurance Administrator have the rule-making authority urged for State Insurance Commissioners, since regulation of information practices within the insurance industry is currently a State function.

PRETEXT INTERVIEWS

As indicated earlier, Factual Service Bureau obtain⟩ ⟨ ⟩me of its

---

[93] *Ibid.*

information through pretext interviews or other false or misleading representations.[94] A pretext interview is one in which the inquirer (l) pretends to be someone he is not; (2) pretends to represent someone he does not; or (3) misrepresents the true purpose of the interview. Mere silence on any or all of these points would not normally constitute a pretext interview. Indeed, an investigator could refuse to identify himself, his client, or the purpose of the inquiry, letting the person of whom the inquiry is being made infer whatever he wishes from such behavior. Nonetheless, an investigator dressed in a white lab coat making inquiries of a clerk in a hospital medical records room would be conducting a pretext interview if he allowed the clerk to assume he was a properly credentialed medical professional.

As pointed out in several chapters of this report, the Commission believes that some investigative practices are unreasonably intrusive, or at least have a high potential for depriving an individual of even a modicum of control over the disclosure of information about himself. An investigator conducting a pretext interview clearly raises that prospect. Thus, out of its desire to prevent unreasonable invasions of privacy resulting from the *techniques* used to collect information about individuals, the Commission recommends:

Recommendation (2):

That the Federal Fair Credit Reporting Act be amended to provide that no insurance institution or insurance-support organization may attempt to obtain information about an individual through pretext interviews or other false or misleading representations that seek to conceal the actual purpose(s) of the inquiry or investigation, or the identity or representative capacity of the inquirer or investigator.

This recommendation would apply to all insurance inquiries—whether for underwriting or first- or third-party claims. The prohibition would be enforceable by the Federal Trade Commission (FTC) against organizations that collect information by means of pretext interviews. An organization would be able to defend itself against an FTC action on the basis that it had taken reasonable steps and instituted reasonable procedures to prevent such activity. The use of pretext interviews should be made a civil offense, punishable by fines and cease and desist orders.

REASONABLE CARE IN THE USE OF SUPPORT ORGANIZATIONS

The reported practices of Factual Service Bureau also raise a legitimate concern about the care with which insurance institutions select and use the services of support organizations. An institution should not be totally unaccountable for the activities of others who perform services for it. The Commission believes that an insurance institution should have an affirmative obligation to check into the *modus operandi* of any support

---

[94] Testimony of Dale Tooley, District Attorney, Denver, Colo., *Medical Records*, Hearings before the Privacy Protection Study Commission, June 11, 1976, pp. 456 - 511.

organizations it uses or proposes to use; and that if an insurance institution does not use reasonable care in selecting or using such organizations, it should not be wholly absolved of responsibility for their actions. Moreover, a like obligation should obtain where one support organization uses the services of another.

Currently, the responsibility of an insurance institution for the acts of a support organization depends upon the degree of control the insurance institution exercises over the support organization. Most insurance-support organizations are independent contractors who traditionally reserve the authority to determine and assure compliance with the terms of their contract. Thus, under the laws of agency, an insurer may be absolved of any liability for the illegal acts of a support organization if those acts are not required by the terms of the contract.[95] In the Commission's opinion, the Factual Service Bureau case illustrates why this is not desirable. Accordingly, to deal with the responsibility of the institution that uses others to gather information about individuals for its own use, the Commission recommends:

Recommendation (3):

That the Federal Fair Credit Reporting Act be amended to provide that each insurance institution and insurance-support organization must exercise reasonable care in the selection and use of insurance-support organizations, so as to assure that the collection, maintenance, use, and disclosure practices of such organizations comply with the Commission's recommendations.

If it could be shown that an insurance institution had hired or used a support organization with knowledge, either actual or constructive, that the organization was engaging in improper collection practices, such as pretext interviews, an individual or the Federal Trade Commission could initiate action against both the insurance institution and the support organization and hold them jointly liable for the support organization's actions.

Fairness

THE REASONABLE PROCEDURES OBJECTIVE

As a general objective guiding the personal-data record-keeping practices of insurance institutions and their support organizations, the Commission recommends:

---

[95] See, e.g., *Milton v. Missouri Pacific Ry. Co.*, 193 Mo. 46, 91 S.W. 949 (1906); *Inscoe v. Globe Jewelry Co.*, 200 N.C. 580, 157 S.E. 794 (1932). However, recent decisions in a few jurisdictions indicate that under certain circumstances, one who contracts with a private investigator may not thereby insulate himself from liability for unlawful acts committed by the investigator by merely arguing that they were outside the scope of the contract. *Ellenberg v. Pinkerton's, Inc.*, 124 Ga. App. 648, 188 S.E. 2d 911 (1972); *Noble v. Sears, Roebuck and Co.*, 33 Cai. App. 3d 654, 109 Cal. Rptr. 269, 73 A.L.R.3d 1164 (1973).

Recommendation (4):

That each insurance institution and insurance-support organization, in order to maximize fairness in its decision-making processes, have reasonable procedures to assure the accuracy, completeness, and timeliness of information it collects, maintains, or discloses about an individual.

Subsection 3(e)(5) of the Privacy Act of 1974 requires each Federal agency to

collect, maintain, use and disclose[96] all records which are used by the agency in making any determination about any individual with such accuracy, relevance, timeliness, and completeness as is reasonably necessary to assure fairness to the individual in the determination.

This provision is a requirement on management wholly independent of the rights the Act gives an individual. For a Federal agency whose administrative procedures are subject to congressional oversight, it is an appropriate requirement.[97] The same, however, cannot be said of its applicability to the private sector.

As pointed out in Chapter 1, the Commission believes that the mix of rights and obligations its private-sector recommendations would establish are in themselves incentive enough to foster the kind of management attention to personal data record-keeping policy and practice that subsection 3(e)(5) of the Privacy Act requires. Thus, the Commission does not recommend that *Recommendation (4)* be incorporated in statute or regulation. Rather it envisages *Recommendation (4)* being implemented automatically as a consequence of the adoption of the other recommendations in this section, particularly *Recommendations (10), (11), (12), (13),* and *(16),* on access, correction, adverse decisions, disclosure of information from proper medical sources, and *Recommendations (5), (6),* and *(17),* on notice and disclosure.

The adoption of these recommendations will promote the maintenance of reasonable procedures by insurance institutions to assure the accuracy, completeness, and timeliness of information and provide a means whereby information collected, maintained, or disclosed may be corrected or updated by the individual.

Fairness in Collection

Notice Regarding Collection from Third Parties

As indicated in the discussion of *Recommendation (1),* the Commission believes that the type of governmental mechanism called for should be used mainly in instances where the forces of the marketplace are not strong

---

[96] The Act's definition of "maintain" includes all four record-keeping functions: collection, maintenance, use, and dissemination.

[97] For more detailed discussion of this requirement, and the problems agencies have had implementing it, see Chapter 13.

enough to induce the elimination of objectionable items from the insurer's scope of inquiry—for example, items that are demonstrably relevant but nonetheless objectionable on the grounds of propriety. To make market forces work to the advantage of the insurance purchaser, however, he must know the type of information that may be developed and considered in the decision-making process for an insurance transaction. Otherwise, he has no way of judging whether to take his business elsewhere. The application form itself serves to apprise the individual of some of the information that will be gathered about him, but as previously pointed out, the application normally gives at best only faint clues as to the type of inquiry that may be made of sources other than the individual himself.

Thus, to minimize the need for public-policy determinations as to the propriety of an insurer's inquiries about an individual, as well as inform the individual of the disclosures that must be made in order to obtain a favorable decision on his insurance application, the Commission recommends:

Recommendation (5):

That an insurance institution, prior to collecting information about an applicant or principal insured from another person in connection with an insurance transaction, notify him as to:

(a)   **the types of information expected to be collected about him from third parties and that are not collected on the application, and, as to information regarding character, general reputation, and mode of living, each area of inquiry;**

(b)   **the techniques that may be used to collect such types of information;**

(c)   **the types of sources that are expected to be asked to provide each type of information about him;**

(d)   **the types of parties to whom and circumstances under which information about the individual may be disclosed without his authorization, and the types of information that may be disclosed;**

(e)   **the procedures established by statute by which the individual may gain access to any resulting record about himself;**

(f)   **the procedures whereby the individual may correct, amend, delete, or dispute any resulting record about himself;**

(g)   **the fact that information in any report prepared by a consumer-reporting agency (as defined by the Fair Credit Reporting Act) may be retained by that organization and subsequently disclosed by it to others.**

Recommendation (5) would not apply to information collected for first- or third-party claims or for marketing purposes where the information is collected prior to the initial application. In all other cases, however, it would provide the individual with information about the scope of inquiry to which he is agreeing: the manner in which the inquiry will be conducted (e.g., through interviews of neighbors and associates) and the disclosures other institutions may possibly make in response to an inquiry from the insurer or an insurance-support organization. Most importantly, it would apprise the individual of the types of uses that may later be made of information without his authorization—for example, of medical-record information acquired by the insurer, or of "adverse information" acquired and retained by an investigative-reporting agency—while at the same time anticipating his need or desire to see and copy, or correct, information developed in the course of the inquiry. Thus, the recommendation would provide the individual with a detailed map of the information flows attendant upon the relationship he proposes to establish with the insurer.

It should be noted, moreover, that the subsection (a) requirement to notify as to "each area of inquiry" when information regarding character, general reputation, and mode of living is to be collected from a third party anticipates a level of specificity finer than currently considered acceptable under the Fair Credit Reporting Act. Furthermore, while the recommendation does not apply to information collected in connection with first- or third-party claims or for marketing purposes prior to the time the individual submits his application, the subsection (d) requirement to notify the individual of those parties to whom the information may be disclosed without his authorization would include notice of the fact that information on first-party property and liability claimants is sometimes disclosed to the loss indexes and the Insurance Crime Prevention Institute.

While unanimously agreeing that the type of notice called for in *Recommendation (5)* is necessary to solve the problems it addresses, the Commission was concerned about its practicality. One insurer, however, drafted an example which showed that the requirements of *Recommendation (5)* could be met by a notice that is neither unreasonably lengthy nor unreasonably complex.

As to implementation, while the Fair Credit Reporting Act governs notice requirements to some extent, Insurance Commissioners can also independently monitor industry compliance through their hearing authority under unfair trade practices laws as well as their authority to approve certain application forms. Finally, *Recommendation (5)* may be self-enforcing because *Recommendations (11)* and *(12)*, if adopted, will give the individual a right to have information beyond the scope of the notice given him deleted from any resulting underwriting or support-organization record about him.

NOTICE AS THE COLLECTION LIMITATION

The notice given pursuant to *Recommendation (5)* will be useless if the insurer's inquiry goes beyond what the notice anticipates. Furthermore, as indicated in the discussion of *Recommendation (3)* on reasonable care in the selection of support organizations, one of the problems with the insurance relationship is the degree to which it is attenuated by the insurer's frequent reliance on independent contractors in gathering information about individuals.

Thus, to assure that there will be consistency between the scope, techniques, and sources described in the *Recommendation (5)* notice and the actual inquiry that takes place, the Commission recommends:

Recommendation (6):

That an insurance institution limit:

(a)   its own information collection and disclosure practices to those specified in the notice called for in *Recommendation (5);* and

(b)   its request to any organization it asks to collect information on its behalf to information, techniques, and sources specified in the notice called for in *Recommendation (5).*

Like the notice recommendation itself, this recommendation does not apply to information collected in connection with first- or third-party claims or for marketing purposes where the information is collected prior to the initial application. Compliance with *Recommendation (6)* could be verified through the correction procedures called for in *Recommendations (11)* and *(12)* as well as Insurance Department examinations. If an individual finds that the insurer has information beyond that specified in the notice, the individual should be able to have it deleted from his record.

INFORMATION FOR MARKETING AND RESEARCH

Subsection 3(e)(3) of the Privacy Act of 1974 requires agencies to advise individuals whether the divulgence of particular items of information is mandatory or voluntary and the consequences of refusing to divulge them. The mandatory and voluntary concepts, however, have little meaning in the private sector, inasmuch as an individual's divulgences are all "voluntary" and an insurance institution can make "mandatory" anything it wishes. As a practical matter, an individual may have little choice but to comply with whatever requests for information are made of him. An example of the trepidation this can cause will be found in the discussion of the Blue Cross-Blue Shield psychiatric claims form in Chapter 7, on the medical-care relationship. Since this is so, insurance institutions should at least indicate on their application forms any requested information which is unnecessary for insurance coverage determination purposes but which is sought for marketing, research, or other purposes. Otherwise individuals will have no way of knowing whether such inquiries are necessary; and thus whether they should bring pressure on the insurer to make the inquiries truly voluntary. Accordingly, the Commission recommends:

Recommendation (7):

That any insurance institution or insurance-support organization clearly specify to an individual those items of inquiry desired for marketing, research, or other purposes not directly related to establishing the individual's eligibility for an insurance benefit or

service being sought and which may be used for such purposes in individually identifiable form.

This recommendation, which would not apply to third-party claim transactions, should be voluntarily complied with by insurers and support organizations. While the determination of what is required to establish eligibility is left to the individual company and will undoubtedly vary to some degree, fairness to the individual requires that he be apprised of those items of information desired, but not required by the company to determine acceptability or price.

AUTHORIZATION STATEMENTS

The authorization forms used by the insurance industry determine what information insurance institutions and their support organizations can obtain from those with whom an individual has a confidential relationship. Many authorization forms now in use are so broad as to constitute an invitation to abuse. Many do not indicate that they will be used by investigative-reporting agency representatives to develop inspection reports or acquire medical-record information to be transmitted to the insurer. Many do not indicate that they will be used to get credit reports, or information from banks and other organizations.

Although today, banks, employers, and some other types of record-keeping organizations may be willing to disclose certain information about an individual without his authorization, the Commission's recommendations with respect to those types of organizations would make obtaining the individual's prior authorization necessary. When that happens, as well as in those situations where record keepers have confidential relationships with individuals today, such as in the medical-care relationship, the record keeper on whom the duty of confidentiality rests will be the final arbiter of what constitutes a valid authorization. As a practical matter, however, such a record keeper may be hard-pressed to refuse to honor a broadly worded authorization if the result is grave inconvenience to the individual or refusal to reimburse the record keeper for services already rendered to the individual. Thus, to set the standards whereby those who have a duty of confidentiality to an individual may properly be asked to disclose information about him to others, the Commission recommends:

Recommendation (8):

That no insurance institution or insurance-support organization ask, require, or otherwise induce an individual, or someone authorized to act on his behalf, to sign any statement authorizing any individual or institution to disclose information about him, or about any other individual, unless the statement is:

(a)   in plain language;
(b)   dated;
(c)   specific as to the individuals and institutions he is authorizing to

>   disclose information about him who are known at the time the
>   authorization is signed, and general as to others whose specific
>   identity is not known at the time the authorization is signed;
> (d) specific as to the nature of the information he is authorizing to
>   be disclosed;
> (e) specific as to the individuals or institutions to whom he is
>   authorizing information to be disclosed;
> (f) specific as to the purpose(s) for which the information may be
>   used by any of the parties named in (e), both at the time of the
>   disclosure and at any time in the future;
> (g) specific as to its expiration date which should be for a
>   reasonable period of time not to exceed one year, and in the
>   case of life insurance or noncancelable or guaranteed renewable
>   health insurance, two years after the date of the policy.

The requirements of *Recommendation (8)* are not as severe as they may
seem. Life and health insurance institutions regularly obtain authorizations
as a part of their applications. Because of the individual's need for
insurance, he exercises little bargaining power over the terms of the
authorization. If a claim is involved, the authorization is obtained as a
condition to considering the claim. It does the claimant little good to refuse
to sign the authorization, for then he must go through the burden of suing
the insurer, and even then much of the information will be available during
discovery. Because insurers can basically dictate the terms of the authorization, the Commission concluded that the terms of the authorization needed
to be specified so that the individual would know what he was agreeing to
have disclosed, and so that those who held information of a confidential
nature would know that they had received a valid authorization from the
individual to release information to others.

Subsection (f) is especially important because it provides the individual with a description of the uses that may subsequently be made of
information obtained about him pursuant to authorization. One particular
example is that an individual would have to be told that information
obtained from a medical-care provider in connection with underwriting may
later be used for claim purposes.

Subsection (c) requires the authorization to be as specific as possible.
It must specifically name those individuals and organizations authorized to
release information about him who are known at the time the authorization
is obtained. But if, for instance, an insurer subsequently learns of an
attending physician whom the individual has not revealed, then the more
general language of the authorization can be used with regard to that
physician. Returning to the individual every time an insurer learned of a
new source would be expensive and, in some cases, distressing to the
individual, since it could delay processing of his application. Moreover, the
subsequently identified source, a physician, for example, would still only be
asked to disclose information of the sort described pursuant to subsection
(d) and for the purpose specified pursuant to subsection (f). In addition, the
individual would ultimately be able to identify every record-keeper contact

by exercising the access rights Commission *Recommendations (10)* and *(13),* below, would give him.

Subsection (g) limits the validity of the authorization to a reasonable period of time not to exceed one year. The only exceptions to this are for life insurance and noncancelable or guaranteed renewable health insurance where an authorization signed in connection with an application would be valid for two years from the date of the policy. Those types of policies, it will be remembered, are contestable for two years after they are issued and during that period an insurer needs to be able to protect itself from fraud or misrepresentation at the time of application.

Recommendation (8) would be implemented through the refusal of a holder of confidential information to release it unless presented with a valid authorization. It has also been suggested to the Commission that the National Association of Insurance Commissioners or the Commission on Uniform State laws might well develop standard authorization forms to achieve and facilitate the desired uniformity. Further, it should be noted that the necessary generality permitted by parts of *Recommendation (8)* need not apply to an insurance institution that obtains an authorization from an applicant, insured, or claimant permitting it to release confidential information to others. In that case, the authorization form can and should be specific as to what information, to whom, and for what purpose.

INVESTIGATIVE INTERVIEWS

As a general policy, the Commission believes that record-keeping institutions should strive as much as possible to collect information about an individual from the individual himself, rather than rely primarily on third-party sources. Furthermore, where an investigative report is being prepared, such a practice should not just be encouraged; it should be required if the individual so wishes.

Although inaccuracies in investigative reports prepared by inspection bureaus were a major stimulus to enactment of the Fair Credit Reporting Act, it has not been possible to determine whether the Act has substantially reduced the error rate. The major purposes of an investigative report are to: (1) verify information supplied by the applicant or his agent; and (2) develop information about the applicant's character, general reputation, and mode of living—lines of inquiry which must perforce involve a certain amount of subjective evaluation. Moreover, as Chapter 8 points out, it has been alleged that some reports get prepared without the investigator ever contacting anyone at all. Whatever the merits of that controversy, requiring an interview with the subject of a report as an affirmative requirement will help to resolve it and, if industry spokesmen are correct about the usefulness of interviews with report subjects, such interviews will improve the quality of the information inspection bureaus transmit to their insurer clients.

Thus, the Commission recommends:

Recommendation (9):

That the Federal Fair Credit Reporting Act be amended to provide that any insur-nce institution that may obtain an investigative report on an applicant or insured inform him that he may, upon request, be interviewed in connection with the preparation of the investigative report. The insurance institution and investigative agency must institute reasonable procedures to assure that such interviews are performed if requested. When an individual requests an interview and cannot reasonably be contacted, the obligation of the institution preparing the investigative report can be discharged by mailing a copy of the report, when prepared, to the individual.

This recommendation would not apply to any investigative report about an individual made in reasonable anticipation of civil or criminal action, or for use in defense or settlement of an insurance claim. Nor would it require an interview in every instance, since the individual would have to request it and presumably would make himself available for the interview. Not all individuals will seek such an opportunity. When an individual requests an interview and cannot be contacted using reasonable procedures, the requirement for an interview can be discharged by mailing a copy of the report to him.

The Commission considered having the interview occur just prior to sending the report off to the insurer, on the theory that the individual would then be in a position to review the information which had been gathered and, if necessary, to correct, amend, or dispute it. However, the Commission concluded that the difficulties involved in making a personal contact at a specific time could work to the disadvantage of the individual anxious to get his insurance application processed. Furthermore, the report is often not prepared until the investigator returns to his office. An alternative, also considered and rejected, would have required that a copy of the report be sent to the individual at the same time it is sent to the insurer. This was rejected because of the cost involved (a copy of every report prepared would have to be sent, regardless of whether the report resulted in an adverse decision) and because the adoption of *Recommendations (10)* and *(13)*, below, would make the report available to the individual on a see and copy basis from either the insurer or the investigative-reporting agency.

In incorporating this requirement into the Fair Credit Reporting Act, it should be made clear that the interview requirement applies to underwriting investigations undertaken by insurers themselves as well as by inspection bureaus.

FAIRNESS IN USE

ACCESS TO RECORDS

Access to records, as a general concept of fair record-keeping practice, should be extended to insurance records. Allowing an individual to see and copy a record kept about him can be advantageous to the insurance institution as well as to the individual. As suggested earlier, the records an insurance institution maintains about individuals are numerous and can serve a variety of functions. Except for medical records (information from which insurers also maintain), an insurance institution's records may contain information on more dimensions of an individual's life than almost any other type of record the Commission has examined. Moreover, several of the Commission's other recommendations depend on the individual being able to have access to insurance records about himself at times other than when an adverse underwriting decision has been made about him. For example, the notice requirement proposed in *Recommendation (5)*, and the limitation on collection practices in *Recommendation (6)*, depend on the individual being able to find out what information has been collected about him. And, as in other areas, the authorization statement an individual is asked to sign allowing an insurer to disclose information about him will be a meaningless piece of paper if he cannot learn what he has authorized to be disclosed.

Currently, an individual does not have a legal right to see or even learn the nature and substance of information maintained about him by an insurer, or by any insurance-support organization not subject to the Fair Credit Reporting Act. Moreover, the FCRA only requires an investigative-reporting agency to disclose to an individual the "nature and substance" of information in a report it has prepared about him. *[15 U.S.C. 1681g(a)(1)]* The Medical Information Bureau voluntarily gives an individual access to the summary data it maintains on him, if he so requests, but the individual has no legal right of access to anything held by an insurer, and thus, may not be able to figure out why the MIB record says what it does, or get the insurer that caused the MIB record to be created to correct errors in it.

To overcome these deficiencies, the Commission recommends:

Recommendation (10):

That the Federal Fair Credit Reporting Act be amended to provide:

(a)   **That, upon request by an individual, an insurance institution or insurance-support organization must:**

    (i)   **inform the individual, after verifying his identity, whether it has any recorded information pertaining to him; and**

    (ii)   **permit the individual to see and copy any such recorded information, either in person or by mail; or**

    (iii)   **apprise the individual of the nature and substance of any such recorded information by telephone; and**

    (iv)   **permit the individual to use one or the other of the methods of access provided in (a)(ii) and (iii), or both if he prefers.**

The insurance institution or insurance-support organization may charge a reasonable copying fee for any copies provided to the individual. Any such recorded information should be made available to the individual, but need not contain the name or other identifying

particulars of any source (other than an institutional source) of information in the record who has provided such information on the condition that his identity not be revealed, and need not reveal a confidential numerical code.

(b) That notwithstanding part (a), with respect to medical-record information maintained by an insurance institution or an insurance-support organization, an individual has a right of access to that information, either directly or through a licensed medical professional designated by the individual, whichever the insurance institution or support organization prefers.

As far as insurance institutions are concerned, it is the Commission's intention that this right of access be to any reasonably described information about the individual. In the case of an applicant, for example, commonly used identifiers such as name and address, coverage requested, and possibly date of application, ought to be enough to identify the record requested. The fact that information on one individual is contained in a record on another would not preclude the first from being able to see and copy it so long as he can provide the requisite identifier. Also, an individual should be able to see and copy information about other people in a record pertaining to himself if it is pertinent to his relationship with the insurer. For example, a husband who has an automobile policy that insures both him and his wife should be able to review his entire file, including any information in it about his wife. Conversely, as an insured, the wife should be able to see anything in the file on either herself or her husband.

The proposed right of access would extend to all records about an individual that are reasonably retrievable. Thus, it would include all information in a credit or investigative report, except that the identity of a non-institutional source (for instance, a neighbor or associate) need not be revealed where such a source provided information on the condition that his identity not be revealed. The individual, however, would have full access to all information such a source provided.

This, it will be noted, is a major departure from current practice wherein an insurer is customarily constrained from disclosing the contents of an investigative report to the individual by provisions in its contract with the inspection bureau. In the future, if the Commission's recommendations are adopted, such contractual constraints will not be possible. Moreover, neither the insurer nor the inspection bureau will be able to withhold the identity of any *institutional* sources.

The proposed right of access would also extend to medical-record information held by an insurer or insurance-support organization, although either organization would have the option of disclosing information to the individual through a licensed medical professional designated by the individual. The medical professional would be obligated to allow the individual to see and copy it upon request by the individual.

Finally, to make his access right convenient to exercise, the recommendation would allow an individual or a licensed medical professional designated by him pursuant to subsection (b), to see and copy records in person or by mail, or to have their nature and substance disclosed by telephone. This, too, is a departure from current practice inasmuch as the recommendation applies to support organizations as well as insurers, and the Fair Credit Reporting Act does not currently require an inspection bureau to provide the individual with a copy of an investigative report.

It should be noted that this recommendation would not apply to any record about an individual compiled in reasonable anticipation of a civil or criminal action, or for use in settling a claim while the claim remains unsettled. After the claim is settled the recommendation would not apply to any record compiled in relation to a third-party claimant (i.e., a claimant who is not a principal insured or policy owner) except as to any portion of such a record which is disseminated or used for a purpose unrelated to processing the claim. The exception for records compiled in reasonable anticipation of civil or criminal litigation would apply regardless of whether the insurance institution or support organization envisions being a plaintiff or defendant (in a civil action) or a complainant in a criminal proceeding. For example, an insurance institution or support organization may be compiling information to prove arson on the part of a first-party claimant. The insurer may have already paid the claim but is considering prosecution. When such an action is no longer reasonably contemplated, the first-party claimant's access right would be established.

When information is compiled in connection with the settlement of a first-party claim, and negotiations are in progress or contemplated, allowing access prior to settlement would unbalance the existing legal rights of both parties. However, once the first-party claim has been settled, the Commission believes that there is no sound justification for continuing to deny access.

The Commission does see the need to distinguish between first- and third-party claimants. *Recommendation (10)* creates a very limited right of access for a third-party claimant. Whereas the first-party claimant has a contractual relationship with the insurer, the third-party claimant, by definition, occupies an adversary role and has not entered into a relationship with the insurer. Only where information compiled in the course of a third-party settlement is used for a purpose other than settling the claim should the claimant be allowed access to such information. The principle involved is that non-claim decisions should not be made about an individual on the basis of records whose contents he cannot know. However, where the individual claimant is in an adversary negotiation with the record keeper, and existing law creates certain rights of access in the course of litigation, an exception to the general right of access recommended by the Commission can be justified. Information can be given to loss indexes and others solely for claim purposes without violating this exception to access by the individual.

Since *Recommendation (10)* would be implemented by amending the Fair Credit Reporting Act, an individual would be able to compel production of a record by an insurance institution or support organization through litigation brought in Federal court or another appropriate court. The right would be similar to the one given a citizen by the Federal Freedom of Information Act. The plaintiff would have to prove that he requested and was denied reasonably described records about himself in the possession of the insurance institution or support organization, and the burden would be on the institution or support organization to present any reason why the statute would not be applicable. Courts would have the power to order the insurance institution or support organization to disclose the particular record or records sought and to award reasonable attorney's fees and other litigation costs to any plaintiff who substantially prevailed.

Systematic denials of access by an insurance institution or support organization could be subject to Federal Trade Commission enforcement, in which the remedy would be an order directing the institution or support organization to produce records upon request by individuals. Once the Federal Trade Commission issued such an order, the insurance institution or support organization would then be subject to the usual enforcement mechanisms available to the FTC to secure compliance with its orders.

An alternative to this approach, in the case of insurance institutions, is to encourage the States to enact amendments to the unfair trade practices sections of their insurance laws to give State Insurance Commissioners the authority to enforce the requirements of this recommendation, and of the correction and adverse decision rights that *Recommendations (11)* and *(13)* would create. If a State failed to enact such legislation, the Federal Trade Commission would then be able to exercise its enforcement proceedings, using its normal enforcement mechanism with respect to systematic failures in that particular State.

An individual would have no right to money damages based solely upon a denial of his access right under *Recommendation (10)*. The burden would be on the individual to reasonably describe the document sought and the insurance institution or support organization could defend on the basis that it cannot reasonably locate or identify the records sought by the plaintiff. For example, the individual could sue for any document developed as the result of an application for insurance if the individual could identify the date and nature of the application. If, however, an individual requested any information that relates to him in a file, but could not, with some specificity, identify the circumstances pursuant to which such a file would have been developed, the insurance institution would not be under an affirmative obligation to search manually through each and every document to locate a possible passing reference to the individual.

The Fair Credit Reporting Act currently creates the following limitation of liability protection:

> Except as provided in Sections 1681n and 1681o of this title, no consumer may bring any action or proceeding in the nature of defamation, invasion of privacy, or negligence with respect to the reporting of information against any consumer reporting agency, any user of information, or any person who furnishes information to a consumer reporting agency, based on information disclosed pursuant to 1681h or 1681m of this title, except as to false information furnished with malice or willful intent to injure such customer. *[15 U.S.C. 1681h(e)]*

The Commission believes that this type of protection should be extended to insurance institutions and support organizations in connection with recorded information furnished pursuant to either *Recommendation (10)* or *Recommendation (13)* concerning adverse underwriting decisions. In addition, because insurers, unlike their support organizations, make decisions about individuals, the Commission believes that they should not be liable to suit for retroactive coverage where an adverse underwriting decision is made on the basis of information which proves to be incorrect. Thus, an insurance institution or support organization should have no liability, including liability for defamation, invasion of privacy or negligence, with respect to information which had been disclosed to an individual, regardless of whether or not that information was created or furnished by the insurance institution or insurance-support organization, unless false information was furnished to third parties with malice or willful intent to injure the individual.

CORRECTION OF RECORDS

Giving an individual the right to see and copy a record created for the purpose of making a decision about him is of little value if it is not accompanied by a right to get erroneous information in the record corrected. Both the Privacy Act and the Fair Credit Reporting Act establish procedures whereby an individual can correct, amend, or dispute inaccurate, obsolete, or incomplete information in a record about himself. The insurance business stands to gain, moreover, from improving the quality of information about individuals available to it. When an individual is denied insurance on the basis of an inaccurate record about himself, the insurer also suffers through the loss of premium income. Finally, given the observed need to strengthen and balance the respective roles of insurer and individual within the context of the insurance relationship, and given the fact that there is information interchange among insurers (particularly as facilitated by inspection bureaus, the Medical Information Bureau, and the loss indexes), it is unrealistic to expect the individual to chase an error through every insurance-related record-keeping organization to which it may have been transmitted. The insurer, the primary record keeper, must assume its fair share of responsibility for that task.

Accordingly, to make the individual's right of access to an insurance record worthwhile, and to improve the quality of recorded information available to underwriters and others who make decisions about applicants and insureds, the Commission recommends:

Recommendation (11):

That the Federal Fair Credit Reporting Act be amended to provide that each insurance institution and insurance-support organization permit an individual to request correction, amendment, or deletion of a record pertaining to him; and

(a)   within a reasonable period of time:

(i)   correct or amend (including supplement) any portion thereof which the individual reasonably believes is not accurate, timely, or complete; and

(ii)   delete any portion thereof which is not within the scope of information the individual was originally told would be collected about him; and

(b)   furnish the correction, amendment, or fact of deletion to any person or organization specifically designated by the individual who may have, within two years prior thereto, received any such information; and, automatically, to any insurance-support organization whose primary source of information on individuals is insurance institutions when the support organization has systematically received any such information from the insurance institution within the preceding seven years, unless the support organization no longer maintains the information, in which case, furnishing the correction, amendment, or fact of deletion is not required; and automatically to any insurance-support organization that furnished the information corrected, amended, or deleted; or

(c)   inform the individual of its refusal to correct or amend the record in accordance with his request and of the reason(s) for the refusal; and

(i)   permit an individual who disagrees with the refusal to correct or amend the record to have placed on or with the record a concise statement setting forth the reasons for his disagreement; and

(ii)   in any subsequent disclosure outside the insurance institution or support organization containing information about which the individual has filed a statement of dispute, clearly note any portion of the record which is disputed, and provide a copy of the statement along with the information being disclosed; and

(iii)   furnish the statement of dispute to any person or organization specifically designated by the individual who may have, within two years prior thereto, received any such information; and, automatically, to an insurance-support organization whose primary source of information on individuals is insurance institutions when the support organization has received any such information from the insurance institution within the preceding seven years, unless the support organization no longer maintains the information, in which case, furnishing the statement is not required; and, automatically, to any insurance-support organization that furnished the disputed information;

(d)   limit its reinvestigation of disputed information to those record items in dispute.

Recommendation (12):

That notwithstanding *Recommendation (11)(a)(i)*, if an individual who is the subject of medical-record information maintained by an insurance institution or insurance-support organization requests correction or amendment of such information, the insurance institution or insurance-support organization be required to:

(a)   disclose to the individual, or to a medical professional designated by him, the identity of the medical-care provider who was the source of the medical-record information; and

(b)   make the correction or amendment requested within a reasonable period of time, if the medical-care provider who was the source of the information agrees that it is inaccurate or incomplete; and

(c)   establish a procedure whereby an individual who is the subject of medical-record information maintained by an insurance institution or insurance-support organization, and who believes that the information is incorrect or incomplete, would be provided an opportunity to present supplemental information of a limited nature for inclusion in the medical-record information maintained by the insurance institution or support organization, provided that the source of the supplemental information is also included.

Although *Recommendations (11)* and *(12)* appear complex, they contain only two key requirements:

- that an individual have a way of correcting, amending, deleting, or disputing information in a record about himself, regardless of whether the record is held by an insurance institution or by a support organization; and

- that the insurance institution or support organization to whom the request for correction, amendment, or deletion is made, shall have an obligation to propagate the correction, amendment, deletion, or statement of dispute in any subsequent disclosure it makes of the information to possible recipients within the previous two years whom the individual designates; and to any insurance-support organization which within the previous seven years has been a regular recipient of the type of information, or which was the source of the information.

Regular recipients would include support organizations such as the Medical Information Bureau, the Impairment Bureau, or the loss indexes. Sources would mainly be investigative-reporting agencies (inspection bureaus).

The obvious objective of the second set of requirements is to allow for a thorough cleansing of industry record systems when inaccurate information is discovered and, in the case of amended or corrected information, to provide measures of the completeness and validity of information used in making decisions about an individual, thereby reducing the number of adverse decisions made on the basis of inaccurate or incomplete information. Furthermore, *Recommendations (11)* and *(12)* also provide two important vehicles for enforcing compliance with *Recommendations (5)* and *(6)* on pre-notice and limits on collection practices.

The requirement to delete information that falls outside the boundaries set by the notice called for in *Recommendation (5)*, not only from the insurer's records but also from the records of any support organization that has collected it, or to which it has been disclosed, not only gives the individual a means of holding the insurer to its declarations regarding the scope of the inquiry to be made about him, but also enhances the insurer's control over the record-keeping practices of its contractors. In addition, by closely wedding the scope of a support organization's inquiry on behalf of each of its clients to each client's specified needs, the net effect of this requirement should be to allow an insurer that spends money on refining its relevance criteria and information collection techniques to avoid subsidizing other insurers that have not done so. At the present time, the relationship between insurer and investigative-reporting agency, for example, is loose enough to allow the reporting agency to use an inquiry on behalf of one insurer to gather information that can be marketed to others. Today, apparently, this is not a serious problem, because there are broad similarities among the kinds of reports insurers order. If *Recommendation (5)* succeeds in making privacy protection policy an element in insurers' competition for customers, however, fairness demands that the more socially responsible insurers not have to subsidize the practices of their less conscientious competitors.

In addition, subsection (d) limits the reinvestigation of disputed information to the items in dispute. The purpose of this provision is to prevent the dispute mechanism from becoming an occasion for a wholly new intrusion merely because of the questioned accuracy of one item.

As to *Recommendation (12)*, the rationale and explanation for it will be found in the discussion of *Recommendation (8)* in Chapter 7 on the medical-care relationship.

Like *Recommendation (10)*, neither *Recommendation (11)* nor *Recommendation (12)* would apply to any record about an individual compiled in reasonable anticipation of a civil or criminal action, or for use in settling a claim while the claim remains unsettled. After the claim is settled, moreover, these recommendations would not apply to any record compiled in relation to a claimant who is not an insured or policy owner, except as to any portion of such a record which is disseminated or used for a purpose unrelated to processing the claim. Nor are these recommendations intended to replace entirely the current Fair Credit Reporting Act reinvestigation and dispute requirements. Although *Recommendation (11)* would extend the current six-month limitation on an inspection bureau's obligation to propagate corrections, amendments, and disputes, it is not intended that this recommendation supplant existing Fair Credit Reporting Act requirements to reinvestigate and record the current status of information (unless the complaint is frivolous) or to delete information which can no longer be verified.

The Fair Credit Reporting Act should be amended to allow an individual to sue to force compliance with *Recommendations (11)* and *(12)* and be entitled to reasonable attorney's fees and other litigation costs if he substantially prevails. This would be the sole remedy in the event an insurance institution or support organization fails to comply with the requirements of *Recommendations (11)* and *(12)*, except that an intentional or willful refusal to comply could result in up to $1,000 in damages. The alternatives for Federal Trade Commission or State regulatory enforcement when there are repeated violations have been discussed above in conjunction with *Recommendation (10)* on access and apply equally here.

ADVERSE UNDERWRITING DECISIONS

An underwriting decision cannot be fair if it is made on the basis of inaccurate information. Both the individual and the insurance institution have a common objective in this regard. Currently, however, an insurer that makes an adverse underwriting decision about an individual is not required, in most cases, to give any clues as to the information that supported it. If the information came from an investigative-reporting agency or a credit bureau, the insurer must identify the agency or bureau and furnish its address but nothing more. Furthermore, as explained earlier, being able to find out from a support organization the "nature and substance" of information it reported to the insurer is no guarantee that the individual will be able to relate what he learns to the decision that was made on the basis of it. The "nature and substance" of an investigative report may sound harmless to a rejected applicant. How is he to know that something in it, if explained in greater detail, might have caused the adverse decision to come out the other way? Or if something in the report is inaccurate, how is he to know whether it was that particular item that caused the adverse decision and thus the one that needs to be followed up?

Because the investigative-reporting agency's sources (including institutional sources) need not be disclosed to the individual, he also has no way of knowing to which sources he should go to get an inaccuracy corrected in a manner which will persuade the insurance institution that information the support organization reported was erroneous. Nor is the insurer under any obligation to disclose its own independent sources, such as the Medical Information Bureau, or the Impairment Bureau, or a source identified *through* the Medical Information Bureau. Finally, if the individual is venturesome enough to try to get inaccurate information corrected, he is expected to make the decision to do so without necessarily knowing what his rights are under the Fair Credit Reporting Act.

Thus, in order to bring insurance practices in line with current or recommended practice in other areas the Commission has examined, the Commission recommends:

Recommendation (13):

That the Federal Fair Credit Reporting Act be amended to provide that an insurance institution must:

(a)   disclose in writing to an individual who is the subject of an adverse underwriting decision:
  (i)   the specific reason(s) for the adverse decision;
  (ii)   the specific item(s) of information that support(s) the reason(s) given pursuant to (a)(i), except that medical-record information may be disclosed either directly or through a licensed medical professional designated by the individual, whichever the insurance institution prefers;
  (iii) the name(s) and address(es) of the institutional source(s) of the item(s) given pursuant to (a)(ii); and
  (iv)   the individual's right to see and copy, upon request, all recorded information concerning the individual used to make the adverse decision, to the extent recorded information exists;

(b)   permit the individual to see and copy, upon request, all recorded information pertaining to him used to make the adverse decision, to the extent recorded information exists, except that (i) such information need not contain the name or other identifying particulars of any source (other than an institutional source) who has provided such information on the condition that his or her identity not be revealed, and (ii) an individual may be permitted to see and copy medical-record information either directly or through a licensed medical professional designated by the individual, whichever the insurance institution prefers. The insurance institution should be allowed to charge a reasonable copying fee for any copies provided to the individual;

(c)   inform the individual of:
  (i)   the procedures whereby he can correct, amend, delete, or file a statement of dispute with respect to any information disclosed pursuant to (a) and (b); and
  (ii)   the individual's rights provided by the Fair Credit Reporting Act, when the decision is based in whole or in part on information obtained from a consumer-reporting agency (as defined by the Fair Credit Reporting Act);

(d)   establish reasonable procedures to assure the implementation of the above.

Recommendation (13) is similar to the recommendation regarding adverse credit decisions in Chapter 2. It is, however, even more of a departure from current practice in that insurers generally have not had to disclose the specific reasons for their adverse underwriting decisions. On the other hand, *Recommendation (13)* differs from its counterpart in the credit area in that, like *Recommendation (10)*, above, it takes account of the fact that not all sources of information used to make an insurance decision about an individual are institutional ones and further, that some adverse insurance decisions may be made on the basis of medical-record information. It is linked to *Recommendations (11)* and *(12)* through *subsection (c)*, which requires that the insurer apprise the individual of its own correction, amendment, deletion, and dispute procedures, and to *Recommendation (4)* in requiring that the insurer establish reasonable implementation procedures.

It should be noted that *Recommendation (13)* applies only to adverse underwriting decisions, which the Commission has defined as follows:

- With respect to life and health insurance, a denial of requested insurance coverage (except claims) in whole or in part or an offer to insure at other than standard rates; and with respect to all other kinds of insurance, a denial of requested insurance coverage (except claims) in whole or in part, or a rating which is based on information which differs from that which the individual furnished; or
- a refusal to renew insurance coverage in whole or in part; or
- a cancellation of any insurance coverage in whole or in part.

Since *Recommendation (13)* would be implemented by amending the Fair Credit Reporting Act, an individual would be able to obtain a court order from a Federal court or other court of competent jurisdiction to force an insurance institution to perform any one of the duties called for if he could prove that the insurance institution had failed to do so. This would include incomplete disclosure of the specific reasons and underlying information. The court would have the power to order the insurance institution to comply and to award attorney's fees to any plaintiff who substantially prevailed. Such an action would be the individual's sole remedy, except that the court should also have the power to award up to $1,000 to the plaintiff if it is shown that the institution intentionally or willfully denied the individual any of the rights *Recommendation (13)* would give him.

As noted in the discussion of *Recommendation (10)*, the Commission believes that a limitation of liability similar to that now provided by the Fair Credit Reporting Act should be extended to insurance institutions as well as insurance-support organizations. The implementation of *Recommendation (10)* would create no liability on the part of an insurance institution or support organization, including liability for negligence, defamation or invasion of privacy, unless the institution or support organization acted with malice or willful intent to harm the individual.

Like *Recommendations (10), (11)*, and *(12), Recommendation (13)* depends primarily for its enforcement upon the individual's assertion of his rights. As noted above, however, the Commission proposes two alternate means of government enforcement where an insurance institution repeatedly or systematically denies the rights granted by *Recommendations (10), (11), (12)*, and *(13)*. One alternative is that the Federal Trade Commission would have the authority to bring enforcement proceedings, using its normal enforcement mechanisms. The other would be for the States to be encouraged to enact amendments to the unfair trade practices sections of their insurance laws which would give State Insurance Commissioners the authority to enforce the requirements of these four recommendations. Should a State enact such legislation, the Federal Trade Commission would then be precluded from exercising its enforcement proceedings with respect to systematic failures in that particular State.

DECISIONS BASED ON PREVIOUS ADVERSE DECISIONS

In the following chapter, on record keeping in the employer-employee relationship, there are several examples of the harm that can result when actions taken against an individual by one record-keeping organization become the basis for decision making by another. The problem, however, is a general one and stems from the tendency of record-keeping organizations to make unwarranted assumptions about the validity and currency of information generated by other record-keeping organizations. Questions are seldom asked about how recorded information came to be and the caveats knowledge of those processes should evoke.

As explained earlier, insurers often ask an applicant whether any other insurer has ever declined him, refused to renew a policy, or insured him at other than standard rates. While life insurers seem to use this information as a guide to finding out more about an applicant, automobile insurers often decline applicants solely on the basis of an affirmative response to the question. In the Commission's opinion, this is grossly unfair. The bare fact of an adverse underwriting decision is an incomplete item of information; the reason for the decision is the important item and it is missing. Indeed, using the mere fact of a previous adverse decision as the basis for rejecting an insurance applicant is one of the clearest examples the Commission found of information itself being the cause of unfairness in a decision made on the basis of it. Thus, the Commission recommends:

Recommendation (14):

That no insurance institution or insurance-support organization:

(a)   make inquiry as to:

   (i)   any previous adverse underwriting decision on an individual, or

   (ii)   whether an individual has obtained insurance through the substandard (residual) insurance market,

unless the inquiry requests the reasons for such treatment; *or*

(b)   make any adverse underwriting decision based, in whole or in part, on the mere fact of:

   (i)   a previous adverse underwriting decision, or

   (ii)   an individual having obtained insurance through the substandard (residual) market.

An insurance institution may, however, base an adverse

underwriting decision on further information obtained from the source, including other insurance institutions.

It will be remembered that in the explanation of *Recommendation (1)*, it was noted that when the fairness, as opposed to the propriety, of an item of information is at issue, one might both prohibit its use and require its collection. In *Recommendation (14)*, however, the Commission proposes that an insurer both cease to inquire and cease to use, the reason being that compliance will be principally monitored through the individual's exercise of his rights pursuant to *Recommendation (13)* on adverse underwriting decisions. State Insurance Commissioners should use their unfair trade practices authority, and their authority to review certain application forms to assure that adverse insurance decisions are no longer based on the mere fact of a previous adverse decision. They should also require that insurers collect information about prior declinations only when the reasons for the declination are also collected. The Commission hopes, however, that once the previous adverse decision problem is well enough and widely enough understood, voluntary measures, facilitated by exercise of the statutory rights proposed in *Recommendation (13)*, will assure universal compliance.

UNDERWRITING DECISIONS BASED ON INFORMATION FROM INDUSTRY DATA EXCHANGES

The Commission found that in life and health underwriting, there is less than perfect adherence to the industry's own rules regarding the use of information obtained from the Medical Information Bureau. According to MIB rules, no adverse underwriting decision is ever supposed to be made solely on the basis of an MIB "flag," but the record clearly indicates that efforts to achieve this have been weak and superficial.[98]

The problem here, of course, is the same one *Recommendation (9)* addresses, except for the fact that in this case the items of information in question are being obtained from an industry data exchange rather than from the individual himself, thereby multiplying by two the points at which errors could be made. Either the insurer that reports an item to the exchange, or the exchange in reporting it to still another company, could report it incorrectly. Because the item is only a flag, moreover, it is by its very nature without context; that is, it is an incomplete item of information. Accordingly, the Commission recommends:

Recommendation (15):

That no insurance institution base an adverse underwriting decision, in whole or in part, on information about an individual it obtains from an insurance-support organization whose primary source of information is insurance institutions or insurance-support organizations; however, the insurance institution may base an adverse underwriting

---

[98] Testimony of MIB, Insurance Records Hearings, May 19, 1976, pp. 244-54; 274-77.

decision on further information obtained from the original source, including another insurance institution.

This recommendation would apply to the Medical Information Bureau and the Impairment Bureau, but not to the loss indexes, since they do not supply information for use in underwriting decisions. In addition, the recommendation refers only to information about a particular individual and, therefore, would not govern the use of information obtained, for example, from a rating organization.

As with *Recommendation (14)*, voluntary compliance with this recommendation will be facilitated by exercise of the statutory rights proposed in *Recommendation (13)*, and also by any action taken by State Insurance Commissioners pursuant to their unfair trade practices authority referred to in the discussion of *Recommendation (14)*.

FAIRNESS IN DISCLOSURE

DISCLOSURES TO INDUSTRY DATA EXCHANGES

Life insurance companies have had a longstanding practice of reporting to the Medical Information Bureau or the Impairment Bureau information about an individual's health, which they have obtained from sources other than a licensed medical-care provider, or the individual to whom the information pertains. The same has been true of property and liability reporting on claimants to the loss indexes. In the case of the MIB and the Impairment Bureau, agents' reports and reports compiled by inspection bureaus, in part on the basis of interviews with neighbors and associates, have been a major source of such information. In the Medical Information Bureau this material was coded as "medical information" that because of source does not meet the requirements of the Fair Credit Reporting Act, and "medical information received from a consumer report, not confirmed by the proposed insured or a medical facility."[99]

As discussed earlier, this is an area in which the MIB Executive Committee took action following the Commission's hearings on the record-keeping practices of insurance institutions and insurance-support organizations. The MIB's action, however, does not affect the existing flow of "health status information" into the Impairment Bureau and the loss indexes. Moreover, as indicated in its discussion of *Recommendation (11)*, the Commission believes that the responsibility for the content of records maintained by industry data exchanges is properly placed on the reporting insurance institutions, since it is they who control the record-keeping policies of the data exchanges.

The chief problem with health status information is its unreliability. It is bad enough to be labeled as a pariah by those society considers qualified to do so, but it violates all canons of fairness to allow such labels to be attached by anyone, regardless of his qualifications. Accordingly, the Commission recommends:

[99] Submission of MIB, "Offical Code List of Impairments - 1962," Insurance Records Hearings, May 19, 1976, p. 1.

Recommendation (16):

That Federal law be enacted to provide that no insurance institution or insurance-support organization may disclose to another insurance institution or insurance-support organization information pertaining to an individual's medical history, diagnosis, condition, treatment, or evaluation, even with the explicit authorization of the individual, unless the information was obtained directly from a medical-care provider, the individual himself, his parent, spouse, or guardian.

This recommendation should be implemented in connection with *Recommendation (17)* concerning the confidential relationship between an individual and an insurance institution or support organization. It would become part of the duty of confidentiality owed to an individual by an insurer or support organization. Although support organizations like the loss indexes have little practical control over the source of medical information sent to them, it is expected that insurance institutions, in order to protect their own interests in not disclosing medical information in violation of subsection (b)(iv) of *Recommendation (17)*, will establish procedures to assure that only medical information obtained from a qualified source is communicated to a support organization or to another insurance institution.

Expectation of Confidentiality

The Commission's third policy objective is to establish and define the nature of the confidential relationship between an individual and the record-keeping institutions with which he can be said to have a relationship. A confidential relationship is one in which there is both an explicit limitation on the extent to which information generated by the relationship can be disclosed to others, and a prior mutual understanding by the parties involved as to what that limitation shall be.

Certain relationships (e.g., doctor-patient, attorney-client) have traditionally carried with them legally enforceable expectations of confidentiality, at least in particular types of circumstances.[100] These protections, moreover, have sprung from the breadth of inquiry and observation on which the success of the relationship depends. If one type of relationship requires more divulgence and probing than another, the latter, so the argument goes, should not be permitted to feed off the former at will. To allow that to happen is not only fundamentally unfair; it is also a violation of the ethics of the first relationship.

One sees this problem vividly today in the record-keeping dimensions of the doctor-patient relationship. It is present, however, in every area of personal-data record keeping where an individual must submit to the collection and recording of intimate details about himself in order to obtain some benefit or service. Furthermore, as the Commission argues in Chapter 9, if society is to solve the problems inherent in the compulsory disclosure of

---

[100] For a discussion of the doctor-patient testimonial privilege to most medical record-keeping situations, see Chapter 7.

The Insurance Relationship   215

information about an individual from one record-keeping relationship to another, it must limit the circumstances in which voluntary disclosures are permitted at the discretion of the record keeper. Otherwise, there is no point in restricting the circumstances under which a government agency, for example, may compel a record keeper to produce information it holds in its records on an individual. To make such restrictions sensible, as well as to assure the individual a role in determining when and to what extent they will be suspended, one must first impose a duty of confidentiality on the holder of the records.

With these considerations in mind, the Commission has concluded that each insurance institution and insurance-support organization should owe a duty of confidentiality to the individual on whom it maintains records. The amount, diversity, and character of the information gathered to establish and facilitate the insurance relationship is such as to warrant establishing such a duty of confidentiality. The insurance relationship, moreover, is extraordinarily important to society. Like the credit, depository, and medical-care relationships considered in other chapters of this report, it is one that is increasingly difficult for an individual to avoid. Yet the relationship cannot be maintained successfully if it is perceived as being inherently unfair or as disregarding the legitimate interests of the individuals who enter into it.

Currently, insurance institutions and their support organizations .voluntarily assume some ethical responsibility for the confidentiality of the information they maintain on individuals. However, they do not uniformly respect the individual's legitimate desire to limit the disclosures they make about him, nor are they able to defend the integrity of their record-keeping relationships with individuals against certain demands made on them by extraneous parties. Thus, to create and define obligations with respect to the uses and disclosures that may be made of records about individuals, legitimate patterns of information-sharing within the industry and threshold conditions for the disclosure of such records to outsiders must be established.

Accordingly, the Commission recommends:

Recommendation (17):

That Federal law be enacted to provide that each insurance institution and insurance-support organization be considered to owe a duty of confidentiality to any individual about whom it collects or receives information in connection with an insurance transaction, and that therefore, no insurance institution or support organization should disclose, or be required to disclose, in individually identifiable form, any information about any such individual without the individual's explicit authorization, unless the disclosure would be:

(a)   to a physician for the purpose of informing the individual of a medical problem of which the individual may not be aware;

(b)   from an insurance institution to a reinsurer or co-insurer, or to an agent or contractor of the insurance institution, including a

sales person, independent claims adjuster, or insurance investigator, or to an insurance-support organization whose sole source of information is insurance institutions, or to any other party-in-interest to the insurance transaction, provided:

(i)   that only such information is disclosed as is necessary for such reinsurer, co-insurer, agent, contractor, insurance-support organization, or other party-in-interest to perform its function with regard to the individual or the insurance transaction;

(ii)   that such reinsurer, co-insurer, agent, contractor, insurance-support organization or other party-in-interest is prohibited from redisclosing the information without the authorization of the individual except, in the case of insurance institutions and insurance-support organizations, as otherwise provided in this recommendation; and

(iii)   that the individual, if other than a third-party claimant, is notified at least initially concurrent with the application that such disclosure may be made and can find out if in fact it has been made; and

(iv)   that in no instance shall information pertaining to an individual's medical history, diagnosis, condition, treatment, or evaluation be disclosed, even with the explicit authorization of the individual, unless the information was obtained directly from a medical-care provider, the individual himself, or his parent, spouse, or guardian;

(c)   from an insurance-support organization whose sole source of information is insurance institutions or self-insurers to an insurance institution or self-insurer, provided:

(i)   that the sole function of the insurance-support organization is the detection or prevention of insurance fraud in connection with claim settlements;

(ii)   that, if disclosed to a self-insurer, the self-insurer assumes the same duty of confidentiality with regard to that information which is required of insurance institutions and insurance-support organizations; and

(iii)   that any insurance institution or self-insurer that receives information from any such insurance-support organization is prohibited from using such information for other than claim purposes;

(d)   to the insurance regulator of a State or its agent or contractor, for an insurance regulatory purpose statutorily authorized by the State;

(e)   to a law enforcement authority:

(i)   to protect the legal interest of the insurer, reinsurer, co-insurer, agent, contractor, or other party-in-interest to prevent and to prosecute the perpetration of fraud upon them; or

(ii)   when the insurance institution or insurance-support

> **organization has a reasonable belief of illegal activities on the part of the individual;**
>
> **(f)   pursuant to a Federal, State, or local compulsory reporting statute or regulation;**
>
> **(g)   in response to a lawfully issued administrative summons or judicial order, including a search warrant or subpoena.**

In contrast to the corresponding recommendations with respect to credit grantors and depository institutions, wherein interpretative responsibilities would be assigned to existing regulatory authorities, the Commission recommends that the responsibility for enforcing the confidentiality duties of insurance institutions and support organizations be left exclusively to the aggrieved individual. The information flows in and out of the insurance industry, while extensive in some areas, appear less dynamic and thus less prone to change than those in the credit area, for example. As a result, there is less need for flexibility in establishing their legitimacy; that is, there is no need for an interpretative rule-making function.

The provisions of the recommended statute, however, should be explicitly drawn to allow an individual to sue an insurance institution or support organization and to obtain actual damages for negligent disclosures that violate the duty of confidentiality, even if there is no showing of an intentional or willful violation. Where an intentional or willful violation of the duty of confidentiality is established, the individual should, in addition to actual damages and court costs, including reasonable attorney's fees, be entitled to general damages of a minimum of $1,000 and a maximum of $10,000. A defense available to the defendant charged with *negligent* disclosure would be that it had established reasonable procedures and exercised reasonable care to implement and enforce those procedures in attempting to protect the interests of the individual. Where it could not meet such a test, the insurance institution or support organization would then be subject to actual damages and court costs, including legal fees, for any violations.

The statute should also make clear that *subsection (b)(iii)* would not apply to any record about an individual compiled in reasonable anticipation of a civil or criminal action, or for use in settling a claim while the claim remains unsettled. After the claim is settled, moreover, *subsection (b)(iii)* would not apply to any record compiled in relation to a claimant who is not an insured or policyowner (i.e., a third-party claimant), except as to any portion of such record that is disseminated or used for a purpose unrelated to processing the claim.

The first premise of the proposed statutory duty is that no record should be disclosed by an insurance institution or support organization without the authorization of the individual to whom it pertains. The Commission would expect, moreover, that the authorization statement used would be specific as to the information proposed to be furnished, to whom, and for what purpose. Nonetheless, as in other areas, the Commission has recognized the need to allow certain types of disclosures to occur without the individual's authorization. These exceptions can be divided into three categories:

- disclosures to protect the individual;
- disclosures the insurance institution or support organization must make in order to perform duties inherent in the insurance relationship or to protect itself from failure by the individual to meet the terms of the relationship; and
- disclosures to governmental authorities.

Subsection (a) of the recommendation falls into the first category. It permits disclosure without authorization to a physician for the purpose of informing the individual of a medical problem about which he may be unaware, and which an insurance institution or support organization may be reluctant to disclose to him directly. Making an exception for such situations seems justified by the benefit to the individual and by the minimal risk to personal privacy it involves, since the physician also stands in a confidential relationship to the individual.

The second category of exceptions concerns disclosures consistent with the insurer's rights and duties in its relationship with the insurance consumer. The duty of confidentiality, primarily for the benefit of the latter, should not unfairly burden the insurer's ability to fulfill its part of the bargain or to protect its own interests. By the mere fact of applying for insurance, maintaining a policy, or presenting a claim, the individual authorizes the insurer to perform certain functions. Thus, under *subsection (b)* of the Commission's recommendation, no authorization is required for disclosures to reinsurers, co-insurers, agents, contractors, insurance-support organizations, or any other party-in-interest, when disclosure is necessary for that person to perform a function concerned with the insurer's relationship with the insured. The insured should nonetheless be notified (see *Recommendation (5)*) that such disclosures may be made and should be able to find out whether or not they have, in fact, been made (see *Recommendation (10)*).

In many cases, individually identifiable information is provided by an insurer to one or more other insurers who act as reinsurers of the first. The individual whose insurance policy is reinsured has no legal relationship with the reinsurer. The only party who has a contractual relationship with the insured is the insurer from whom the individual purchased the policy. Reinsurance is common within the insurance industry, and sometimes involves the transfer of individually identifiable information. Currently, however, the individual has no knowledge of this type of disclosure.

It would serve no purpose to require an applicant to expressly authorize the dissemination of information about him to a reinsurer. The individual who refused to authorize the disclosure would simply be denied the insurance. The reinsurer, moreover, would have the same duty of confidentiality as the original insurer and be subject to the same requirements for holding information in confidence.

The reinsurance situation is similar to other party-in-interest situations in which the Commission believes individual authorization should not be required for information disclosure. For example, the amount of one insurer's claim payment may be related to another's payment. In this case, where a pro-rata liability or other coordination of benefits clause exists, each insurer must be considered a co-insurer and should, therefore, be allowed to share necessary information, subject to the same restrictions as to notice and confidentiality outlined above. Other exceptions based on the party-in-interest concept would include cases involving subrogation,[101] as well as cases involving insurers who were potentially being defrauded by the same person.

All parties-in-interest referred to in *subsection (b)* would either already be bound by or would assume the same duty of confidentiality as the provider of the information—that is, they would not be permitted to redisclose the information without the individual's authorization, unless, in the case of any party-in-interest that is an insurance institution or insurance-support organization, the disclosure would be otherwise authorized under this recommendation. Only information necessary for the recipient to perform its function should be disclosed. Thus, for example, an independent claims adjuster should only be given the information needed to properly settle a claim. As already noted, *subsection (b)(iii)*, which requires notice and a way for an individual to find out whether a particular disclosure had been made, would not apply to cases expected to involve litigation or to claims situations. *Subsection (b)(iv)* incorporates *Recommendation (16)* as the Commission urged that it should, above.

One special concern of insurance institutions and insurance-support organizations is to detect and deter fraud. Privacy requirements should not be used to restrict an insurer's capacity to protect its interests, especially where fraud may be involved. Thus, no authorization is required under *subsection (b)* for the disclosure of information to the Insurance Crime Prevention Institute or other support organizations that operate as surrogates of the insurer in seeking to prevent fraud. Authorization is also not needed for disclosure to one of the loss indexes or other insurers when the purpose is to deter and detect insurance fraud. Conversely, *subsection (c)* could allow the loss indexes to continue to disseminate information to their subscribers without individual authorization. To require otherwise would be tantamount to destroying the loss indexes, since those intent on fraud would naturally refuse to agree to the disclosure.

Currently, "self-insurers" may subscribe to the loss indexes. These subscribers are neither insurance institutions nor insurance-support organizations within the Commission's or insurance regulatory officials' definitions. They are companies and governments that have chosen to retain some or all of their exposure to loss rather than to transfer it to an insurer. Since they are not insurance institutions or insurance-support organizations, they are not subject to the Commission's recommendations on such organizations. Nevertheless, the information from the loss indexes may continue to flow to self-insurers and should, therefore, be subject to a duty of confidentiality as provided in *subsection (c)(ii)*.

The third category of exceptions concerns disclosures to government. The Commission is aware that, for public policy reasons, information must be disclosed by insurance industry parties to law enforcement officials under

---

[101] Subrogation is the substitution of one party in place of another with reference to a lawful claim or right.

certain circumstances. Such disclosures would be permitted, provided they comply with the Commission's recommendations regarding government access to private-sector records, explained in Chapter 9.

One voluntary disclosure that is permitted without an authorization is to law enforcement officials when an insurance institution or insurance-support organization reasonably concludes, from information generated in its relationship with him, that an individual has violated the law or is suspected of fraud in connection with the insurance coverage. Certainly in this instance, the insurer should not be required to get the authorization of the individual.

Furthermore, insurance institutions are required to release information to State insurance departments which regulate the insurance industry. Insurance institutions and insurance-support organizations must also respond to Federal, State, and local compulsory reporting statutes and regulations. They have no choice but to disclose information when required by government under these circumstances. A requirement of authorization by the individual would be meaningless. The Commission recognizes, however, that insurance institutions, like other record keepers, should have some obligation to inform an individual that information will be routinely reported to government. Finally, insurance institutions and support organizations must respond to a lawfully issued administrative summons or judicial order, such as a subpoena or search warrant. While they have no choice but to comply with such legal process, and while the primary obligation to assure protection of an individual's rights should rest with government, as explored in Chapter 9, the insurance record keeper has certain responsibilities—primarily to assure the facial validity of the particular form of compulsory process served on it, and to limit its compliance to the specific terms of the order. If, for example, a subpoena requires disclosure of information on a certain date, an insurance institution or support organization should not disclose until that date. Restricted response of this type will permit the individual whose records were sought to exercise those rights the Commission recommends be granted in the context of government access.

*   *   *   *   *   *   *

Insurance protection is vital to most Americans. Much personal information is provided or developed through the process of providing needed insurance protection, properly pricing it, and in servicing insurance contracts, including the investigation and settlement of claims. The Commission believes that the recommendations in this chapter respect this need for information and strengthen the relationship between insured and insurer while promoting its three public-policy objectives.

GLOSSARY OF TERMS

Individual:

any natural person who is a past, present, or proposed named or principal insured (including any principal insured under a family or group policy or similar arrangement of coverage for a person in a group), policyowner, or past or present claimant.

Insurance Institution:

an insurance company (including so-called service plans like Blue Cross and Blue Shield and any other similar service plan), regardless of type of insurance written or organizational form, including insurance company regional, branch, sales, or service offices (or divisions or insurance affiliates), or insurance company solicitors; or agents and brokers.

Insurance-Support Organizations:

an organization which regularly engages in whole or in part in the practice of assembling or evaluating information on individuals for the purpose of providing such information or evaluation to insurance institutions for insurance purposes.

Insurance Transaction:

whenever a decision (be it adverse or otherwise) is rendered regarding an individual's eligibility for an insurance benefit or service.

Adverse Underwriting Decision:

(1) with respect to life and health insurance, a denial of requested insurance coverage (except claims) in whole or in part, or an offer to insure at other than standard rates; and with respect to all other kinds of insurance, a denial of requested coverage (except claims) in whole or in part, or a rating which is based on information which differs from that which the individual furnished;

(2) a refusal to renew insurance coverage in whole or in part; or

(3) a cancellation of any insurance coverage in whole or in part.

Institutional Source:

an institutional source is any person who provides information as part of his employment or any other connection with an insurance institution.

Medical-Record Information:

information relating to an individual's medical history, diagnosis, condition, treatment, or evaluation obtained from a medical-care provider, from the individual himself, or from his spouse, parent, or guardian for the purpose of making a non-medical decision (e.g., an underwriting decision) about the individual.

Medical-Care Provider:

a medical professional or medical-care institution.

Medical Professional:

any person licensed or certified to provide medical services to individuals, including but not limited to, a physician, dentist, nurse, optometrist, physical or occupational therapist, psychiatric social worker, clinical dietitian, or clinical psychologist.

Medical-Care Institution:

any facility or institution that is licensed to provide medical-care services to individuals, including, but not limited to, hospitals, skilled nursing facilities, home-health agencies, clinics, rehabilitation agencies, and public-health agencies or health-maintenance organizations (HMO's).

Appendix **B**

Excerpts from H.R. 10076 Relevant to the Insurance Industry

95TH CONGRESS
1ST SESSION

H. R. 10076

IN THE HOUSE OF REPRESENTATIVES

NOVEMBER 11, 1977

Mr. PREYER (for himself, Mr. KOCH, and Mr. GOLDWATER) introduced the following bill; which was referred jointly to the Committees on Agriculture, Banking, Finance and Urban Affairs, Education and Labor, Government Operations, Interstate and Foreign Commerce, the Judiciary, and Ways and Means

Note: *Page numbers for this bill are reprinted as they occur in the original text.*

A BILL

To protect the privacy of individuals from governmental and nongovernmental intrusion, and for other purposes.

1   *Be it enacted by the Senate and House of Representa-*

2   *tives of the United States of America in Congress assembled.*

TABLE OF CONTENTS

VI—O

2

TABLE OF CONTENTS—Continued

TITLE III—PERSONAL RECORDS

3

TABLE OF CONTENTS—Continued

TITLE VIII—EDUCATIONAL PRIVACY RIGHTS

1   SHORT TITLE

2   SECTION 1. This Act may be cited as the "Omnibus

3   Right to Privacy Act of 1977".

4 FINDINGS AND PURPOSES

5 SEC. 2. (a) The Congress finds that—

6 (1) the right to privacy is a personal and funda-
7 mental right protected by the Constitution of the United
8 States;

9 (2) the free flow of information, while essential
10 to a democratic society, must be balanced by protection
11 of the right to personal privacy;

12 (3) there is an accelerating trend toward the ac-
13 cumulation in records of more and more personal details
14 about an individual;

15 (4) the privacy of an individual is directly affected
16 by the collection, maintenance, use, and dissemination
17 of personal information by Federal, State, and local agen-
18 cies, and by private sector organizations;

19 (5) more and more records about an individual are
20 collected, maintained, used, and disseminated by agen-
21 cies and organizations that have no direct relationship
22 with the individual;

4

1 (6) an individual must be able to exercise more
2 direct control over personal information;

3 (7) the opportunities for an individual to secure

4   employment, insurance, credit, medical care, education,

5   right to due process, and other important societal benefits

6   are endangered by the misuse of information; and

7   (8) neither law nor technology now gives an

8   individual the tools he needs to protect his legitimate in-

9   terests in records kept about him by Federal, State, and

10   local agencies and by private sector organizations.

11   (b) The purpose of this Act is to—

12   (1) create a proper balance between what an in-

13   dividual is expected to reveal to recordkeepers and what

14   he seeks in return;

15   (2) open up recordkeeping operations in ways that

16   will minimize the extent to which recorded information

17   about an individual is itself a source of unfairness in any

18   decision about him made on the basis of it; and

19   (3) to create and define obligations with respect to

20   the uses and disclosures that will be made of recorded

21   information about an individual.

22 # TITLE I—FEDERAL INFORMATION PRACTICES

23 # BOARD

24 ### SHORT TITLE

25   SEC. 101. This title may be cited as the "Federal In-

26   formation and Privacy Board Act of 1977".

120

INSURANCE INSTITUTIONS AND PRIVACY

Sec. 605. The Fair Credit Reporting Act is further amended by inserting after chapter 3 thereof (as added by section 604 of this Act) the following new chapter:

"Chapter 5

"Sec. 671. (a) (1) Except as provided by subsections (b) and (c), each insurance institution and insurance support organization, upon request by an individual, shall—

"(A) inform the individual, after verifying his identity, whether it has any recorded information pertaining to him; and

"(B) permit the individual to see and copy any such recorded information, either in person or by mail, and

121

apprise the individual of the nature and substance of any such recorded information by telephone;

"(2) The individual may use the method of disclosure that he prefers. The insurance institution or insurance-support organization may charge a reasonable fee for any copies provided to the individual. Any such recorded information should be made available to the individual but need not contain the name or other identifying particulars of any source of information (other than an institutional source)

10 in the record who has provided such information on the con-
11 dition that his or her identity not be revealed and need
12 not disclose a confidential numerical code.

13 "(b) Notwithstanding subsection (a), an individual
14 who is the subject of medical-record information maintained
15 by an insurance institution or an insurance-support organiza-
16 tion has a right of access to that information, including a right
17 to see and copy it, either directly or through a licensed medi-
18 cal care professional designated by the individual, whichever
19 the insurance institution or support organization prefers.

20 "(c) The disclosure requirements of subsection (a)
21 and subsection (b) are not applicable with respect to any
22 record about an individual compiled in reasonable anticipa-
23 tion of a civil or criminal action, or for use in settling a claim
24 while the claim remains unsettled; or after the claim is set-

122

1 tled, to any record compiled in relation to a claimant who is
2 not an insured or policy owner except as to any portion of
3 such a record which is disseminated or used for a purpose
4 unrelated to processing the claim after such time as a
5 proceeding may no longer be contemplated.

6 "SEC. 672. (a) Except as provided by subsection (b),
7 each insurance institution and insurance support organiza-
8 tion shall permit an individual to request correction, amend-

9 ment, or deletion of a record pertaining to him and within

10 a reasonable period of time—

11   "(1) (A) (i) correct or amend (including supple-

12   ment) any portion thereof which the individual reason-

13   ably believes is not accurate, timely, or complete; or

14   "(ii) delete any portion thereof which is not within

15   the scope of information which the individual was origi-

16   nally told would be collected about him; and

17   "(B) furnish notification of the correction amend-

18   ment or deletion to any person or organization specifi-

19   cally designated by the individual which has within two

20   years prior thereto received any such information; and,

21   automatically to any insurance support organization

22   whose primary source of information on individuals is

23   insurance institutions when the support organization has

24   systematically received any such information from the

25   insurance institution within the preceding seven years,

123

1   unless the support organization no longer maintains the

2   information, in which case, notification is not required;

3   and automatically to any insurance support organization

4   that furnished the information corrected or amended; or

5   "(2) inform the individual of its refusal to correct or

6 amend the record in accordance with his request and of
7 the reason for the refusal and—

8   " (A) permit an individual who disagrees with
9   the refusal to corrèct or amend the record to have
10 placed on or with the record a concise statement
11 setting forth the reasons for his disagreement;

12   " (B) in any subsequent disclosure outside the
13 institution containing information about which the
14 individual has filed a statement of dispute, clearly
15 note any portion of the record which is disputed and
16 provide a copy of the statement along with the in-
17 formation being disclosed;

18   " (C) furnish notification of the statement to any
19 person or organization specifically designated by the
20 individual which has within two years prior thereto
21 received any such information; and, automatically
22 to an insurance support organization whose primary
23 source of information on individuals is insurance in-
24 stitutions when the support organization has syste-
25 matically received any such information from the in-

124

1 surance institution within the preceding seven years,
2 unless the support organization no longer maintains

3   the information, in which case, notification is not re-

4   quired; and automatically to any insurance support

5   organization that furnished the information corrected

6   or amended; and

7   "(D) limit its reinvestigation of disputed infor-

8   mation to those record items in dispute.

9 "(b) The disclosure requirements of subsection (a) are

10 not applicable with respect to any record about an individual

11 compiled in reasonable anticipation of a civil or criminal ac-

12 tion, or for use in settling a claim while the claim remains un-

13 settled; or after the claim is settled, to any record compiled in

14 relation to a claimant who is not an insured or policyowner

15 except as to any portion of such a record which is dissemi-

16 nated or use for a purpose unrelated to processing the claim

17 after such time as a proceeding may no longer be

18 contemplated.

19 "SEC. 673. Except as provided by section 672 (b) and

20 notwithstanding section 672 (a), if an individual who is the

21 subject of medical record information maintained by an insur-

22 ance institution or insurance support organization requests

23 correction or amendment of such information, the insurance

24 institution or insurance support organization shall—

25   "(1) disclose to the individual or to a medical care

125

1   professional designated by him the identity of the

2   medical care provider who was the source of the medical

3   record information, and

4   " (2) if the medical care provider who is the source

5   of the information agrees that it is inaccurate or in-

6   complete, the insurance institution or insurance support

7   organization maintaining it shall make, within a reason-

8   able period of time, the correction amendment re-

9   quested; and

10   " (3) establish a procedure whereby an individual

11   who is the subject of medical record information main-

12   tained by an insurance institution or insurance support

13   organization and who believes that the information is

14   incorrect or incomplete, shall be provided an opportunity

15   to present supplemental information of a limited nature

16   for inclusion on or with the medical record information

17   maintained by the insurance institution or support orga-

18   nization: *Provided,* That the source of the supplemental

19   information is also included.

20   "SEC. 674. Each insurance institution and insurance sup-

21   port organization shall develop and maintain reasonable pro-

22   cedures to assure the accuracy, completeness, and timeli-

23 ness of information it collects, maintains, or discloses about

24 an individual.

25   "SEC. 675. No insurance institution or insurance support

126

14 organization may disclose to another insurance institution or

15 insurance support organization information pertaining to

16 an individual's health, with or without the authorization of

17 the individual, unless that information was obtained from a

18 medical care provider or the individual, his parent, spouse, or

19 guardian.

20   "SEC. 676. No insurance institution or insurance support

21 organization may—

22   "(1) make any inquiry respecting—

23   "(A) any previous adverse underwriting de-

24   cision on an individual, or

25   "(B) whether an individual has obtained insur-

14   ance through the substandard (residual) insurance

15   market,

16   unless the inquiry also requests the reasons for such

17   treatment; or

18   "(2) make any adverse underwriting decision based,

19   in whole or in part, on the mere fact of—

20   "(A) a previous adverse underwriting decision,

21   or

22   " (B) an individual having obtained insurance

23   through the substandard (residual) market.

24   However, the insurance institution may base an adverse

127

1   underwriting decision on further information obtained

2   from the source, including other insurance institutions.

3   "SEC. 677. (a) Except as provided by subsection (d),

4   any insurance institution that obtains an investigative report

5   on an applicant or insured individual shall inform him that

6   he may, upon request, be interviewed in connection with the

7   preparation of the report.

8   " (b) Insurance institutions and agencies preparing in-

9   vestigative reports shall institute reasonable procedures to

10   assure that any interviews referred to in subsection (a) are

11   performed if requested.

12   " (c) When an individual requests an interview under

13   this section and the insurance institution is unable to contact

14   such individual to schedule the interview, then, in lieu of com-

15   plying with subsection (a), the insurance institution shall

16   mail a copy of the investigative report to the individual.

17   " (d) Subsections (a) and (c) are not applicable in the

18   case of any investigative report about an individual made in

19   reasonable anticipation of a civil or criminal action or for use

20   in defense or settlement of a claim.

21   "SEC. 678. (a) Each insurance institution shall disclose,

22   in writing, to any individual who is the subject of an adverse

23   underwriting decision the following:

24   "(1) The specific reasons for the adverse decision.

128

1   "(2) The specific item of information in plain lan-

2   guage that support the reason given.

3   "(3) The name and address of any institutional

4   source of the items given pursuant to paragraph (2).

5   "(4) The individual's right, upon request, to see and

6   copy all information used to arrive at the adverse deci-

7   sion concerning the individual to the extent recorded in-

8   formation exists, but such information need not contain

9   the name or other identifying particulars of any source

10   of information (other than an institutional source) who

11   has provided such information on the condition that his

12   or her identity not be revealed; however, an individual

13   who is the subject of medical record information main-

14   tained by an insurance institution should have a right of

15   access to that record, including a right to see and copy it

16   (for a reasonable charge), either directly or through a

17   licensed medical care professional designated by the indi-

18   vidual, whichever the insurance institution or support

19   organization prefers.

20   " (5) Inform the individual of the procedures

21   whereby he may correct, amend, or file a statement of

22   dispute with respect to any such information.

23   " (6) The individual's rights provided by chapter 1

24   of the Fair Credit Reporting Act when the decision is

129

1   based in whole or in part on information obtained from

2   a consumer reporting agency.

3   " (b) Insurance institutions shall establish and maintain

4   reasonable procedures to assure their compliance with subsec-

5   tion (a).

6   "SEC. 679. No insurance institution may base an ad-

7   verse underwriting decision, in whole or in part, on informa-

8   tion it obtains from an insurance support organization whose

9   primary source of such information is insurance institutions

10   or insurance support organizations; however, the insurance

11   institution may base an adverse underwriting decision on

12   further information obtained from the source, including

13   another insurance institution.

14   "SEC. 680. (a) Except as provided by subsection (b),

15   before collecting information about an insured individual

16   or applicant from another person in connection with an

17   insurance transaction, the insurance institution shall notify,

18   in writing, the insured individual or applicant of:

19   "(1) The types of information expected to be

20   collected about him from third parties and that are not

21   collected in an application, and, as to information re-

22   garding character, general reputation, and mode of

23   living, each area of inquiry.

H.R. 10076——9

130

1   "(2) The techniques that may be used to collect

2   such types of information.

3   "(3) The types of sources that are expected to be

4   asked to provide each type of information about him.

5   "(4) The types of parties to whom and circum-

6   stances under which information about the individual

7   may be disclosed without his authorization, and the

8   types of information which may be disclosed.

9   "(5) The procedures as established by statute by

10   which the individual may gain access to any resulting

11   record about himself.

12   "(6) The procedures whereby the individual may

13   correct, amend, delete or dispute any resulting record

14   about himself.

15   "(7) The fact that information in any report pre-

16   pared by a consumer reporting agency may be retained

17   by that organization and subsequently disclosed by it to

18   others.

19   "(b) Subsection (a) does not apply to information col-

20   lected respecting third- or first-party claims, or to information

21   collected for marketing purposes and obtained prior to an

22   application for insurance by the individual with respect to

23   whom such information relates.

24   "SEC. 681. (a) Each insurance institution shall limit—

25   "(1) its own information collection and disclosure

131

1   practices to those specified in the notice contained in

2   section 680; and

3   "(2) its request to any institution it asks to collect

4   information on its behalf to the information techniques

5   and sources contained in the notice provided in section

6   680.

7   "(b) Subsection (a) does not apply to information col-

8   lected respecting third- or first-party claims, or to information

9   collected for marketing purposes and obtained prior to an

10 application for insurance by the individual with respect to

11 whom such information relates.

12 "SEC. 682. Each insurance institution and insurance sup-

13 port organization exercise reasonable care in the selection and

14 use of insurance support organizations.

15 "SEC. 683. (a) Any insurance institution or insurance

16 support organization clearly specify to an individual those

17 items of inquiry desired for marketing, research, or other
18 purposes not directly related to establishing the individual's
19 eligibility for an insurance benefit or service being sought
20 which may be used for such purpose in individually identifi-
21 able form.

22 "(b) Subsection (a) does not apply with respect to
23 information collected respecting third-party claims.

24 "Sec. 684. No insurance institution or insurance support
25 organization may attempt to obtain information about an

132

1 individual through pretext interviews or other false or mis-
2 leading representations which seek to conceal the actual pur-
3 pose of the inquiry or investigation.

4 "Sec. 685. (a) No insurance institution or insurance
5 support organization shall disclose, or be required to dis-
6 close, in individually identifiable form any information about
7 any individual without the authorization of such individual,
8 unless the disclosure is—

9 "(1) to a physician for the purpose of informing the
10 individual of a medical problem of which the individual
11 may not be aware;

12 "(2) from an insurance institution to an insurer, re-
13 insurer, or coinsurer or to an agent or contractor of the
14 insurance institution or insurance support organization,

15   including a sales person, independent claims adjuster, or

16   insurance investigator, or to any other party-in-interest

17   to the insurance transaction: *Provided*, That—

18   "(A) only such information is disclosed as is

19   necessary for such insurer, reinsurer, coinsurer,

20   agent, contractor, or other party-in-interest to per-

21   form its function with regard to the individual;

22   "(B) such insurer, reinsurer, coinsurer, agent,

23   contractor, or other party-in-interest is prohibited

24   from redisclosing the information without the

25   authorization of the individual; and

133

1   "(C) the individual is notified at least initially

2   concurrent with the application that such disclosure

3   may be made and can find out if in fact it has been

4   made;

5   "(3) to any insurance support organization or in-

6   surance institution: *Provided*, That—

7   "(A) the primary function of the disclosure is

8   the detection or prevention of insurance fraud in

9   connection with loss settlements;

10   "(B) only such information is disclosed to the

11   insurance support organization as is necessary for

12   the support organization to perform its function;

13   however, further provided that in no instance shall

14   health information be disclosed unless it was ob-

15   tained from the individual, his spouse, parent, or

16   guardian or a medical care provider;

17   "(C) if disclosed to a self-insurer, the self-

18   insurer assume the same duty of confidentiality

19   with regard to that information which is required

20   of insurance institutions and insurance support

21   organizations; and

22   "(D) any insurance company which receives

23   information from an index bureau is prohibited

24   from using such information for other than claim

25   purposes;

134

1   "(4) to the insurance regulator of a State or its

2   agent or contractor, for an insurance regulatory purpose

3   statutorily authorized by the State;

4   "(5) to a law enforcement authority to protect the

5   legal interest of the insurer, reinsurer, coinsurer, agent,

6   contractor, or other party-in-interest to prevent and to

7   prosecute the perpetration of fraud upon them;

8   "(6) to a law enforcement authority when the

9   insurance institution or insurance support organization

10 has a reasonable belief of illegal activities on the part of
11 the individual;

12   "(7) pursuant to a Federal, State, or local compul-
13 sory reporting statute or regulation; or

14   "(8) in response to a lawfully issued administrative
15 summons or judicial order, including a search warrant or
16 subpena.

17   "(b) Subsection (a) (2) (C) does not apply to any
18 record about an individual compiled in reasonable anticipa-
19 tion of a civil or criminal action, or for use in settling a claim
20 while the claim remains unsettled, or after the claim is settled,
21 to any record compiled in relation to a claimant who is not an
22 insured or policyowner except as to any portion of such a
23 record which is disseminated or used for a purpose unrelated
24 to processing the claim after such time as a proceeding may
25 no longer be anticipated.

135

1   "SEC. 686. No insurance institution or insurance support
2 organization may ask, require, or otherwise induce an indi-
3 vidual or someone lawfully authorized to act in his behalf
4 when the individual is a minor, legally incompetent, or de-
5 ceased, to sign any statement authorizing any individual or
6 institution to disclose information about him, or about any
7 other individual, unless the statement is—

8   "(1) in clear and concise language;

9   "(2) dated;

10   "(3) specific as to the individuals and institutions

11   whom he is authorizing to disclose information about him

12   who are known at the time the authorization is signed

13   and general as to others whose specific identity is not

14   known at the time the authorization is signed;

15   "(4) specific as to the nature of the information he

16   is authorizing to be disclosed;

17   "(5) specific as to the individuals or institutions to

18   whom he is authorizing information to be disclosed;

19   "(6) specific as to the purpose for which the infor-

20   mation may be used by any of the parties named in para-

21   graph (5) both at the time of the disclosure and at any

22   time in the future; and

23   "(7) specific as to its expiration date which should

24   be for a reasonable period of time not to exceed one year,

136

1   and in the case of life insurance, two years after the date

2   of the policy.

3   "Sec. 687. (a) The Federal Trade Commission shall

4 prescribe such regulations as may be necessary to carry out

5 this chapter.

6   "(b) The Federal Trade Commission shall enforce this

7   chapter. For the purpose of the exercise by the Federal

8   Trade Commission of its functions and powers under the

9   Federal Trade Commission Act, a violation of this chapter

10 shall be deemed a violation of a requirement imposed under

11 that Act. All of the functions and powers of the Federal

12 Trade Commission under the Federal Trade Commission Act

13 are available to the Commission to enforce compliance by

14 any person with this chapter, irrespective of whether that

15 person is engaged in commerce or meets any other juris-

16 dictional tests in the Federal Trade Commission Act.

17   "Sec. 688. For purposes of this chapter, the term—

18   "(1) 'individual' means a natural person;

19   "(2) 'record' means any collection or grouping of

20 information about an individual which is retrieved by

21 the name of the individual or by policy number;

22   "(3) 'insurance institution' means an insurance

23 company (regardless of type of insurance written or or-

24 ganizational form) including insurance company re-

137

1   gional, branch, sales, or service offices (or divisions),

2   or insurance company solicitors; or agents and brokers;

3   "(4) 'insurance support organization' means an or-

4   ganization which regularly engages in whole or in part

5   in the practice of assembling or evaluating information

6   on individuals for the purpose of providing such informa-

7   tion or evaluation to insurance institutions for insurance

8   purposes;

9   "(5) 'adverse underwriting decision' means (A)

10   with respect to life and health insurance, a denial of

11   requested insurance coverage (except claims) in whole

12   or in part, or an offer to insure at other than standard

13   rates; and with respect to all other kinds of insurance,

14   a denial of requested coverage (except claims) in whole

15   or in part, or a rating which is based on information

16   which differs from that which the individual furnished;

17   (B) a refusal to renew insurance coverage in whole or

18   in part; or (C) a cancellation of any insurance cover-

19   age in whole or in part;

20   "(6) 'institutional source' means any person who

21   provides information as part of his employment or any

22   other connection with an insurance institution; and

23   "(7) 'medical record information' refers to infor-

24   mation obtained from a medical care provider (including

138

1   licensed physicians, medical practitioners, hospitals,

2   clinics) related to an individual's medical history, diag-

3   nosis, condition, treatment, or evaluation.".

Appendix C

The Goldwater-Koch Bill as a Solution to Privacy Problems

Harold D. Skipper, Jr.

It appears likely that legislation which significantly affects insurer information practices will be enacted in the near future. Activity at the state level is already gaining momentum.[1] At the federal level, Representatives Barry Goldwater, Jr. (R-California) and Edward Koch (D-New York) introduced a bill which is directed specifically at regulating certain information practices of insurers and the organizations which provide support services to insurers. Members of the seven-member Privacy Protection Study Commission (PPSC), the Congressmen introduced their bill, H.R. 8288, on July 12, 1977, the day the report of the PPSC was released.

The bill uses much of the language of the Privacy Commission's recommendations, and it obviously is an attempt by its sponsors to implement these recommendations. It should not be surprising, therefore, that many persons conclude that H.R. 8288 represents the legislative end-product of and faithfully captures the intent of the PPSC recommendations.

The purpose of this paper is to show where H.R. 8288 does not follow the PPSC implementation strategy and, more importantly, the PPSC intent. No attempt is made to analyze the impact of the Privacy Commission's recommendations. They will serve as a standard against which the provisions of H.R. 8288 are judged.

Reprinted with permission from the *Insurance Counsel Journal*, Copyright © July 1978, pp. 299-308.

Overview

A key philosophical difference exists between the PPSC recommendations and H.R. 8288. The PPSC took the position that a single implementation approach for all seventeen of its insurance recommendations was neither needed nor desirable. They stated a preference that seven of the recommendations (numbers 2, 3, 9, 10, 11, 12, and 13) be implemented by amendment to the Federal Fair Credit Reporting Act (FCRA). Of the remaining ten recommendations, the Commission stated a preference for other federal law in two of its recommendations (numbers 16 and 17), for some form of individual state action on five (numbers 1, 5, 6, 8, and 14), and for no explicit governmental-related implementation (i.e., for voluntary compliance) on the remaining three recommendations (numbers 4, 7, and 15).

H.R. 8288 provides that a new "Chapter Three" should be added to the FCRA. The new chapter would implement sixteen of the Commission's seventeen recommendations; a significant departure from the Privacy Commission's preferred implementation strategy. Philosophically, the authors of H.R. 8288 appear to believe that compliance will not be achieved voluntarily for certain recommendations, and that individual states (primarily state insurance regulators) or federal agencies other than the Federal Trade Commission (FTC) will not enforce privacy protections adequately.

Contrasts Between H.R. 8288 and the Privacy Commission's Recommendations

In the following discussion, each of the Privacy Commission's seventeen insurance recommendations will be paraphrased and the equivalent section of H.R. 8288 contrasted with the recommendation.[2] Along with the notation of key differences, comments will be presented about the implications of these differences.

1. *Governmental Mechanisms.* The Privacy Commission's first recommendation was that governmental mechanisms should exist for individuals to question the propriety of information collected or used by insurance institutions and to bring such objections to the appropriate public policy body. The Commission's preference for implementing this recommendation was to have state insurance commissioners serve as the collectors of such questions and, perhaps, also to have them determine whether or not the collection and use of certain information should be proscribed.[3]

The Goldwater-Koch bill makes no mention of this recommendation. However, this is the only insurance recommendation which is not incorporated in H.R. 8288.

2. *Pretext Interviews.* The Commission recommended that the FCRA be amended to provide that no insurance institution or insurance support

organization (ISO) "may attempt to obtain information about an individual through pretext interviews or false or misleading representations that seek to conceal the actual purpose(s) of the inquiry or investigation, or the identity or representative capacity of the inquirer or investigator."[4]

The language of Section 684 of H.R. 8288 is almost identical to the language of the Commission's recommendation. The exception is that the bill does not include the recommendation's tag-on of "or the identity or representative capacity of the inquirer or investigator." Thus, it appears that the wording of the bill is less stringent than that of the Commission's recommendation. One could argue that concealment or misrepresentation of identity or representative capacity would not be a violation of Section 684.

The omission of this last phrase is probably inadvertent. As it is written now, Section 684 contains the identical wording of the penultimate draft of the Commission's recommendation. To present the bill on the floor of Congress the day the Privacy Commission's report was released, it may have been necessary to draft the bill based on an earlier draft of the Commission's recommendation.[5]

3. *Reasonable Care in the Use of Support Organizations.* The Privacy Commission's third policy recommendation was that the FCRA should be amended to provide that each insurance institution and ISO must exercise reasonable care in the selection and use of ISOs "so as to assure that the collection, maintenance, use, and disclosure practices of such organizations comply with the Commission's recommendations."[6]

Section 682 of the Goldwater-Koch bill would implement this recommendation. The only significant difference in wording between the Commission's recommendation and Section 682 is that the above quoted phrase is omitted from H.R. 8288. With this omission, the exact meaning of "reasonable care" appears to be unclear. A "reasonable care" standard should be "reasonable" in relation to something. The tag-on "so as to assure . . ." appears desirable and needed.

4. *Reasonable Procedures.* The Commission recommended that insurance institutions and ISOs have reasonable procedures to assure the accuracy, completeness, and timeliness of information they collect, maintain, or disclose about an individual. This recommendation was considered to be a "general objective" to be strived for by insurance institutions and ISOs. Further, the Commission report observed that compliance would be automatic and self-enforcing because such compliance would be a self-serving by-product of the other Commission recommendations. The Commission stated flatly: "the Commission does not recommend that *Recommendation 4* be incorporated in statute or regulation."[7]

Section 674 of the Goldwater-Koch bill attempts to do exactly what the Commission said should not be done. It would codify the Commission's recommendation by amending the FCRA to require "reasonable procedures." Since the FTC is responsible for enforcing the FCRA, presumably it would establish what constitutes reasonable procedures. This section of H.R. 8288, if enacted into law, would seem to require the FTC to have a direct hand in insurer information practices. Historically, this has been the almost exclusive purview of state insurance regulators. H.R. 8288 departs significantly from what the Privacy Commission felt was the most desirable approach to handling this recommendation.

5. *Collection Notice.* The fifth recommendation of the Privacy Commission was that insurance institutions, prior to collecting information about "an *applicant or principal insured* from another person in connection with an insurance transaction, notify him as to: . . ." (emphasis added) the types of information expected to be collected about him from third parties, the techniques that may be used to collect the information, the sources that are expected to provide the information, and other procedures. The Commission felt that insurance commissioners could monitor insurance industry compliance with this recommendation and that, to a large extent, the recommendation would be self-enforcing because Recommendations 11 and 12 would give an individual the right to have deleted from any record information collected beyond the scope of a notice.[8]

Section 680 of the Goldwater-Koch bill states "before collecting information about an *insured individual or applicant* from another person in connection with an insurance transaction, the insurance institution shall notify, in writing, the insured individual or applicant of. . . ." (Emphasis added.) Following this is a listing of requirements almost identical to those outlined in the Privacy Commission's recommendation. Just as the Privacy Commission felt that its recommendation should not apply to information collected in connection with first- or third-party claims or marketing, so too does Section 680 exclude such information from the notice requirement.

The first obvious difference between the PPSC recommendation and Section 680 is the implementation mechanism. The Commission did not recommend amendment to the FCRA as it felt this recommendation would be largely self-enforcing. Further, by the use of the term "insured individual" instead of "principal insured," Section 680 seems to require that the notice be given literally to every individual who may be insured under an insurance policy. Thus, under the Family Automobile Policy it appears that a notice would have to be given to every individual within a given household, an unnecessary and, perhaps, undesirable requirement from the consumer's viewpoint.

The term "insurance transaction" appears in the PPSC recommendation as well as Section 680. While the Privacy Commission defined the term in its report as meaning "whenever a decision (be it adverse or otherwise), is rendered regarding an individual's eligibility for an insurance benefit or service," the term is undefined in H.R. 8288.[9] Hopefully, this is a mere oversight but it is obvious that such a term must be defined if insurers are to comply with the recommendation.

Similarly, Section 680 uses the undefined terms "third- or first-party claims." While these terms are generally understood within the property and liability insurance industry, it is not at all clear that the terms should be used in a law unless they are defined clearly.

Finally, although the Commission felt this recommendation should generally not be applied in loss settlements, it did state that the notice should include an explanation of any disclosures of information which would be made in connection with these claim transactions. Section 680 overlooks this PPSC preference.

6. *Notice as the Collection Limitation.* The Commission's sixth recommendation is an extension of the previous recommendation. It provides that an insurance institution limit its own information collection and disclosure practices to those specified in the notice called for in Recommendation 5 and limit its request to any organization that it asks to collect information on its behalf to information, techniques, and sources specified in the notice. Also this recommendation does not apply to claims and marketing. The Commission felt that, as with Recommendation 5, this recommendation would be largely self-enforcing because of the rights given an individual through Recommendations 11 and 12. The Commission also believed that insurance department examinations would lend additional strength to this requirement.[10]

Section 681 of H.R. 8288 is a faithful translation of the Commission's recommendation. The definitional problem regarding first- and third-party claims arises again. Moreover, it appears that implementation through the FCRA means that the FTC would necessarily become involved in insurer information collection practices.

7. *Information for Marketing and Research.* The Commission's seventh recommendation was that any insurance institution or ISO clearly specify to an individual those items of inquiry which elicit information desired for marketing, research, or other purposes not directly related to establishing the individual's eligibility for an insurance benefit or service. This recommendation does not apply to third-party claim transactions. The Commission preferred that insurers and ISOs voluntarily comply with this recommendation.

Section 683 of the Goldwater-Koch bill would have the Commission's recommendation enacted into law. It would require insurers and others to delineate fully those "items of inquiry desired for marketing, research, or other purposes. . . ."[11] To enforce this section it seems apparent that the FTC must serve as a sounding board for insurers and others in determining those items which are to be so labeled. Other items, by definition, must be related to establishing an individual's eligibility for the insurance benefit or service being sought. In other words, they must be relevant to the insurance transaction. One can infer that to enforce this provision of H.R. 8288, the FTC would have to be satisfied that the requested information was relevant. It is a small step to require FTC approval of relevancy standards. The FTC will occupy a significantly expanded role in insurer regulation if this section is enacted into law.

8. *Authorization Statements.* The Commission's eighth

recommendation was that no insurance institution or ISO ask an individual to sign any statement authorizing anyone to disclose information about him or her, or about any other individual, unless the statement is very specific as to the purpose, scope, and other matters. The Commission felt that this recommendation should be implemented "through the refusal of a holder of confidential information [e.g., a physician] to release it unless presented with a valid authorization."[12] The Commission also implicitly endorsed the concept that the National Association of Insurance Commissioners or the Commission on Uniform State Laws might develop standard authorization forms.[13]

Section 686 of H.R. 8288 would implement this recommendation by amendment to the FCRA which would spell out the minimum standards necessary for authorization statements. Some of the wording in Section 686 appears unnecessary but of greater importance is the omission in this section of part of the Privacy Commission's recommendation. The Commission stated that any authorization should be specific as to its expiration date, and that this date should not exceed one year from the date of the policy except "in the case of life insurance or noncancellable or guaranteed renewable health insurance . . ." in which case the expiration date could be two years from the date of the policy. Section 686 allows the same type of time limit but is silent on allowing a two-year expiration period on noncancellable or guaranteed renewable health insurance. Thus, the one-year period would apply in those cases.

Congressmen Koch and Goldwater introduced numerous bills to enact the Privacy Commission's recommendations in other areas. One of these bills, H.R. 8283, would amend the Social Security Act to provide for confidentiality of personal medical information created or maintained by certain medical care institutions. Section 182 (f) (1) of this bill provides that no medical care institution should disclose personal medical information about an individual pursuant to an authorization from the individual unless the authorization, among other things, is valid, "only for a specified and reasonable period of time (which may not exceed one year). . . ." Thus, according to H.R. 8283, it would be useless for a life insurer or an organization conducting an investigation for a life insurer to request information from a medical care institution[14] with an authorization which was more than a year old. This holds even though H.R. 8288 would allow the insurer to utilize such an authorization. This contradictory wording should be resolved.

9. *Investigative Interviews.* The Privacy Commission's ninth recommendation was that the FCRA be amended to provide that any insurance institution that may obtain an investigative report on an applicant or insured inform the individual that he or she may, upon request, be interviewed in connection with the report's preparation. The Commission further recommended that if an individual who had requested an interview could not be contacted after a reasonable effort, the obligation of the organization preparing the report could be discharged by the organization mailing a copy of the report to the individual. This

recommendation does not apply to any investigative report about an individual made in reasonable anticipation of a civil or criminal action or for use in defense or settlement of an insurance claim. Finally, the Commission suggested that the FCRA, in this connection, be amended to make clear that the interview requirement applied to underwriting investigations undertaken by insurers themselves as well as those undertaken by consumer reporting agencies.[15]

Section 677 of H.R. 8288 would implement this recommendation. There are two problems as this section is now worded. First, the bill has the exact language of the Commission's recommendation and hence it speaks to an "investigative report" and "agencies preparing investigative reports." Such language is new to the FCRA and H.R. 8288 does not define these terms. Presumably, an "investigative report" is the same as a "consumer investigative report." However, this is not clear from the bill, and the intent could be otherwise. If the two are synonymous, the wording should be corrected. If they are different, the distinction should be made clear. Similarly, "agencies preparing investigative reports" appears to mean "consumer reporting agencies," provided the term consumer reporting agencies is redefined to include insurance institutions and others who prepare investigative consumer reports. If this is not the intent, the terms should be clearly defined.

Second, subsection (c) of Section 677 provides that when an individual requests an interview "and the *insurance institution* is unable to contact such individual to schedule the interview, then, in lieu of complying with subsection (a), the *insurance institution* shall mail a copy of the investigative report to the individual." (Emphasis added.) To place the obligation on the insurance institution to mail the report is out of phase with the intent of the Privacy Commission's recommendation. Hopefully, the inclusion of the term insurance institution in the two places above is an oversight and either the phrase "agency preparing the investigative report" or the term "consumer reporting agency" should have been inserted in place of insurance institution.

10. *Access to Records.* The Commission's tenth recommendation was that the FCRA be amended to provide that upon request by an *individual*, an insurance institution or ISO must: "(i) inform the *individual*, after verifying his identity, whether it has *any recorded information* pertaining to him; and (ii) permit the individual to see and copy any such recorded information, either in person or by mail. . . ."[16] Other particulars are listed. The institution could disclose "medical record information" either directly, or through a licensed "medical care professional" designated by the individual, whichever the disclosing organization preferred. The proposed right of access would not apply to any record about an individual compiled in reasonable anticipation of a civil or criminal action or for use in settling a claim while the claim remained unsettled. After the claim was settled, the access right would not apply to any record compiled about a third-party claimant except as to any portion of such a record which was disseminated or used for purposes unrelated to the claim.

It is important to note that in the Commission's recommendation, the term "individual" has a specific meaning. It is "any natural person who is a past, present or proposed named or principal insured (including any principal insured under a family or group policy or similar arrangement of coverage for a person in a group), policyowner, or past or present claimant."[17] Thus, the Commission's recommendation would allow access only to those individuals who enjoyed a significant, usually legal, relationship with insurance institutions and ISOs.

Section 671 of H.R. 8288 would implement the Commission's tenth recommendation. The wording of this section is almost identical to the wording of the Privacy Commission's recommendation. Importantly, the terms emphasized above ("individual" and "any recorded information") are retained in this section. However, the intent is substantially different from that of the Privacy Commission. The difference arises because Section 688 of H.R. 8288 defines "individual" as "a natural person." Thus, an insurance institution or ISO would have to search literally every file in its possession to be able to "inform the individual" if it has "any recorded information" pertaining to him. Further, complete access rights would accrue to the individual. If this is, indeed, the intent of Section 671, one must seriously question the desirability and feasibility of establishing the detailed search capability which would be required. A computer would be essential and, importantly, such a law would seem to encourage the creation of sophisticated, computerized record-retrieval and identification systems. Conceivably this could be more of a threat to, than a protection of, privacy.

Subsection (b) of Section 671 is a codification of the PPSC's suggested medical record information exception. The wording is almost identical to that of the Privacy Commission's recommendation, including the use of the term "medical care professional." The Privacy Commission defined the term but it is undefined in H.R. 8288.

Similarly, Section 671 allows the PPSC's suggested exception to access rights in claim or litigation situations. Subsection (c), which codifies this exception, states that:

> the disclosure requirements . . . are not applicable with respect to any record about an individual compiled in reasonable anticipation of a civil or criminal action, or for use in settling a claim while the claim *remains unsettled*; or after the claim is settled, to any record compiled in relationship to a claimant who is not an insured or policyholder except as to any portion of such a record which is disseminated or used for a purpose unrelated to processing the claim after such time as *a proceeding* may no longer be contemplated. (Emphasis added.)

A problem that is common to both the Privacy Commission's recommendation and this bill is that of defining what constitutes a "settled claim." It appears appropriate to have a definition or explanatory regulations.

The wording of the last portion of Subsection (c) appears to be in error. The use of *proceeding* appears related to an exception in earlier drafts of the Commission's recommendations which dealt with proceedings in connection with civil or criminal litigation.

11. *The Correction of Records.* The Privacy Commission's eleventh recommendation was that the FCRA should be amended to provide that each insurance institution and ISO permit an individual to request correction, amendment, or deletion of information in a record pertaining to that individual. This recommendation is lengthy and contains numerous other provisions and exceptions. Generally the exceptions noted in the preceding recommendation dealing with the right of access apply here also.[18]

Section 672 of H.R. 8288 would implement the Commission's eleventh recommendation. It provides that "each insurance institution and insurance support organization shall permit an *individual* to request correction, amendment, or deletion of a *record* pertaining to him. . . ." (Emphasis added.) The interaction of the terms "individual" and "record" make for a section which is not inconsistent with the intent of the Privacy Commission. This is because Section 688 defines a record as meaning "any collection or grouping of information about an individual which is retrieved by the name of the individual or by policy number." This is in contrast to that previously discussed regarding Section 671 on access rights where the term "any recorded information" rather than "record" was used.

The Commission's recommendation allows an individual to request correction, amendment *and* deletion. The wording of Section 672 would allow an individual to request correction, amendment *or* deletion. There seems to be no great justification for allowing an individual to request only one of the three options.

Section 672 would require that the insurance institution or ISO "*furnish notification* of the correction[,] amendment or deletion to any person or organization specifically designated by the individual. . . ." (Emphasis added.) The Commission's recommendation was that the insurance institution or ISO not merely furnish notification of the correction, amendment, or deletion but rather should "*furnish the* correction, amendment, or fact of a deletion." (Emphasis added.) This same discrepancy appears in another area of this section. The H.R. 8288 approach, from a privacy protection viewpoint, appears less desirable than that recommended by the Privacy Commission.

The Privacy Commission recommended that in connection with a reinvestigation of disputed information by an insurance institution or ISO the investigating organization limit its investigation to those record items in dispute. The Privacy Commission's limitation would apply regardless of whether the insurance institution or ISO accepted the correction, amendment, or deletion. Section 672 would require that the limitation on reinvestigation of disputed information apply only in cases where the insurance institution or ISO refused to accept the correction, amendment, or deletion. Thus, presumably, when an individual challenged the quality of information contained in a record about him or her and the insurance institution or ISO agreed to the correction, it could initiate a reinvestigation with no limitations. From a privacy protection viewpoint, there seems to be little justification for this difference.

This section also contains the problems mentioned earlier in the *Access to Records* discussion regarding what constitutes a "settled claim" as well as the problem of "a proceeding."

12. *Correction of Records–Medical.* The Commission's twelfth recommendation was closely allied to the eleventh in that it provided a correction procedure when medical record information was involved. An individual who is the subject of medical record information maintained by an insurance institution or ISO must be able to request correction or amendment of such information and the insurance organization must be required to disclose various procedures and to make the requested corrections. Provision is made for dealing with "medical professionals" as well as "medical care providers."[19]

Section 673 provides that an *individual* has certain rights with respect to medical record information. Again, the term individual as defined means this section would apply to "any natural person." This is not consistent with the recommendation of the Privacy Commission. Further, this section does not provide for the exceptions about records compiled in reasonable anticipation of a civil or criminal action or for records used in settling a claim while the claim remained unsettled. Therefore, the claimant, litigant, or defendant could utilize this correction procedure in a way which could hinder an investigation. Identities of "medical care providers" would have to be disclosed and, importantly, if the individual could find another medical care provider to disagree with the information provided by the first, the insurance institution or ISO would be required to make the requested correction or amendment. In a claim situation, this could be quite disruptive.

The Privacy Commission defined the terms "medical care provider" and "medical professional." The terms are undefined in H.R. 8288.

13. *Adverse Underwriting Decisions.* The Commission's thirteenth recommendation was that the FCRA be amended to provide that an insurance institution must disclose in writing to an individual who is the subject of an adverse underwriting decision the specific reasons for the decision and the necessary supporting information. Other requirements are also levied on insurance institutions when an adverse underwriting decision occurs.[20]

Section 678 captures the wording and intent of the Privacy Commission recommendation except for two areas. The Privacy Commission stated that an insurance institution should disclose to an individual who is the subject of an adverse underwriting decision: "the specific item(s) of information that support(s) the reasons given [for the adverse decision] . . ., except that medical record information may be disclosed either directly or through a licensed medical professional designated by the individual, whichever the insurance institution prefers. . . ."[21] The equivalent H.R. 8288 section provides that the insurance institution should disclose "the specific item of information in plain language that support[s] the reason given." The omission of the allowance for more than one item or reason is not crucial but the absence of the medical record exception is a significant departure from the Privacy Commission's recommendation. Section 678 would require, for example, a life insurer to disclose directly to an individual any medical record information even though the insurance institution may be aware that the information is unknown to the individual. The approach of allowing the insurance institution to disclose such information through a medical professional seems not only desirable but also consistent with the medical record exception discussed above with respect to one's right of access.

14. *Decisions Based on Previous Adverse Decisions.* Recommendation fourteen of the PPSC stated that no insurance institution or ISO make an inquiry as to previous adverse underwriting decisions or as to whether an individual had obtained insurance through the substandard insurance market unless the inquiry also requested the reasons for such treatment. Moreover, even in the situations where reasons were requested, an insurance institution or ISO should not make an adverse underwriting decision based on such incomplete information. The Commission's clear preference for implementation of this recommendation was for state insurance commissioners to use their authority to force compliance.[22]

Section 676 of H.R. 8288, on the other hand, would have this recommendation implemented by amendment to the FCRA. The Commission felt that the regulatory agency (insurance commissioners) could foster compliance of this recommendation by using their powers to approve insurance (application) forms. Presumably, under H.R. 8288, the FTC would have some authority over the approval of such forms. Further, to enforce adequately this recommendation, the FTC must become involved in the underwriting processes of insurance companies. This seems inconsistent with the desire of the PPSC and the traditional role of state insurance regulation.

15. *Underwriting Decisions and Industry Data Exchanges.* Recommendation fifteen of the PPSC was that no insurance institution base an adverse underwriting decision on information about an individual obtained from an ISO whose primary source of information is insurance institutions or other ISOs. This recommendation was aimed at the practice of some Medical Information Bureau (MIB) member insurers utilizing the code provided by the MIB as the sole basis for some adverse underwriting decisions. Recognizing that the MIB historically has exercised little control over its member insurers and that, further, the access and correction rights would probably do much to alleviate this problem, the Commission felt that voluntary compliance was sufficient as an implementation strategy.[23]

Ignoring the Commission's stated preference for voluntary compliance, Section 679 of H.R. 8288 would have the recommendation implemented by amendment to the FCRA. Again, the FTC presumably must involve itself in underwriting practices in order to police this recommendation.

16. *Disclosures to Industry Data Exchanges.* The Commission's sixteenth recommendation was that federal law be enacted to provide that no insurance institution or ISO may disclose to another, information pertaining to an individual's health unless the information was obtained directly from a medical care provider or the individual.[24]

Although the Commission did not recommend that the federal law be in the form of amendment to the FCRA, Section 675 of the Goldwater-Koch bill would provide for such implementation. It would appear that the FTC would be the enforcement arm.

17. *Expectation of Confidentiality.* The Commission's seventeenth insurance recommendation was that Federal law be enacted to provide that each insurance institution and ISO be considered to owe a duty of confidentiality to any individual about whom it collected or received information and that, therefore, numerous limitations on disclosure without authorization be enacted.[25]

Section 685 would implement this recommendation. This section is fraught with problems. (It is this author's belief that the problems stem from the fact that, as mentioned earlier, this bill had to be drafted prior to the release of the Privacy Commission's report. The wording of Section 685 is virtually identical to that of the Privacy Commission's penultimate draft of this recommendation. The Privacy Commission's recommendation underwent significant changes in June 1977 before the report was released in July 1977. Conversation with the staff of Congressman Goldwater support this view.[26])

As currently worded, this section would allow one insurer to share information with another without authorization, provided the other insurer was rendering a decision about the individual. From a privacy protection standpoint, this is weak.

Section 685 would allow disclosures from the MIB to a member insurer without authorization if the insurer was using the information for claim purposes. This represents less protection for the consumer than is currently provided by the MIB's own rules.

Other problems include the use of such undefined terms as "coinsurer," "health information," "index bureau," "loss settlements," "claim purposes," and "self-insurer." While many of these terms have meanings that are commonly understood within the insurance business, some of them need to be defined in any new law, especially to the extent the term has a meaning different from that commonly understood within the insurance business.

Summary and Conclusion

Appendix I gives a summary of the key differences between H.R. 8288 and the insurance recommendations of the Privacy Protection Study Commission. H.R. 8288 departs from the preferred PPSC implementation approach in 9 of the 17 insurance recommendations. Since the PPSC recommendations are tailored to a particular implementation strategy (and vice versa), major disruptions and changes in meanings and results of the recommendation occur when the recommendations are implemented in other ways. This paper has attempted to demonstrate that, in certain areas, these changed meanings and results could result in undesirable consequences. If enacted into law, H.R. 8288 seems to require unprecedented Federal Trade Commission involvement in insurance practices and procedures. Much of what is commonly believed to be the exclusive province of state insurance regulators would be taken over by the FTC. At the least, one could infer that the Congressional intent as enunciated in McCarren-Ferguson would undergo a significant change if H.R. 8288 is enacted. This issue should be faced squarely and debated on its merits rather than have the matter decided in an indirect manner.

Besides differing with the PPSC on implementation strategy in over half of the recommendations, H.R. 8288 is riddled with definitional and other problems. The Chairman of the PPSC, David Linowes, in a recent paper given before the National Conference on Privacy and the Insurance Industry stated: "our [the PPSC] recommendations reflect our concern with balancing the protection of individual privacy with the legitimate information needs of your industry. We believe they also reflect our awareness of various regulatory mechanisms already in place—particularly at the State level—and seek to strengthen, rather than replace, such mechanisms."[27] Chairman Linowes also stressed that the Commission had sought to keep government involvement in privacy matters to a minimum.[28] H.R. 8288 does not reflect this intent.

Appendix I: H.R. 8288 Provisions versus Privacy Protection Study Commission Recommendations

PPSC Rec. No.	PPSC Rec.	PPSC Implementation	H.R. 8288 Implementation	H.R. 8288 Sec. No.	Major Problems (other than implementation)
1	Govt. Mech.	Ins. Comm.*			
2	Pretext Interviews	FCRA	FCRA	684	—bill omits concealment of identity or representative capacity of inquirer
3	Reasonable Care-ISO	FCRA	FCRA	682	—bill has no standard for reasonable care
4	Reasonable Procedures	Vol.	FCRA	674	—who determines reasonable procedures
5	Collection Notice	Ins. Comm.*	FCRA	680	—every insd. receives notice —undefined terms
6	Limits on Collection	Ins. Comm.	FCRA	681	—undefined terms
7	Info. Collection	Vol.	FCRA	683	—who determines relevancy
8	Authorization	Ins. Comm.*	FCRA	686	—expiration on health apps. —contradiction with H.R. 8283
9	Interview	FCRA	FCRA	677	—burden on insurers, should be on CRA —undefined terms
10	Access	FCRA	FCRA	671	—bill allows access by anyone —undefined terms
11	Correction	FCRA	FCRA	672	—bill requires notification only —bill omits part of reinvestigation limitation
12	Corrections Med.	FCRA	FCRA	673	—bill allows anyone to request correction —disruptive to litigation & claims
13	Reasons	FCRA	FCRA	678	—bill omits med. exception
14	Previous Decisions	Ins. Comm.	FCRA	676	—bill requires FTC involvement in underwriting
15	Data Exchange	Vol.	FCRA	679	—bill requires FTC involvement in underwriting
16	Health Info.	Fed. Law	FCRA	675	—FTC involvement
17	Confidentiality	Fed. Law	FCRA	685	—bill allows privacy abuses —undefined terms

*Other approaches considered okay; although state action seems to be the preferred approach.

1. W. Lee Burge, "Information Needs and the Insurance Industry: Where to From Here," remarks and discussion at the Georgia State University National Conference on Privacy and the Insurance Industry, October 13, 1977 (*Proceedings* forthcoming).

2. Much of the content of each recommendation will of necessity be omitted. For a more detailed discussion of the more significant insurance recommendation see: Harold Skipper, "Recommendations of the Privacy Protection Study Commission of Importance to Life and Health Insurers," *Best's Review*—Life/Health edition, Vol. 78, August 1977, p. 20; and Harold Skipper, "Recommendations of the Privacy Protection Study Commission of Importance to Property and Casualty Insurers," *Best's Review*—Property/Casualty edition, Vol. 78, October 1977, p. 16.

3. The Privacy Protection Study Commission, *Personal Privacy in an Information Society*, pp. 188-89 (Washington, D.C.: U.S. Government Printing Office, 1977) [hereinafter cited as *Personal Privacy*].

4. Ibid., p. 190.

5. A telephone conversation on November 18, 1977 with Joseph Overton, Congressman Goldwater's Legislative Assistant, supported this view.

6. *Personal Privacy*, p. 191.

7. Ibid., p. 192.

8. Ibid., pp. 193-194.

9. Ibid., p. 221.

10. Ibid., p. 195.

11. Both the PPSC recommendation and H.R. 8288 speak of "items of inquiry desired for. . . ." The items of inquiry are not that which is desired but rather the information *elicited from* the items of inquiry is that which is desired.

12. *Personal Privacy*, p. 198.

13. Ibid.

14. H.R. 8283 defines 'medical care institution' as "any facility or institution that lawfully provides medical-care services, and include [sic] a hospital, skilled nursing facility, intermediate care facility, home health agency, and a health maintenance organization." Sec. 1181 (b) (1).

15. *Personal Privacy*, pp. 198-199.

16. Ibid., p. 200 (emphasis added).

17. Ibid., p. 221.

18. Ibid., pp. 204-208.

19. Ibid., pp. 206-208, 222.

20. Ibid., pp. 209-211.

21. Ibid., p. 209.

22. Ibid., pp. 211-212.

23. Ibid., pp. 212-213.

24. Ibid., pp. 213-214.

25. Ibid., pp. 215-217.

26. Telephone conversation of November 18, 1977 with Joseph Overton, Legislative Assistant to Rep. Barry Goldwater, Jr.

27. "The Changing Concept of Privacy," paper and discussion. (*Proceedings* forthcoming).

28. Ibid.

(*Note*: Since this article was prepared, a new bill, H.R. 10076, was introduced into the U.S. House. This bill, the "Omnibus Right to Privacy Act of 1977," is co-sponsored by Congressmen L. Richardson Preyer, Barry Goldwater, Jr., and Edward Koch. Section 605 of this bill is identical to H.R. 8288 and, therefore, this article applies to that portion of the bill.)

7840